POLITICIZING THE INTERNATIONAL CRIMINAL COURT

POLITICIZING THE INTERNATIONAL CRIMINAL COURT

The Convergence of Politics, Ethics, and Law

Steven C. Roach

ROWMAN & LITTLEFIELD PUBLISHERS, INC.
Lanham • Boulder • New York • Toronto • Plymouth, UK

ROWMAN & LITTLEFIELD PUBLISHERS, INC.

Published in the United States of America
by Rowman & Littlefield Publishers, Inc.
A wholly owned subsidiary of The Rowman & Littlefield Publishing Group, Inc.
4501 Forbes Boulevard, Suite 200, Lanham, Maryland 20706
www.rowmanlittlefield.com

Estover Road, Plmouth PL6 7PY, United Kingdom

British Library Cataloguing in Publication Information Available

Library of Congress Cataloging-in-Publication Data
Roach, Steven C.
Politicizing the International Criminal Court : the convergence of politics, ethics, and law / Steven C. Roach.
p. cm.
Includes bibliographical references and index.
ISBN-13: 978-0-7425-4103-0 (cloth : alk. paper)
ISBN-10: 0-7425-4103-7 (cloth : alk. paper)
ISBN-13: 978-0-7425-4104-7 (pbk. : alk. paper)
ISBN-10: 0-7425-4104-5 (pbk. : alk. paper)
1. International Criminal Court. 2. International criminal courts—Moral and ethical aspects. 3. International criminal courts—Political aspects. 4. International cooperation. I. Title.
KZ6311.R63 2006
345'.01—dc22

2005035979

Printed in the United States of America

∞™ The paper used in this publication meets the minimum requirements of American National Standard for Information Sciences—Permanence of Paper for Printed Library Materials, ANSI/NISO Z39.48-1992.

For Erica

Contents

Preface and Acknowledgments

When I first began to teach on the issue of U.S. opposition to the International Criminal Court (ICC) in the spring of 2002 at Colorado State University at Pueblo, I never imagined that my teachings would become the starting point for extensive research on the issue, much less a full-length book on the topic. At this time, it will be remembered, the ICC had not yet entered into force (it would on July 1, 2002); nor had the Bush administration's war on the ICC, or its disengagement from the ICC, officially commenced. Still, I was struck by the vast majority of students in my introductory class on world issues who had raised their hand when I asked them if the ICC constituted a threat to U.S. national security.

Some time after my short tenure at Colorado State University, Pueblo, I had the opportunity to present a paper on U.S. opposition to the ICC at the 99th American Political Science Annual Meeting in Philadelphia (September 1–5 of 2003)in which I addressed the larger issue of whether the United States could learn to share power with another global organization, that is, to enter into a sort of global *cohabitacion*. In doing so, I began to see U.S. opposition in rather Machiavellian terms, albeit without the prudence that Machiavelli had so valued as a measure of power. U.S intransigence also struck me as the supreme form of disenchantment with the ICC's jurisdictional authority. In essence, the United States had created its own iron cage rationalization of (a warlike) international society, in which its own citizens and other persons could now be deprived of due process afforded under international law and the U.S. Constitution. Perhaps it was this image that also revealed the tacit and (ir)rational aim of violating international law, as evidenced by the reports of human rights abuses committed by the United States at the Abu Ghraib prison and Guantanamo Bay (according to confirmed eyewitness reports).

Whether or not this is true, for academicians it underscores the following problem: the failure to merge together their substantive and descriptive analyses of the politics of law and the global political order. However, the growing scholarship on the topic of the politics of law provides signs of a rich and evolving theoretical framework for studying the interaction between politics of international law, beginning with the theory of legalization, authored by Robert Keohane, Anne-Marie Slaughter, Andrew Moravschik, Kenneth Abbot, and Duncan Snidal, and Christian Reus-Smit's theoretical analysis in *The Politics of International Law*, followed by more case specific theoretical analyses of the ICC, including the works by Jason Ralph, Caroline Fehl, Thomas W. Smith, Antonio Franceschet, to name only a few. With these latter cases, it has become evident that the ICC will serve as a dynamic context for understanding the intersection of politics, power, and ethics; and for that matter, the ongoing synthesis between political science and international law. If we are to work toward synthesis, we will need to draw on legal scholarship, theory, and empirical science in ways that allow us to substantiate the political dimension of the ICC.

It is this ethical and political challenge that will invariably require an interdisciplinary approach to explain the moral and political trajectory of the Court, or rather its complex role in global politics or global civil society (e.g., the Darfur crisis). Putting together these conceptual pieces of the ICC's political agency will nonetheless require the formulation of political strategies designed to enhance and sustain its role in promoting accountability and international peace and security. This book, then, is an attempt to gather together and assemble some of these pieces. It is by no means an exhaustive analysis of the Court's ethical and political structure; only an initial and modest cut into what I believe will become an increasingly important context for understanding the transformation of international law.

I am thus indebted to many who have assisted in the writing of this book. Much, if not all of the editorial assistance came from my wife, Erica, to whom this book is dedicated. Her honesty, unmitigated love, patience, and, above all, Dutch sensibilities have always been the sequine of lights linking my personal and academic lives, even in the dimmest of times. I am also very grateful to the acquisitions editor, Renée Legatt, for her professional and down-to-earth advice in moving this manuscript to publication.

Many parts of the chapters were presented at conferences and other scholarly forums, where I received valuable comments and related suggestions from Mark Amen, George Andreopolous, John Barkdull, Michael Forman, Mark Gibney, Gary Herbert, David Kinsella, Richard Mansbach, Paul Passavant,

Rob Piro, and Tony Smith, among others. I also received helpful written comments from Tom Farer, Amy Eckert, and several anonymous reviewers and benefited a great deal from discussions with my students in my international human rights class at the University of South Florida.

I would like to thank the following publishers for granting me the permission to reprint articles that comprise a substantial part of the book manuscript: Taylor & Francis (Routledge), Palgrave Macmillan, Lynne Rienner, and Blackwell Publishing. Parts of chapter 9 were originally published in *Alternatives: Global, Local, Political* 30, no. 4 (Sept–Dec 2005). Copyright © 2005 by Lynne Rienner Publishers. Used with permission. Parts of chapter 8 and chapter 9 were originally published with *International Politics* 43, no. 1 (2006). Copyright © 2006 by Palgrave Macmillan. Used with permission. A substantial portion of chapter 8 appeared in *International Studies Perspectives* 6, no. 4 (November 2005). Copyright © 2005 by Blackwell Publishing. Used with permission. The same applies to chapter 7, which appeared in *Political Studies* 53, no. 1 (March 2005). Copyright © 2005 by Blackwell Publishing. And lastly, parts of chapter 5 appeared in *Journal of Human Rights* 4, no. 4 (December 2005). Copyright © 2005 by Taylor & Francis Publishers.

In short, this book is an attempt to weave together the topics of these different articles into a cohesive framework for understanding the political dimension of the ICC. In this way, it is also possible to see this book, with its nine chapters, as part of an unfolding story about international criminal accountability in global politics.

Steven C. Roach
University of South Florida
December 2005

Introduction: The Global Politics of Criminalizing Violence

> It is impossible to know a man's soul, both the wit and will, before he writes laws and enforces them. I believe that he who rules in a state and fails to embrace the best men's councils, but stays locked in silence and vague fear, is the worst man there.
>
> —Sophocles, *Antigone*

WHILE THE ESTABLISHMENT of the International Criminal Court (ICC) in July 1998 constituted a millennial event in legal history, its development as an international institution remains, for many social scientists, a novel political process. The ICC, I argue in this book, is a political institution. More than that, it is a complex institution whose political dimension needs to be understood as a constructive (albeit formative) component of global politics. The central aim of this book is to probe the theoretical and empirical parameters of this evolving dimension so that we may begin to link the formative development of the ICC with an internal form of politicization. I propose that such an internal form of politicization will allow the ICC to counter external attempts to politicize it, whether this involves the political agenda of a state hegemon, or the geopolitical interests of the U.N. Security Council permanent members.

Legal purists will no doubt be troubled by these claims. But it is also true that the politics of the ICC takes us far beyond the negotiating table and bargaining strategies that took place at the Rome Conference. In fact, the ICC raises a crucial set of questions for legal theorists and social scientists alike. How will its actions (e.g., rulings, judgments, and actions) be shaped by global politics and vice versa? What empirical case studies will address the evolving political dimension of the ICC? And, perhaps more important, which theories will allow us to best understand the intersection of ethics, power, and politics of the ICC?

How we address these questions will depend on our willingness to challenge conventional and non-conventional assumptions concerning the interaction of law and politics. As we shall see, the ICC's dynamics make it possible to establish the connections between different theories that allow us to understand the changing dimensions of global politics and security. Indeed, the implications of the ICC for studying the changing parameters of global politics are intriguing, to say the least. Not only might the employment of a plurality of theories shed light on the convergence of legal and social scientific views, but it might also yield new knowledge of the complex interaction between politics and law.

Nonetheless, one of the critical starting points for understanding the politics of international criminal law is prevention, or the creation of a global deterrent effect. The ICC Statute, for instance, eliminates all existing national amnesty laws that have provided immunity to perpetrators of gross human rights violations. This is certain to mean some withering of the culture of impunity in war-torn societies. But whether it will continue to prevent an outbreak of future cases of gross human rights abuses remains unclear. This is because deterrence remains an indeterminative effect, or rather, a psychological and emotive claim to justice. The essence of deterrence, it could be said, is not learned prevention, but the fear of being punished. In its purest form, then, deterrence can be characterized as the *rule* of fear, as illustrated by the eye-for-an-eye criminal justice system in Singapore.

Indeed, it is precisely this fear that leads to what Cesare Beccaria referred to as the "timid credulity of the people" or the potential regression of civility to barbarism.[1] In this way, the emotive quality of deterrence, if taken to its extreme, may help to facilitate dictatorial and repressive forms of rule in non-states parties, which may, in turn, challenge the high civil standards of fairness embodied in the ICC Statute (a defendant's civil and political rights). Extending the deterrent effect to the global level, then, requires us to address the tradeoffs between domestic and international legal criminal systems and military enforcement and the protection of international human rights.

Complicating matters further is the absence of a reliable enforcement mechanism at the international level. This is one main reason why the efficacy of the rule of law is often analogized to the rule of state sovereignty, since only the state possesses a standing army to enforce the rule of law. However, to say that the rule of law cannot exist in some demonstrable form at that international level—nor continue to evolve within some concrete normative framework—is to ignore the implications of the continuing trend toward global governance. In fact, as we shall see, the erosion of state sovereignty will continue to require a subtle balance between global and state prerogatives. In the case of international collective intervention into humanitarian emergencies, new rules and principles will need to be devised that replace the traditional rules of the U.N. Charter (non-intervention and the sovereign equality of states) and that challenge conventional notions of global power.[2]

Juridical Power and Political Legitimacy

Power, as understood in this book, is defined as the ability of institutions or collective bodies to enforce the norms, rules, and principles encoded and embedded in international law. By embedded, then, I am assuming that morals and normative considerations shape the decisions and judgments that define the application of law, but that such considerations also incorporate the influence of NGOs, social movements, and states. Juridical power, by extension, refers to the capacity to administer and enact the rules of procedure and norms (of the ICC Statute), and the motivational intent to secure and preserve the governing values, principles, and norms of societal order. As one of the most well-known theorists of juridical power during the early twentieth century, Max Weber argued that legal institutions administered and applied the rules of procedure independently of the moral convictions and values that had given rise to these rules. Weber reasoned that legal domination reflected an autonomous bureaucratic authority, which required strict abidance by the citizens of the state, thus diminishing individual freedom in modern society (or what Weber described metaphorically as the iron cage of modern society).[3]

As I will discuss in chapter 5, the ICC's juridical power is neither dominant nor strict. Rather, it is flexible insofar as it lacks a centralized enforcement mechanism and is dependent upon state cooperation (and its legitimacy) to implement and enforce its rules of procedure. The task of understanding the nature and scope of the ICC's juridical power, therefore, will depend on public perception of its fairness and efficacy of norms and the role of NGOs in promoting and upholding the ICC's legal standards of fairness.[4] In this respect, NGOs and the inclusion of other organizational entities figure to provide important vehicles for shaping the juridical power of the ICC.

With the increasing importance of NGOs, it becomes all the more important to consider the ICC's political legitimacy, or how the ICC will justify and rationalize its power in terms of its ability to promote and maintain international peace and security, whether this is through deterrence or action aimed at stopping the violence caused by the targeted perpetrator. Indeed, the political legitimacy of the ICC will require various political strategies and policies to address the political overtones of the exercise of the ICC Prosecutor's discretionary power consistent with its legal standards and rules of fairness.[5] This of course raises a central issue: whether such political strategies will unduly politicize the ICC.

Again, we need to be clear about what we mean by the term politicization, and whether this runs counter to the ICC's fairness and its role in global politics. Many, for instance, have argued that the politicization of the ICC will take the form of the intrusion of geopolitical interests in the ICC's judgment over matters related to peace and security (i.e., crime of aggression). Others insist that the ICC's juridical power will lead to the potential 'tyranny' of judicial authority at the international level.[6] Whether or not these concerns are rooted in false political or legal pretenses, they do underscore the increasing importance of the legitimacy deficit in legal institutions, or rather how international legal institutions will require strong forms of legitimacy to function effectively and efficiently. As most legal scholars would probably agree, the ICC's legitimacy cannot be entirely separated from its role in promoting international peace and security. Yet the dilemma we face in this regard is this: if the ICC's political legitimacy requires active enforcement to ensure that its demands are met, then how will it extricate this source of its political legitimacy from Western coercion or military power?

One way of resolving this dilemma, is to distinguish between the ICC's actions directed towards a political and moral end, and the actions of states and/or other international organizations that will constrict the ICC's judicial power. I will explain more clearly what I mean by this qualitative distinction between the internal and external forces of the ICC's development in the following section. Here, it is important to stress the relationship between the ICC's evolution and its political dimension. In this book, I distinguish between two stages of political development of the ICC: 1) A preformative and 2) formative phase. Whereas the former refers to the politics of the ICC's implementation or the bargaining and negotiating that took place at the Rome Conference and resulted in the important changes to and the full implementation of the ICC Statute, the latter refers to the actions and operations of the ICC as a fully implemented, international legal institution.

As such, the date of the ICC's entry into force (July 1, 2002) marks the official start of the formative phase. It is also during this phase that we have seen the United States launch its virtual war against the ICC, or its concerted attempts to disengage itself from the formative development of the ICC. The formative phase, then, represents the evolution of the ICC's capabilities as a flexible and effective institution in global politics. Such capacities, as we shall see, will encompass a range of political strategies or policy arrangements, including negotiating and bargaining with national governments (non-state parties that are non-compliant or reluctant to abide by the ICC's terms of surrender), strategically oriented amendments to the ICC Statute designed to counter the effects of hegemonic interests, and a cooperative arrangement between the ICC and the U.N.

I do wish to stress here that such political strategies represent hypothetical starting points for understanding the ICC's political development. As such, they are not intended to resolve the political tensions between the exercise of the Prosecutor's discretionary power and non-compliance by non-states parties. Here it should be noted that the current ICC Prosecutor, Luis Moreno Ocampo, recently announced in December of 2004 that he had selected his first case involving the gross human rights abuses committed during the civil war between the rebels of the Lord's Resistance Army (LRA) and the Uganda national government. More recently, the U.N. Security Council referred the situation of the humanitarian crisis in the Darfur region of Sudan to the ICC (April 2005). In response to the ICC's referral, Ocampo announced that his office had gathered enough evidence to indict various individuals for the crime of genocide, which took place between April of 2003 and 2005. However, the Sudanese government, although pledging to conduct its own investigation into the matter, has showed few if any concrete signs that it will comply with the ICC.

Given the political uncertainties of these cases, it is important that we delve into the constructive dimensions of the politics of the ICC. Constructivism, as we shall see in chapter 4, provides some insight into this formative stage of the ICC's evolution, as does pragmatic ethics (chapter 3).[7] But applying these and other theoretical approaches to the ICC will also depend on our ability to analyze the complex nature of the ICC's political dimension.

Politics and the Political

In this book, I adopt a working distinction between the politics of the ICC, which generally refers to the negotiations, contestation, and bargaining related to the implementation of policies and rules of the ICC; and the political, which characterizes the tactical design of the ICC's (and international criminal tribunals) enactment of juridical authority.[8] Politics, in this sense, refers to the means by which international criminal courts validate their actions and moral principles. In the case of the ICTY, politics can be characterized by the contested decisions of the Office of the Prosecutor to investigate a sensitive case (high profile leaders), or rather the active pursuit of political policies aimed at ending the Balkan War. As Rachel Kerr notes in the context of the ICTY, "Politics is manifested in a series of maneuvers in pursuit of a given interest or policy. Both law and politics operate in the context of an organized political community—the state with a prescribed sovereign authority, the executive—and a designated Legislature and Judiciary."[9]

By comparison, the political refers to the Security Council's rationale for establishing the International Criminal Tribunal for the Former Yugoslavia (ICTY) and the International Criminal Tribunal for Rwanda (ICTR). Such a rationale can be defined by the need to address a breach in peace and security in accordance with Chapter VII of the Charter. In the context of the Nuremberg and Tokyo tribunals, the political might also underscore the political lesson associated with victor's justice. The political in this sense is not simply strategic in nature; it reflects a highly dynamic and unwieldy concept, which is "constitutive of social order in which new social practices are instituted (5–6)."

For Christian Reus-Smit, the political represents a dynamic set of features of moral deliberation. Here, he interprets political deliberation as constituting four integrated types of reason: idiographic, purposive, instrumental, and ethical. According to him, the idiographic refers to identity construction or the question of "who am I in the world"; the purposive, "to what and how should I contribute to the world"; and the ethical, "how I should act."[10] Reus-Smit's primary aim here is to show that structural realism and institutionalism (positivist approaches that separate fact from value or politics from morality) ignore the political constitutivity of law. In his view, new standards of legitimacy such as human rights or women's and children's rights will continue to shape the political deliberation of institutions in multiple, and often contradictory ways. What this suggests is the increasingly complex interaction of politics, ethics, and power, which, for our purposes, will require delicate analytical maneuvering.

Neutralization, Politicization, and the Role of Ethics

To manuever effectively in this respect, we will need to make a second distinction between *internal* and *external politicization.* As already noted, such a distinction is based on the differing goal oriented actions (one belonging to the ICC's use of its own institutional resources; the other to outside action) and the formulation of certain political strategies consistent with the ICC's rules and standards of fairness. Again, to say that the Court should never become politicized is to ignore its role in enforcing international peace and security.[11] On the other hand, it is important that we prevent geopolitical interests from intruding on the operations of the ICC. As noted above, I employ external politicization to refer to the politicization of the Court by Western interests, or in this case, the determination of the U.N. Security Council permanent members of when an act of aggression has taken place.

By comparison, internal politicization reflects the role of the ICC's institutional mechanisms (Assembly of States Parties and the many forms of checks and balances on the Prosecutor's power) in formulating political and policy strategies. These can range from the Prosecutor's negotiation with states to institutional reengineering, as well as the adoption of certain amendments to counteract outside resistance. It is always possible that powerful states within the ICC may use their power to shape these political strategies, thus blurring the line between internal and external politicization. But this should be considered a mitigating factor at best, since the institutional mechanisms of the ICC, such as the Assembly of States Parties presuppose strong, internal forms of accountability, checks and balances, and consensus formation. Again, what I am proposing is that the ICC's internal politicization constitutes an essential component of its formative development as a fair and representative legal institution.

Given this distinction, it is possible to see the politics of the ICC as operating along a continuum between *strict neutrality* (legalism) and *external politicization* (politicized instability). Those (legal purists) who adhere to the strict notion of legal neutrality treat law as a detached body of rules and procedures. The application of law, in this case, is based on the rigid separation of rules and values, whereby rules and norms are applied independently of the moral and political concerns that have shaped these rules. Many international legal scholars of the ICC can be said to be mixed or diluted purists in this sense, insofar as they maintain that the neutrality of the Court remains fundamental to the Court's effectiveness, legitimacy, and capacity to overcome the uncertainties of state noncompliance.[12] For these scholars, the evolution of the ICC will proceed on a basis in which international criminal accountability becomes entrenched in societies *via* constitutional or legislative changes. Social expectations of domestic law, therefore, will ultimately converge with perceptions of the Court's fairness and norm efficacy, thereby removing the politicized barriers (or differences between international and domestic law) to the effective enforcement of its proscriptive norms against genocide, crimes against humanity and war crimes.[13]

For radical critical theorists or Postmodernists, however, such rationalization of the law exposes the underlying contradictions of juridical power.[14] Power, they claim, does not operate in an empty vacuum; it confers legitimacy onto the values and interests sustaining and promoting this order, and, in the process, marginalizes the voices and beliefs of private and individual agents.[15] In this way, politics and power become intertwined in a diffuse web of relations among states, individuals, and private entities in which the legitimization of power expresses the subjugation of beliefs and values (of developing states) to imperial interests. Politicization, therefore, can be understood as constituting both a cause and effect of imperialism; it represents how the most powerful states have employed and manipulated the law to serve their own interests.

But the problem with this radical interpretation of power is that it focuses only on external politicization and its attendant restrictions or controls on freedom and difference. But internal politicization, as I have proposed, represents the participatory elements of the ICC, and how these elements represent the ability of states, individuals, and NGOs to shape the ICC's policies and political strategies for countering forms of external politicization. In this manner, I argue that radical critical theory overlooks the inclusive and dynamic function of the ICC's internal politicization and how ethics mediate between the application of power and the political objectives informing the application of this power. As we shall see, there are various ethical influences at work here, including the pragmatic character of the ICC, and the political cosmopolitanism associated with the universal morality of the ICC. Nevertheless, the importance of considering ethics in this sense is that it allows us to normalize the causal connection between legitimacy and power politics, that is, to conceive of the inclusivity of the values, beliefs, and views of other agents in the ICC.

The Concept of Political Legalism

The distinction between internal and external politicization, therefore, enables us to steer a path between radical critical theory and legal formalism, or strict legalism and external politicization. It demonstrates, in other words, how the application of rules and institutional mechanisms remain essential to countering the repressive effects of juridical power. In this way, it forms a flexible component of our understanding of the politics of criminalizing violence and provides the reflexive basis of what I call *political legalism.* By political legalism, I am referring to an informed and flexible adherence to the legal rules and principles of the ICC Statute, resulting in the self-directed and engaged application of these rules. A self-directed application of the rules refers to the calculated and designed pursuit of policies and political strategies aimed at facilitating the [ICC's] moral and ethical objective of holding accountable the worst perpetrators of gross human rights violations. From this perspective, a self-directed application of the rules is both dynamic and open-ended, and is intended to represent the possibilities of the constructive intersection of politics, ethics, and power.

There are two underlying assumptions of political legalism. First, non-state party resistance or opposition generates political effects that are constitutive of the political strategies and ethics needed to counter these effects. This means that ethics and politics will play a key role in the development of the ICC, since they will substantiate the measures needed to reduce the political tensions and conflict between the ICC and the state. Here it is possible to identify several functional types of ethics that figure to shape the Court's power and legitimacy, including pragmatic, discursive, and cosmopolitan ethics. I should stress that not all non-states parties are likely to resist the Court. However, those that do, will, as I will show, constitute an important political element of the active and engaged legalism of the ICC.

Second, the procedural neutrality of the ICC remains a limited and problematic source of legitimizing the ICC's legalized authority. It is crucial that we realize that the tensions between the ICC and non-states parties stems from the conflict between its perceived neutrality and its external politicization. Indeed, only in a perfect and non-conflictual world can we expect the ICC's legal impartiality to provide the exclusive source of its legitimacy.

Given this framework of political legalism, I shall address two central issues in the book: 1) Whether the ICC can continue to evolve as an effective player in global politics or in criminalizing international violence and 2) whether we can understand its political dimension as constitutive of a new global political order.

Organization

In addressing these issues, I have divided the book into three main parts. The first assesses the historical and legal parameters of ICC. The second offers theoretical analyses of the intersection of the politics, ethics, and power by drawing on various political and international theories. The third applies the theoretical conclusions of the second part to three areas of international politics—namely, U.S. opposition to the ICC, the potential conflict between Islamic and international criminal law, and the relationship between the ICC and the U.N. Security Council.

In chapter 1, I discuss the lessons of various past and current mechanisms to criminalize international violence, including the Nuremberg and Tokyo Military Tribunals, the International Criminal Tribunal for the Former Yugoslavia (ICTY), and the International Criminal Tribunal for Rwanda (ICTR). As we shall see, the legacy of the Nuremburg and Tokyo Military Tribunals paved the way for the adoption of sweeping legal mechanisms, including the Genocide Convention, Geneva Conventions/Protocols, and the International

Law Commission. Although the momentum generated from these tribunals would prove short-lived, the end of the Cold War would mark a new starting point for implementing proscriptive norms against genocide, crimes against humanity, and war crimes. In particular, the U.N. General Assembly would instruct the International Law Commission (ILC) to complete a final draft statute of the ICC, a document that would specify the elements of genocide and crimes against humanity, both of which would be central to the establishment of the ICC. Moreover, the establishment of two international criminal tribunals by the Security Council would provide important models upon which to design and define the parameters and the scope of the ICC Statute.

Moving on to the legal dynamics of the ICC, chapter 2 discusses the legal principles and political issues surrounding the application of the complementarity principle and the ICC's rules of procedure. The aim of this chapter is to lay the legal groundwork for understanding the political legalism of the ICC. The central issue I address here is whether the ICC's automatic jurisdiction via the territorial principle is a constructive alternative to universal (forms of) jurisdiction. I argue that the combination of the ICC's complementarity principle and automatic jurisdiction represents an important and valid alternative to universal jurisdiction. To support my argument, I analyze the legal and political problems surrounding universal jurisdiction (e.g., the Belgium statute) and examine the applicability of the universality principle in the case of the ICC. I then move on to assess the ICC's governing structure, including the guidelines for exercising discretionary power, the internal accountability mechanisms of the ICC, and the narrowing of the gap between domestic and international law.

As we shall see, these procedural mechanisms are certain to facilitate negotiations between the ICC and other organizations (U.N.). However, they also raise many issues as to how the ICC will deal with the effects that cannot be effectively contained by the strict application of these procedural mechanisms. In other words, how will the ICC assert its juridical authority against state noncompliance or resistance? And how will this reflect the struggle for political legitimacy, or rather the development of the ICC's self-governing capabilities vis-à-vis other institutions? The former question forms the basis of our theoretical discussion of the ICC (chapters 3–5); the latter is addressed more directly in part 3. Still, it is crucial to stress here that this gray area of (the future of) the ICC's internal political development will depend on its capacity to deal with political tensions between the assertion of its juridical authority and the non-compliance of non-states parties. This is not to say that international pressures such as U.N. economic sanctions, NGO protests, and media reporting will fail to have a significant impact on non-compliance. Rather, it underscores a substantive political challenge of the ICC in which the ICC's internal political development will complement, or in some cases, supplant the *dependency* of the Court on these pressures to enforce its decisions and judgments.

To be sure, there are many different ways in which the ICC's politics will intersect with ethics and power. Chapter 3 discusses this intersection by examining the theoretical implications of the ICC's juridical authority for legalization theory, which provides a (empirical) theoretical framework for integrating international relations and international law. The limitations of legalization theory offers us an important starting point for inquiring into the casual function of pragmatic ethics in the ICC. The last section of the chapter theorizes about the pragmatic character of the ICC, or the evolutionary traits of the ICC's pragmatism. Here I draw on John Dewey's theory of value and public law to show how experience and intelligence will play an important role in governing the effects or consequences of its actions, or case by case selection (situation). The main limitation of Dewey's theory is that it fails to show how the pragmatic character of a global legal institution, such as the ICC, challenges or even operates outside the scope of traditional assumptions of societal order. If the ICC, in other words, is an autonomous structure of a global society, then, how does the difference between state and world society explain the unique features of its global juridical authority, or rather its dynamic role in constructing a world society?

In chapter 4, I address this question by proposing that the ICC's global juridical authority constitutes not just an institutional context for invoking ethical standards, but a novel ethical structure within the global realm. The chapter begins with a critical examination of Buzan's theoretical analysis of the transition from international to world society, arguing that the limitations of his state centric analysis underestimates the constitutive and regulative dimension of the ICC's global juridical authority. To move beyond these limitations, I draw on Weber's and Habermas's theories of societal rationalization, as well as various critical international relations theories of world society. The aim here is to show how the shift from state societal order to a world one requires a discursive analysis of the ICC's flexible juridical power.

The issue I take up in chapter 5 is whether we can conceive the ICC's autonomous juridical structure as a novel form of political cosmopolitanism. Here I draw on value pluralism and cosmopolitanism to understand the relationship between the ICC's universal morality and ethical particularism (meta-ethics). I address the following question: How does the ICC's weak cosmopolitanism provide the basis for understanding its political cosmopolitanism? A central theme of the chapter is the ICC's cosmopolitan intent, or its willingness to uphold new moral standards of legitimacy (gender crimes). I argue that the cosmopolitan intent of the ICC needs to be viewed as an important determinant of its flexible juridical power. As we shall see, the self-directed application of the ICC's rules offers an important and novel dynamic of the ICC's political cosmopolitanism, since it allows us to understand the convergence of the ICC's moral autonomy and its internal political development.

Turning to the case studies of the third part of the book, I articulate the empirical parameters of the concept of political legalism, by formulating various political strategies or hypothetical policy frameworks of the ICC. In chapter 6, for instance, I assess the parameters and strategic fronts of the U.S. opposition (or war on) to the ICC by contextualizing two of the central pragmatic assumptions raised in chapter 3. First, the ICC is an imperfect or fallible institution which cannot fully govern the effects and consequences of its own rulings on international society. Second, the evolving capacity to govern these consequences reflects the self-directed application of the ICC's rules. The aim of this chapter is to link this pragmatic character of the ICC with the political and legislative capabilities of the Assembly of States Parties (its legislative organ). It does so by formulating a policy framework of strategic accommodation designed to integrate the legislative capacity of the Assembly of States Parties with the statutory power of the ICC.

The purpose of chapter 7 is to address the more conventional strategy of mutual accommodation by examining the moral implications of Arab state (non-states parties) resistance for the ICC's evolution. One of the central issues explored is how state politics, while providing an important vehicle for narrowing the gap between domestic and international law, engenders and even intensifies conflict between Islam and the ICC. In this way, the normative aim of the chapter is to show the compatibility between the ethics of Islamic law (*Shariah*) and the ICC Statute provisions, by focusing on the conflictual role played by Islamic fundamentalist state politics. It should be stressed here that while the immunity of Israel from the ICC remains a matter of concern for Arab states, it is not the exclusive factor engendering the political conflict between Arab states and the ICC.

Nonetheless, chapter 7 will return us to the pre-formative stage of the ICC's political development, or the various disagreements between Arab states and Western states that surfaced at the Rome Conference and Preparatory Commission meetings. Here I claim that, given these differences, more mutual accommodation will be needed to resolve these and future conflicts between Islamic and international law accompanied by further cultural adaptation to the ICC Statute. It is out of this process of cultural adaptation, I argue, that the relationship between Islam and serious international crimes will evolve.

In chapter 8, I address a more salient and revealing feature of the ICC's political legalism: a cooperative arrangement between the ICC and U.N. Security Council. The key issue examined here is whether the U.N. Security Council and ICC can mutually reinforce their legitimacy as political institutions by working together to coordinate an effective response to humanitarian emergencies. Accordingly, I analyze the structural and policy implications of the report of the International Commission on Intervention and State Sovereignty (December 2001) for a cooperative relationship between the ICC and Security Council. In addition, I address the rather broad issue as to whether humanitarian-based criteria for military intervention, coupled with other proposed U.N. Security Council reforms (e.g., increased membership, global jury mechanisms), is sufficient to overcome the obstacles posed by the geopolitical interests of the U.N. Security Council, as well as fears of the high costs of intervention. I argue that the ICC needs to be seen as an important source of legitimacy of Security Council action and vice versa and that a cooperative relationship between the Security Council and ICC would involve mutual political and moral benefits for both governing institutions.

The concluding chapter focuses on the wider implications of the ICC's global juridical power and the evolution of the concept of political legalism for a new global political order. As such, the "political" of global order refers to an evolving normatized notion of decisionism at the global level: an emerging fusion of decisionism and cosmopolitanism or what I will refer to as *decisionist ethics.* I derive this normative form of ethics from Carl Schmitt's concept of political sovereignty by reinterpreting the dialectical content of his thought in terms of global (structural) change. From this vantage point, the enduring ethical challenge becomes one of linking the ICC's political evolution with the revolutionary content of a human rights enforcement regime.

Notes

1. Cesare Beccaria, *On Crimes and Punishments* (New York: On Crimes and Punishment, The Library of Liberal Arts), 65.

2. See, *e.g.*, B.S. Chimni, "A New Humanitarian Council for Humanitarian Interventions?" *The International Journal of Human Rights* 6, no. 1 (Spring 2002): 103-112; Lori Fisher Damrosch, "The Inevitability of Selective Response? Principles to Guide Urgent International Action," in Albecht Shnabel and Ramesh Thakur, eds., *Kosovo and the Challenge of Humanitarian Intervention: Selective Indignation, Collective Action, and International Citizenship* (New York: United Nations Press, 2000), 405-419. It should be noted that many have argued for an ethics of self-restraint to temper the overzealous invocation of these new rules. For a discussion of the moral and ethical implications of such restraint for U.S. foreign policy, see John A. Vasquez, "Ethics, Foreign Policy, and Liberal Wars: The Role of Restraint in Moral Decision Making," *International Studies Perspectives* 6, no. 3 (August 2005): 307-316; part II of Amitai Etzioni, *From Empire to Community* (New York: Palgrave Macmillian, 2004); Terry

Nardin, "The Moral Basis of Humanitarian Intervention," *Ethics and International Affairs* 16 (2002): 57-70.

3. Max Weber, *Economy and Society*, Vol. 2 (Berkeley: University of California Press, 1978).

4. See Christian Reus-Smit, "Introduction," in Christian Reus-Smit, ed. *The Politics of International Law* (Cambridge: Cambridge University Press, 2004).

5. For an excellent discussion of this issue, see Allison Marston Danner, "Enhancing the Legitimacy and Accountability of Prosecutorial Discretion at the International Criminal Court," *American Journal of International Law* 97 (2003): 510-552.

6. See Henry Kissinger, "The Pitfalls of Universal Jurisdiction," *Foreign Affairs* 80, no. 3 (2001): 86; For a legal perspective on the implication of the ICC juridical authority for world order, see Madeleine Morris, "Complementarity and Conflict: States, Victims, and the ICC," in S. B. Sewall and Carl Kaysen, eds. *The United States and the International Criminal Court* (Lanham: Rowman & Littlefield Publishers, Inc., 2000).

7. See, e.g., Friedrich Kratochwil, *Rules, Norms, and Decisions: On the Conditions of Practical Reasoning in International Relations and Domestic Affairs* (Cambridge: Cambridge University Press, 1989); John Ruggie, *Constructing the World Polity* (New York: Routledge, 1998).

8. See David Wippman, "The International Criminal Court," in Christian Reus-Smit, ed. *The Politics of International Law* (Cambridge: Cambridge University Press, 2004), 158.

9. Rachel Kerr, *The International Criminal Tribunal for the Former Yugoslavia* (Oxford: Oxford University Press, 2004), 6.

10. Reus-Smit, "The Politics of International Law," 25.

11. On this point, see Bruce Broomhall, *International Justice & the International Criminal Court: Between Sovereignty and the Rule of Law* (Oxford: Oxford University Press, 2003). As Broomhall argues, "taken to its logical extreme, routine enforcement of international criminal law would call for a qualitatively different approach to the deployment of coercive power, that is to the management of international peace and security; but such deployment remains a pre-eminently 'politicized' area of international law. . . . the best remaining hope for entrenchment of international criminal law as a regular feature of the international system is the development of a deeply rooted culture of accountability that leads to a convergence of perceived interests and of behavior on the part of States responsible for enforcing this law (3)."

12. M. Cherif Bassiouni, "The Universal Model: The International Criminal Court," in M. Cherif Bassiouni, ed. *Post-Conflict Justice* (Ardsley, NY: Transnational Publishers, 2003), 813-828; John Charney, "International Criminal Law and the Role of Domestic Courts," *American Journal of International Law* 95 (2001): 120-124; Mark Ellis, "The International Criminal Court and Its Implication for Domestic Law and National Capacity Building," *Florida Journal of International Law* 15, no. 2 (2002): 216-242; Roy Lee, ed. *The International Criminal Court: Issues, Negotiations, Results* (The Hague: Kluwer Publishers, 1999); Antonio Cassese, The Statute of the International Criminal Court, *European Journal of International Law* 10 (1999): 141-171; Anthony Arend, "Toward an Understanding of International Legal Rules," in Robert J. Beck, Anthony Clark Arend, and Robert D. Vander Lugt, eds. *International Rules: Approaches*

from International Law and International Relations (New York: Oxford University Press, 1996), 289-310.

13. For a detailed analysis of this process, see e.g., Thomas Risse, Stephen C. Ropp, and Kathryn Sikkink, eds. *The Power of Human Rights* (Cambridge: Cambridge University Press, 1999). See also Bassiouni, "The Universal Model: The International Criminal Court," in M. Cherif Bassiouni, ed. *Post-Conflict Justice*; and Broomhall, *International Justice & the International Criminal Court: Between Sovereignty and the Rule of Law.*

14. I distinguish between radical and critical theorists in terms of postmodernism, which rejects the foundations of truth, and critical theory that actively seeks to promote the foundational, enlightenment ideals of solidarity, equality, reason, freedom, and autonomy. Postmodernism, while concerned with the subversive qualities of resistance and freedom, rejects the pursuit of these ideals on the grounds that they constitute a teleological or linear design.

15. See, e.g., Michel Foucault, *Power/Knowledge: Selected Interviews & Other Writings 1972-1977*, Colin Gordon, ed. (New York: Random House Publishers, 1999); Jacque Derrida, *Spectres of Marx* (London: Routledge, 1994); Jenny Edkins, *Poststructuralism and International Relations: Bringing the Political Back In* (Boulder, CO: Lynne Rienner, 1999); Nigel Purvis, "Critical Legal Studies in Public International Law", *Harvard International Law Review* 32, no.1 (Winter 1991): 81-128; David Kennedy, "A New Stream of International Law Scholarship," in *International Rules: Approaches from International Law and International Relations,* Robert J. Beck, Anthony Clark Arend, and Robert D. Vander Lugt, eds. (New York: Oxford University Press, 1996), 230-252; Michael Dillon, "Criminalising Social and Political Violence Internationally," *Millennium: Journal of International Studies* 27 no. 3 (1998).

I

HISTORY AND LEGAL STRUCTURE

1

Historical Background: From the League of Nations to the Rome Conference

> Punishment is then the prerogative of the victor and the celebrations of the Vae Victis! In all its ruthlessness and cruelty—which explains how war itself (including the warlike cult of sacrifice) has produced all the forms in which punishment appears throughout history.
>
> —Nietzsche, *Genealogy of Morals*

THE MOST ESSENTIAL FEATURE of the evolution of international criminal law is the link between state sovereignty and accountability. Throughout the twentieth century, state sovereignty has provided one of the most enduring obstacles for advancing international criminal law. While the establishment of the ICC challenges the link between sovereignty and impunity, it does reveal the continuing importance of state cooperation and compliance. But whatever the obstacles that state compliance poses, the ICC can be seen as the culmination of a long struggle to ensure that the worst perpetrators of gross human rights abuses will be held to account for their crimes.

The roots of this long struggle can be traced to the Hague Conventions and later to the League of Nations, whose failure to contain national aggression would ultimately lead to the establishment of the United Nations. As this would suggest, politics has played a key role in determining the scope and application of international criminal law. And while the establishment of the ICTY may have eliminated the notion of victors' justice that characterized the political elements of the juridical authority of the Nuremberg and Tokyo military tribunals, the politics of international criminal courts has arguably become more complex and intermeshed with power and ethics.

The primary aim of this chapter is to document and analyze the role of politics in the criminalization of international violence. In doing so, we will be tracing the newly emergent tensions between a global civil order and gross human rights violations, and the changing relationship between the criminalization of international violence and state sovereignty. As we shall see, the changing relationship between state sovereignty and international criminal law is key to understanding the underlying complexity of the politics of the ICC. To show this, the first section focuses on the tensions between absolute state sovereignty and individual accountability which surfaced during the Interwar Period. The second goes on to assess the parameters of the Nuremberg and Tokyo military tribunals, which arguably reinforced the link between politics and international criminal justice. And lastly, the third section concludes with an assessment of the post-Cold War period and the events and actions that led up to the establishment of the ICC, including the PrepCom meetings and the Rome Conference.

The Interwar Period

At the turn of the twentieth century, the most powerful nation states held two important conventions to discuss the customs of war and the adoption of new rules concerning the conduct of war. The Hague Conventions for the Peaceful Settlement of International Disputes (1899) (1907) represented the first such set of international efforts to proscribe war crimes and to protect civilians during times of war. As the main precursors to the permanent international criminal court of justice, the two conventions proved instrumental in exposing the problems and prospects for establishing consensus on binding international rules of warfare.

At the 1899 conference for instance, which was attended by twenty-six nation states, negotiations focused primarily on the establishment of rules and elements of war crimes, as well as judicial mechanisms needed to adjudicate and enforce these rules and elements in *specific* cases. In discussing the terms of adjudication, state delegates focused on two central issues: whether the adjudicatory court should become a permanent mechanism, and if there should be various obligations imposed on the judges to adjudicate specific disputes.[1] Most notably, the latter issue called attention to the need for a list of disputes that would define the scope of discretionary power and settle the question of the court's competence, or rather, who would be in charge of investigating such disputes. However, after Germany voted against obligatory arbitration, the participating members of the conference elected to establish a "phantom" court, one with no obligatory adjudication.

At the 1907 Convention for the Peaceful Settlement of International Disputes, state delegates once again took up the issue of obligatory arbitration—this time with strong support from the United States, Great Britain, and Russia. However, after several meetings in which the delegations discussed various proposals for obligatory and mandatory obligations, the state delegations failed to reach agreement on the terms of obligatory arbitration.[2] Along with this failure to establish obligatory arbitration, the participating delegates were unable to decide if the international court should become permanent. Accordingly, state delegations failed to resolve one of the most critical issues discussed at the convention: whether an international court of justice should be obliged to adjudicate disputes involving state violations of the rules of war set forth in the convention.

The League of Nations would later address this issue by establishing a Permanent International Court of Justice. As the main judicial organ of the League, the Permanent Court of Justice would be in charge of settling disputes between states. Meanwhile, the League of Nations or the Allied powers (the architect of the League Covenant) drew up proposals containing various international rules of individual culpability for human rights abuses and aggression (for starting wars with no legitimate pretext). This latter judicial priority arose from the growing concern of the effects of systematic violence of WWI, including the use of mustard and chemical gas, armored tanks, and airplane bombing. All of these factors would prove instrumental in the Turkish state's ability to conduct its campaign of genocide against the Armenians, in which an estimated 1.5 million Armenians were believed to have been killed by Turkish authorities.[3] Note that the common aim of implementing both courts was to prevent states from waging aggressive wars. In this respect, it could be argued that the need for permanent arbitration provided the incipient rationale for implementing the general principle of individual criminal responsibility, and linking together individual and state responsibility for gross human rights abuses.[4]

Nonetheless, to incorporate the rules and procedures of the international criminal court into the Versailles Treaty (signed on June 28, 1919), the Allied powers appointed a Special Commission on the War and Enforcement of Penalties to discuss the responsibilities for the cause of the war.[5] The commission adopted a mandate that called for the investigation into violations of the customs of war, individual criminal accountability for members of the Central Powers, and "the constitution and procedure for a tribunal to try such offenses."[6] In the commission's report to the preliminary peace conference, the draftees concluded: 1) that the perpetrators of the violence and war should be held personally responsible for causes of the war; 2) that a high tribunal be implemented to try the enemies for offenses perpetrated during the war; and

3) that the commission adopt a long list of war crimes to try the enemies, including massacres, systematic terrorism, rape and torture of civilians, and pillage in order to prosecute the Turkish perpetrators of the Armenian genocide.[7]

These recommendations were subsequently presented to the Allied powers, who, as alluded to earlier, were responsible for drafting the final version of the Treaty of Versailles. To the surprise of many, the Allied powers elected to incorporate the list of war crimes, followed by the decision to establish a special tribunal to investigate and prosecute (only) the German Kaiser, William II of Hohenzollern. As the key institutional feature of article 227 of the Treaty, the special tribunal, with its restricted legal scope, represented a vastly scaled down version of the commission's initial recommendation to hold all relevant enemies accountable for war violations and human rights abuses.[8]

Notwithstanding the League's interest in instituting the principle of international criminal accountability, most states rejected the inclusion of crimes against the laws of humanity. In particular, the United States contended that the laws of humanity ran counter to the idea of devising rules to guard against violations of customary law. In their view, there was "no fixed universal standard of humanity;" hence no legal or substantive basis for holding state leaders accountable in an international criminal court.[9] Still, it was not U.S. objections that proved decisive in undermining the Court's existence, but the Netherlands' decision to provide safe haven to the Kaiser. Indeed, when the Dutch government refused to turn over the Kaiser to the Court, the League could do little to coerce, much less persuade the Netherlands to reverse its decision. The Netherlands' action effectively signaled the demise of a special international criminal tribunal.

The failure to establish a viable court represented one of many early setbacks for the League, including, most notably the unwillingness of the U.S. Senate to ratify the League of Nations. Despite these initial setbacks, continued interest and discussion in an international criminal court during the Interwar Period eventually led to the establishment of an Advisory Committee of Jurists, an *ad hoc* international criminal court.[10] However, when the League Council Committee's recommendations for creating a new international criminal court failed to receive the required support by the League Council, the League elected to rescind its plans for an *ad hoc* international criminal court.

The Council would later take up the issue of a new international criminal court at the Convention for the Creation of an International Court. But by this time (during the late 1930s), the League had already suffered several moral defeats, including its failure to prevent and stop the Japanese invasion of Manchuria (1932), and Mussolini's decision to invade Abyssinia (1936).[11] Both events served to weaken the credibility of the League Commission and, for that matter, its ability to enforce its key provisions for promoting international peace and security. The result was that only 13 member states signed the convention; well below the needed number to establish the Court.

In short, the failure to implement an international criminal court during the Interwar Period underscored several factors of the League's overall ineffectiveness. First, the norm of state sovereignty remained absolute, meaning that no other state nor international body could *ipso facto* violate the norm of non-intervention (without that state party's consent). More than anything, this underscored the rather restrictive nature of international customary law,[12] in which the governing doctrine of legal positivism reinforced the notion of an amoral and "mechanical" legal order.[13] As Tom Campbell notes of legal positivism: "[It is] the practice of law as the mechanical application of rules without thought to consequences for human well-being and social justice in particular cases."[14] In effect, legal positivism reinforced the separation between the "is" and "ought," or morality and the neutral application of rules. As we shall see in chapter 4, positivism remained the prevailing methodological framework for justifying legal domination, or the juridical authority of legal institutions (the application and enactment of state law).

Still, the idea that a set of rules should remain "distinguishable from common morality," limited one's understanding of the morality and ethical convictions underlying the application of state sovereignty, or, in this case, the state's responsibility to abide by the incipient proscriptive norms against war crimes.[15] Perhaps in this way, legal positivism could be seen as the source of the League's formalistic detachment from political conflict: its unwillingness to take an active moral position against the above episodes of national aggression.

Another limiting factor concerned the problematic notion of a new democratic world order. Here it could be argued that the great powers' plans (e.g., France and Britain) to spread democracy and civilize underdeveloped areas of the former Ottoman Empire, amounted to nothing more than a veiled attempt to promote their own power interests. At the very least, such determination suggested a particular type of immunity from the effects of establishing this order. In this way, the League failed to establish the universal basis of punishing the transgressors of humanitarian norms. And while it may have incorporated the democratic right to self-determination[16] into the Convenant, such a right continued to remain a highly contestable source of legitimacy, since it only addressed the democratic aspirations of formerly oppressed minority groups; and not other groups from different geographical areas.[17] Thus, the League in this sense exposed the tensions between geopolitics and the universal morality of a world democratic order. Indeed, it is important to ask as to how such morality and democracy could ever be universal, especially if the League's principles applied only to those peoples living in the developing regions of the world.

Finally, it could be argued that the great powers never actually believed that an international criminal court would prevent war. In fact, as Leyla Sadat notes, many believed that an international criminal court "would start war by encouraging states to take aggressive action, knowing that some state leaders might be reluctant to intervene to defend the interests of the victim or invading state."[18] Whether or not this disguised their deep-seeded fear of the court's jurisdictional controls over its own military personnel remains unclear.

In sum, the failure to establish an international criminal court during the Interwar years reflected the paradoxical nature of the moral pretensions of the great powers. For while the great powers wished to construct a democratic and humane world order, they also remained reluctant to endorse the authority of the international criminal tribunal. The solution, then, was to find a way of suspending this political factor, that is, of bringing together the power and politics of the great powers in such a way as to harness the enforcement of the morality of international criminal law to their political interests.

International Military Tribunals: Deferred Lessons of Victor's Justice, or Precedent?

Such a solution would eventually be realized in the establishment of two international military tribunals to investigate and prosecute the perpetrators of serious crimes committed during World War II. Both the International Military Tribunal (IMT) and the International Military Tribunal for the Far East trial (IMTFE) provided important precedents for the evolution of international criminal law. However, it was the IMT that attracted the most media attention, while the IMTFE received relatively little, if any press. This may have had as much to do with the Nuremberg Trial becoming a show trial, as it did with the disorderly manner in which the IMTFE was conducted.[19] And yet, the IMTFE, which took place in the Japanese town of Ichigay, ended up prosecuting nearly all of the 28 defendants put on trial for crimes (with the exception of Matsui and Oshima). Perhaps more remarkable was the fact that the IMTFE tried 19 members of the professional military and 9 civilians.[20]

Certainly the most important issue in this respect was whether the IMTFE would put the Japanese Emperor, Hirohito, on trial. Despite initial concern and growing pressure by U.S. officials, General Douglas MacArthur cabled a statement to U.S. authorities in Washington, arguing that Hirohito's trial would further destabilize the country.[21] MacArthur concluded that the available evidence of the Emperor's non-engagement with the wartime policy would ultimately exonerate him. This was enough to convince U.S. officials not to prosecute Hirohito, which eliminated one of the most potentially politically sensitive trials of the ICTFE. As we shall see, reducing such potential political tensions also justified many of the decisions for limiting the juridical scope of the IMT.

The Establishment of the International Military Tribunal for Nuremburg

The four Allied powers established the IMT on August 8, 1945.[22] The London Accord, which implemented the IMT, contained 33 articles which set forth the structure of the military tribunal and listed the elements of war crimes, crimes against humanity, and crimes against peace. One of the issues that surfaced at the meetings in London was whether only Nazis and Italians would be targeted for investigation and prosecution.[23] Discussion of the issue revolved around the proposal to investigate certain Soviet leaders for crimes committed on the Eastern Front during the latter phase of World War II. When the other Allied leaders continued to press the issue of Soviet culpability, however, the Soviet leaders threatened to pull their troops from the areas of the Allied occupation. Taking the threat seriously, the United States, France, and Britain soon agreed that the IMT's jurisdiction would extend only to Nazi and Italian officials.

Equally critical was the legal issue of how the Allied powers would act as a legitimate transitional sovereign power in Germany. As Quincy Wright notes, "the great powers still needed to observe the following basic principles of international justice: the fair and equal treatment of German prisoners or perpetrators, fair retribution, good faith."[24] It was in this respect, however, that the newly implemented United Nations Charter, which established the conditions for the suspension of state consent or the norm of non-intervention, provided an important link between the tribunal and universal jurisdiction.[25] In effect, the Allied powers could enact the Charter as a "legislative act" to investigate and prosecute certain individuals "with whatever tangible evidence that would show that they violated the principle of the law of nations."[26]

The legitimacy of the U.N. thus offered a unique opportunity to test and even push the (validity of) boundaries of international criminal law. At the very least, this seemed to encourage Robert Jackson, the chief IMT Prosecutor, to address the difficult issue regarding the inviolability of state sovereignty and the concomitant need to assess the relationship between the universality of heinous crimes and state *irresponsibility*.[27] Jackson, for instance, writes that

> inherently criminal acts cannot be defended by showing that those who committed them were engaged in a war, when war itself is illegal. The very minimum legal consequences of the treaties making aggressive wars illegal is to strip those who incite or wage them of every defense the law ever gave, and to leave war makers subject to judgement by the usually accepted principle of the law of crime . . . Only sanctions which reach individuals can peacefully and effectively be enforced. Hence the principle of the criminality of aggressive war is implemented by the charter with the principle of personal responsibility. Of course, the idea that a state any more than a corporate corporation commits crime is a fiction.[28]

As this passage suggests, aggression could, under certain circumstances, constitute an individual crime. Since the leaders of the state drew up the policies and made the decisions that resulted in acts of aggression, it meant that responsibility could be directly traced back to the policies devised by these rulers or state commanders.

This, however, raised an even more pressing issue of how to identify and adopt the definition and elements of crimes consistent with international legal principles. Initially, this proved a major sticking point. For it required that the new element of the crime of aggression and systematic violence committed by the German government against its own peoples be reconciled with the valid application of principles of *ex post facto* and *nullem crimen sine lege*, both of which posit that a court cannot exercise jurisdiction over crimes that did not exist at the time that they were committed. Thus, while aggression existed as a violation of international law, the Nazi acts of aggression renewed the debate over whether to adopt a list of crimes against humanity, similar to those proposed by the special commission at the Paris Peace Accords.[29] In this respect, as Richard Overy writes: "the framing of charges against the Nazis required international law to be written backwards."[30]

In the end, IMT officials agreed that the Nazi atrocities were not only a part of the campaign to launch an aggressive war, but also symptomatic of the wanton and inhumane acts committed by former state leaders and officials against civilians. The challenge, then, was to figure out a way of inter-linking the plans for aggression with these other heinous crimes.

Conspiracy and the Elements of Crimes

The IMT Prosecutor's solution to this problem was to treat the various crimes committed by the Nazis as a *master plan* of conspiracy to wage an aggressive war, one that could be traced back to January 30, 1933.[31] The advantage of this legal strategy was that it allowed the IMT prosecutor to eliminate a key problem of the prosecution: namely, the claim by defendants that they were taking commands by a higher authority over which they had no control.[32] Under the master plan, the prosecutor could establish guilt without having to define and specify the elements of these crimes. The plan, as Overy notes, "entirely removed the need to define new categories of crimes for other policies pursued by the regime, since the charge of conspiracy only required documented evidence to substantiate involvement and knowledge of those being prosecuted."[33] As such, the conspiracy charge constituted the common and overarching (purposive) element of the four separate categories of crimes, including a common conspiracy to wage aggressive war, crimes against peace, war crimes, and crimes against humanity.[34]

It should be noted that the conspiracy element also eliminated the possibility that military officials could claim that they were misled by the single perpetrator of the crimes, most notably Adolf Hitler himself. In this respect, as George Finch explains, the conspiracy charge eliminated a potentially important *reductio ad absurdum*. For had these Nazi officials been permitted to make these claims, accountability for their criminal acts would have also been "buried with Hitler himself."[35] Given this legal strategy, the Tribunal was able to codify several (albeit general) elements of a crime and to establish the procedures for investigating and prosecuting these crimes. Most important, it represented an event in which politicians, legal scholars, practitioners, and policymakers sought to link state irresponsibility with the duty to try those accused of heinous crimes in an international criminal court. As Robert Woetzel states: "the principles laid down by such a tribunal even if they are not recognized as generally valid, can be cited as precedents by later courts and thus prove to be generally valid after continued practice."[36] The result was that Nuremburg moved beyond the formal limitations imposed by absolute state sovereignty by providing exceptions to the sovereign rule of law, and by helping to define the universality of these crimes.

Still, the IMT left open the question as to whether the international community would elect to establish a permanent international criminal court that would target individual perpetrators regardless of nationality. As we saw, the decision to give in to the Soviet threat exposed the problematic link between power and politics. The IMT also revealed the arbitrary nature of victors' justice: the (political) need to teach a lesson to the Nazis or any other future aggressors. While this does not diminish the legal fact that the Nazis had committed gross human rights violations, it does suggest that Western political interests and power would continue to shape the environment, out of which international criminal law would evolve.

The Cold War: Good Intentions and Failed Objectives

The success of the IMT and IMTFE inspired policymakers to adopt new provisions of human rights and to establish new rules and laws prohibiting genocide and war crimes. Certainly, the two most notable legal documents in this respect were the Universal Declaration of Human Rights (UDHR), which codified several key political, civil and social rights into international law; and the Convention on Genocide, which defined and enumerated the acts of the crime of genocide. Both documents provided arguably important momentum for the U.N. General Assembly's (GA) plans to establish a permanent international criminal court.[37] A key feature of their plans was the International Law Commission's (ILC) study of the feasibility and desirability of establishing an international criminal court. Here the GA considered having the court become part of the criminal chamber of the International Criminal Court of Justice (ICJ) (formerly the Permanent International Court of Justice), so that it could administer the subject matter of the recently completed Draft of the Code of Crimes Against Peace and Security of Mankind (1947).

It did not take long for the Commission to issue its first resolution concerning the court; it voted 8-1 in favor of the desirability of the draft code.[38] The majority vote, it could be said, reflected the collective determination to challenge the procedural justice of the international system of sovereign states. Clearly, the spectacle of the Holocaust was still fresh in the minds of policymakers. Indeed, it had seemed to convince many that the implementation of the international principle of criminal accountability via the proscriptive norm against genocide, was not just a political requirement, but a supreme moral necessity.

Given this determination, the GA proceeded to form the Committee on the International Criminal Jurisdiction, which would be in charge of drafting a statute for an international criminal court. One of its key recommendations was that the court be established as a multilateral treaty.[39] At its summer meeting in 1953, the Committee elected to add some minor revisions to the 1951 draft. In doing so, however, it effectively laid the basis for a new international criminal court. But before the final 1953 Committee report could be completed, the GA suspended the final vote on the adoption of the draft, declaring that it [the GA] would need to adopt a resolution on the definition of the crime of aggression before further studies could be resumed.

The decision proved most unfortunate, since it nullified any short-term plans for an international criminal court. An underlying reason for this was the heightening tensions between the United States and the Soviet Union. Indeed, the politics of the Cold War essentially meant that both the Soviet Union and the United States had tacitly declared each other as hostile enemies or potential aggressors. This, in turn, reflected the disempowerment or virtual irrelevance of the U.N as the principal player for promoting international peace and security. Nevertheless, it would take the General Assembly nearly 30 years to adopt resolution 3314 on the crime of aggression. And while the resolution specified the general acts of aggression, it failed to resolve the more pressing issue of how the U.N. Security Council would determine when an act of aggression had occurred. As we shall see in chapters 6 and 7, this would provide the basis for one of the U.S. key objections to the ICC Statute, and the political conflict between Arab and Western states at the Rome Conference.

By the late 1980s, the General Assembly would request the ILC to complete the Draft Code of Crimes. Paradoxically, the General Assembly's decision to request the ILC to address the feasibility of an international criminal court arose from the growing concern within the GA regarding the international crime of drug trafficking. Such a concern was highlighted by a resolution proposed by Trinidad and Tobago in the Assembly in 1989, which called on the ILC to study an international enforcement mechanism to combat illicit trafficking in narcotic drugs. Nonetheless, the resolution signaled a new willingness to hold accountable perpetrators of gross human rights violations, which like drug trafficking, amounted to crimes that were universally condemned by all members of the international community.[40]

The Post-Cold War: Institutionalizing Individual Criminal Accountability

A New Sense of Urgency

In 1991, therefore, the General Assembly created a working group to study the question of establishing a permanent court with international criminal jurisdiction,[41] declaring that the group "should seek a mandate to draft a statute that would be in principle distinct from the draft Code of Crimes Against Peace and Security of Mankind."[42] The commission discussed various issues of the ICC's structure, including the court's permanent status as a full-time standing court and whether the jurisdiction of the ICC would be based on state consent, as opposed to compulsory jurisdiction. Having recognized the special importance of an independent international court, the commission, in its 1993 final report, agreed that the Court's jurisdiction would not be compulsory, and that an official prosecutor would be needed to investigate and prosecute perpetrators of the core crimes of genocide, crimes against humanity, and war crimes (and aggression).

In the following year, the commission completed a draft statute, containing 60 articles that defined the structure of the Court, and enumerated the substantive elements of crimes.[43] The Commission then submitted the draft statute to the General Assembly, which proceeded to schedule Preparatory Committees to clarify the Statute in preparation for a future conference that would establish the Court. In the meantime, the U.N. Security Council would become busy with its own plans for implementing and enforcing the principle of international criminal accountability.

Ad Hoc International Criminal Courts: Precedent and Lessons

As is well-known, the Security Council decided to invoke its Chapter VII powers of the U.N. Charter to establish the International Criminal Tribunal for the Former Yugoslavia (ICTY). What was the primary goal of the ICTY? Some have argued that it was about the larger objective of deterring future perpetrators, while others have contended that it provided an alternative security option to sending troops into Yugoslavia. Both of course are quite plausible; however, if there was one common objective, it was to take action to redress or stop the ethnic conflict and inter-communal violence that had occurred in the Balkan region. Given the increasing number of confirmed eyewitness reports of unlawful detentions and mass killings in Bosnia-Herzegovina, many leaders and policymakers had become convinced that the lack of international (and domestic) accountability had produced a culture of impunity. This provided the rationale for the unprecedented decision by the U.N. Security Council to establish the ICTY pursuant to Chapter VII of the Charter in 1993 (and International Criminal Tribunal for Rwanda [ICTR] in 1994). To the extent that this option would save lives and reduce military costs, it would also provide a cost-effective alternative to military intervention, not to mention a novel invocation of the Security Council's Chapter VII powers. Beyond this, the ICTY would also offer an efficient and effective ad hoc juridical framework for investigating and prosecuting the perpetrators of crimes that took place during the Yugoslavia war (1991–1995) and within the 1991 borders of the former Yugoslavia.

The ICTY Statute, which sets forth the Office of the Prosecutor, Judiciary (a chamber of judges and appeals chamber), and Registry (see Article 11 of the ICTY Statute), contains 34 articles, four of which enumerate the categories of crimes: grave breaches of the 1949 Geneva Conventions, violations of the laws and customs of war, crimes against humanity, and genocide. Accordingly, it empowers the Prosecutor to investigate the core crimes of genocide, crimes against humanity, and war crimes, and it allows the Prosecutor to conduct its judicial affairs independently of the Security Council and to focus on the individualization of guilt of the perpetrators.[44] The aim of the individualization of guilt, for instance, is to distinguish the guilt of individuals from their communities, thereby limiting the perception of collective guilt and arguably facilitating reconciliation. Whether or not the ICTY has accomplished this task of reconciliation remains a open-ended issue, since many Serbs continue to see the ICTY as biased against the Serbs.

Still, for many, the politics of the ICTY represents the pursuit of policies that are designed to reinforce the perception of its fair and impartial application of the rules of procedure for investigating and prosecuting genocide, crimes against humanity, and war crimes.[45] From this perspective, the ICTY provides a crucial historical turn in international criminal justice since it eliminates the politics of victors' justice, while also constituting an arguably important deterrent effect, which has arguably withered the culture of impunity in the region.[46]

But it is also true that the ICTY Prosecutor's discretionary power has generated political tensions between states and the ICTY. Here the Serbs, as already mentioned, have contended that the ICTY has targeted a disproportionate number of Serbs, the most important being Slobodan Milosevic.[47] Notwithstanding the validity of these claims, the development and application of the ICTY's authority underscores several problems and limitations of *ad hoc* international criminal courts.

First, international criminal tribunals have become costly and arguably inefficient. The ICTR, for instance, continues to lack the resources to prosecute many of the perpetrators of genocide. As such, the judiciary continues to face the daunting task of trying several thousands of offenders of gross human rights atrocities with limited financial resources. By contrast, as of April 2005, the ICTY's total operating budget had reached nearly $650 million. Certainly, one of the ways that the ICTY, and the ICC, for that matter, can reduce such costs is to encourage more plea bargains.[48] On the other hand, as the Jean Kambanda case illustrates, the charges of genocide may well outweigh any concessions for pleading guilty.[49] What is more, because international criminal tribunals operate on a temporary and/or indefinite time basis, they must operate efficiently within the given budgetary and time constraints.

Second, the regional focus of the jurisdiction of international criminal tribunals means that *ad hoc* international criminal courts can only target crimes that occur within a designated or defined territory or region. The main consequence of this is that international criminal tribunals may become ensnared in the heated tensions between and among ethnic groups, as the Serbian accusations of bias seem to indicate. In the case of the Kosovo War, for instance, the ICTY's indictment of Milosevic, during the height of the war (1999), raised concern that the ICTY had become allied with NATO's political objectives.[50] The growing international legal pressure to investigate the atrocities committed by NATO forced Louis Arbour to establish a special commission to investigate the accusations that NATO military personnel had committed war crimes. Although the commission concluded that there was no substantial evidence to show that NATO commanders had committed gross human rights violations, it was evident that the ICTY, if it was to eliminate the political overtones of bias, would need to take a difficult, albeit balanced approach to investigating and prosecuting the perpetrators of violence. In short, it would need to spend far more time and money to investigate the main perpetrators, regardless of nationality. Only recently has it begun to seriously pursue this objective, as highlighted by its recent indictment of the leader of the Kosovar Liberation Front.

Lastly, and perhaps most important, *ad hoc* international criminal courts reveal the contradictions of state sovereignty. The idea here is that the permanent members of the Security Council would never have consented to allowing the investigation of their own generals; and that the permanant members, in this case, have used the ICTY to promote their own geopolitical interests. From this, it follows that the permanent member states will use their own veto power to block the prosecution of any of its own military personnel stationed in the area. It is precisely this factor, of course, that weakens the legitimacy of sovereignty, by allowing the permanent members of the Council to trump the territorial integrity of state sovereignty when their own sovereign interests are threatened.[51] Given this factor, the ICC provides an arguably more autonomous, less entrenched legal institution, insofar as it is rooted in treaty law or state consent.

The Rome Conference

Turning to the formal establishment of the ICC, there were several key events that marked the continuing political resolve to implement the ICC. Indeed, by 1996, plans were already well underway to establish a permanent international criminal court. One of the underlying objectives of the ILC's final draft Statute of the ICC was to ensure that the Court's jurisdiction would not preempt state sovereignty. As already suggested, the ILC commission anticipated that few states would agree to sign a treaty in which their own state sovereignty would be subordinated to the jurisdiction of the ICC. The commission also believed that state consent would remain a volatile issue, notably because states parties would object to the Court's jurisdiction over their own nationals.

In the end, policymakers agreed that the international criminal court would be established by international treaty law. Such an option was preferred to other options including amending the U.N. Charter—which many believed would take too long to implement—and a U.N. Security Council resolution (through Chapter VII powers), which some argued would present too many conflicts of interests, including the Security Council's permanent control over the judiciary process. As a result, the Court's jurisdiction would have to be judiciously balanced against state sovereignty, in which it was determined that the Court's jurisdiction would have to remain compatible with the state's ability and willingness to try the worst perpetrators of gross human rights violations. The solution, then, was to ensure that states would assume *prima facie* jurisdiction over crimes committed within their territorial boundaries, but that the ICC could intervene when it deemed that national courts remained unable and/or unwilling to try such offenders.

But the 1995 ILC Draft Statute, while providing the framework principles and many rules of procedure and evidence and elements, also left many technical and social issues unresolved. For instance, there was the question of the edification of the statute. The ILC final draft statute still needed to be clarified in a way that was not only presentable to the state delegations of the upcoming conference, but also agreeable in nature.[52] Accordingly, the General Assembly called for the creation of a Preparatory Committee to resolve these issues with the aim of holding a conference that would hopefully establish an international criminal court. In the ensuing three years, the committees met twice in 1995 and 1996, and once in 1997. Among their main accomplishments were the reduction in the number of brackets of the statute (which included options) and a widely consolidated text. By the end of 1997, the General Assembly announced that the United Nations Diplomatic Conference of Plenipotentiaries on the Establishment of an International Criminal Court would take place during the summer of 1998, in Rome, Italy.

The Rome Conference brought together 168 state delegations and several delegates from international organizations, including international bodies and non-governmental organizations. It highlighted the quasi-legislative process of diplomacy, or the ways and means by which state delegations compromised and debated over the validity of new elements of crimes. The legislative format of the conference prompted some delegates to view the conference as more of a parliamentary body of decision-making than an international conference of delegates.[53]

While a detailed discussion of the major issues of the conference remains beyond the scope of this chapter, it is important to note a few of the key issues that divided many of the state delegations, including the jurisdiction of the Prosecutor, the Prosecutor's *proprio motu* powers (the right to initiate an investigation and prosecution), and the role of the Security Council.[54] While many state delegations, including the United States, Russia, and China and many Middle Eastern countries strongly opposed the Prosecutor's *proprio motu* powers on the grounds that it would violate international law, it was agreed, in the end, that an independent prosecutor was needed as a condition for maintaining and promoting the independence of the ICC *vis-à-vis* the Security Council.

The issue of the role of the Security Council also tended to divide developing and developed countries. In particular, many developing state delegations believed that any integral role of Security Council's powers would politicize the court, since it would allow the permanent members to use their veto to block the investigation and prosecution of certain perpetrators, namely, their own. Despite concerns of Security Council interference in the Court, state delegates agreed to adopt a provision that would allow the Security Council to refer situations to the Court and to defer cases on a 12-month renewable basis (with a Security Council resolution). In sum, the Rome Conference provided a historic opportunity for not just developed states, but also developing states to actively shape international criminal law. In the end, 128 participating state delegations voted to adopt the final draft, while seven dissented. Yet, it would be left up to the Preparatory Commission to finalize a complete list of elements of crimes and the rules of procedures and evidence.[55]

Here, it should be noted that because of the short duration of the Rome Conference, there simply was not enough time to adopt all the necessary procedures and rules to render the Court fully operable. Thus, it was agreed that a fully functioning court would require a draft text on the complete list of the rules of procedure and evidence which, along with the elements of crimes, would be drawn up by June 30, 2000. The commission also agreed that the draft report on the elements of crimes would be turned over to the Assembly of States Parties, the legislative body of the ICC.

Clearly, the task of adopting a draft statute on the elements of crimes presented the most formidable challenge for the PrepCom. This was because many of the elements in the Draft Statute were new to international criminal law, including, as mentioned earlier, crimes against humanity, most notably, forced pregnancy (see article 7(2)(f)). Moreover, conflicts between international and national criminal law forced the commission to address the most efficient means possible to reconcile the gap between these two systems. Such a gap encompassed a wide range of issues, including "the investigation and prosecution of crimes, the pretrial regime, disclosure of evidence, the fundamental notions of justice, fair trial, and the rights of the accused."[56] Perhaps more importantly, the gap revealed the extent to which states feared that adding any new elements would change the provisions of the Statute.

In short, the Preparatory Commission provided the much needed debate for resolving some of the issues raised at the Rome Conference. Yet, when the Court entered into force, many political tensions were left unresolved, including the role of the Security Council. Addressing these tensions, as we shall see in the next chapter, will require a flexible framework for understanding the political effects of the Prosecutor's discretionary power.

Conclusion

As we saw in this chapter, the establishment of the ICC followed a long history of failed attempts to institutionalize the principle of international criminal accountability. By documenting and analyzing the emergence of the ICC, I sought to link the politics of state sovereignty with the (decisions) formal implementation of the ICC. In the following chapter, I will critically examine some of the legal parameters of the ICC and attempt to link the ICC's procedural framework with its political character. In doing so, I will show how the evolution of the ICC will turn on its internal politicization. This holds many vital policy and political implications for the evolution of the criminalization of international violence, not the least of which is whether the ICC can fully overcome the political limitations of victors' justice.

Notes

1. David D. Caron, "War and International Adjudication: Reflections on the 1899 Peace Conference," *American Journal of International Law* 94, no. 4 (2002): 19–20.
2. Caron, "War and International Adjudication," 21.
3. For a detailed account of the Armenian genocide, see Peter Balakian, *The Burning Tigris: The Armenian Genocide and America's Response* (New York: Harper Collins Publishers, 2003).
4. Nadya Leila Sadat, "The Evolution of the ICC: From the Hague to Rome and Back Again," in Sarah B. Sewall and Carl Kaysen, eds. *The United States and the International Criminal Court* (Lanham, MD: Rowman and Littlefield Publishers, 2000), 42.
5. See the Report presented to the Preliminary Peace Conference by the Commission on the Responsibility of the Authors of the War and on Enforcement of Penalties, 1919.
6. M. Cherif Bassiouni, "World War I: The War to End All Wars and the Birth of a Handicapped International Criminal Justice System," *Denver Journal of International Law and Policy* 30 (2002): 251–52.
7. Bassiouni, "World War I," 251–52. It should be noted here that the "laws of humanity" appears in the preamble of the 1907 Hague Convention. Crimes against the "Laws of Humanity" would ultimately become known as crimes against humanity.
8. Article 227 reads: "A special tribunal will be constituted to try the accused, thereby assuring him the guarantees essential to the right of defense. It will be composed of five judges appointed by each of the following Powers: namely, the United States of America, Great Britain, France, Italy and Japan."
9. M. Cherif Bassiouni, "World War I: The War to End All Wars and the Birth of a Handicapped International Criminal Justice System," 264.

10. Lela Nadya Sadat, *The International Criminal Court and the Transformation of International Law: Justice for the New Millenium* (Ardsley, NY: Transnational Publishers, 2002), 24.

11. For a discussion of these events surrounding the League of Nations minority rights program, see Steven C. Roach, *Cultural Autonomy, Minority Rights, and Globalization* (Burlington, VT; Aldershot, Hampshire, England: Ashgate Publishing Inc., 2005). It should be noted here that Mussolini's actions amounted to a clear-cut violation of Articles 12, 14, and 15, which stipulated that all members be required to consult the Council and court before declaring or committing war against another nation. Insisting that their invasion was justified under Article 22 of the covenant, which stipulated that the "advanced nations were responsible for advancing the ideals of freedom," the Italian government demanded that the League recognize the special importance of their mission.

12. International customary law can be defined as "an informal, unwritten body of rules that derives the practice of states together with *opinio juris*—a belief, on the part of the governments, that the practice is required by law or is at least of relevance to its ongoing evolution." See Michael Byers and Simon Chesterman, "Changing the rules about rules? Unilateral humanitarian intervention and the future of international law," in J.L. Holzgrefe and Robert Keohane, eds. *Humanitarian Intervention: Ethical, Legal, and Political Dilemmas* (Cambridge: Cambridge University Press, 2003), 179.

13. Tom Campbell, *Prescriptive Legal Positivism: Law, Rights and Democracy* (New York: UCL Press, 2004), 1 and 4. Campbell distinguishes legal positivism from prescriptive legal positivism, referring to legal positivism in the following terms: "the benefits of the rule of law require that the laws in question are existing general rules . . . that are sufficiently clear and specific to enable members of society to agree whether or not the rules have been followed or breached, even when they disagree about the desirability of the rules in question."

14. Campbell, *Prescriptive Legal Positivism*, 1 and 4.

15. Terry Nardin, "International Pluralism and the Rule of Law," in Ken Booth, Tim Dunne, and Michael Cox, eds. *How Might We Live?* (Cambridge: Cambridge University Press, 2001), 103.

16. The Covenant did recognize the right of self-determination in the context of development and the moral goal of civilizing undeveloped areas of the world, including the territories of the former Ottoman Empire, Asia and Africa. As Article 22 (2, 3, 4) of the Covenant declares: "Certain communities formerly belonging to the Turkish Empire have reached a stage of development where their existence as independent nations can be provisionally recognized subject to the rendering of administrative advice and assistance . . ."

17. See Article 22(1) of the League Covenant, which reads: "To those colonies and territories, which as a consequence of the late war have ceased to be under the sovereignty of the States which formerly governed them, and which are inhabited by peoples not yet able to stand by themselves under the strenuous conditions of the modern world, there should be applied the principle that the well-being and development of such peoples form a sacred trust of civilization, and that securities for the performance of this trust should be embodied in this covenant."

18. Sadat, *The International Criminal Court: The Transformation of International Law*, 25.

19. Arnold C. Brackman, *The Other Nuremberg: The Untold Story of the Tokyo War Crimes Trials* (New York: Morrow, 1987).

20. Brackman, *The Other Nuremberg: The Untold Story of the Tokyo War Crimes*, 61.

21. Brackman, *The Other Nuremberg: The Untold Story of the Tokyo War Crimes*, 61.

22. See The Agreement for the Prosecution and Punishment of Major War Criminals of the European Axis, Charter of the International Military Tribunal, August 8, 1945, art. 1, 8 U.N.T.S.

23. The issue was largely prompted by the eyewitness reports of Soviet brutality against Nazi soldiers toward the end of the war. It should be noted that many Soviet generals ruthlessly ordered the execution of German soldiers and suspected civilians during and just after the war.

24. Quincy Wright, "The Law of the Nuremberg Trial," *American Journal of International Law* 41, no. 1 (January 1947): 52.

25. Under the U.N. Charter, state consent was no longer required to validate the application and binding nature of international legal provisions and procedures. Since the U.N. Charter was not a multilateral treaty, but an organizational body vested with the powers to make and enforce international law, its resolutions (Security Council) were considered binding on all states involved.

26. See Robert K. Woetzel, *The Nuremburg Trials in International Law* (New York: Stevens & Sons Limited, 1992), 91–92.

27. Concerning the need to confront this difficult challenge posed by absolute state sovereignty, George Finch writes: "the circumstances that such (aggressive acts) may have been permitted or required by Nazi law either within Germany or in the countries invaded by the enemy is no bar to punishment of them by military authorities of the Allies now in control of the government of Germany. They (allies) are not bound to respect the laws of the defeated enemy which are repugnant to their principle of law, justice, and individual rights." George A. Finch, "The Nuremburg Trial and International Law," *American Journal of International Law* 41, no. 1 (January 1947): 24.

28. Quincy Wright, "The Law of the Nuremberg Trial," *American Journal of International Law* 41, no. 1 (January 1947): 64.

29. See, e.g., the Hague Conventions (1907), Geneva convention (1925), Kellog-Briand Pact (1928), and the Paris Pact (1939).

30. Richard Overy, "The Nuremberg Trials: International Law in the Making," in Phillipe Sands, ed. *From Nuremberg to the Hague* (Cambridge: Cambridge University Press, 2000), 17.

31. Overy, "The Nuremberg Trials," 16.

32. Here it should be noted that the final list of 22 perpetrators, included some, though not all, of the most notorious Nazi criminals, including Goering. Of these 22, 14 received the death penalty, seven received life sentences, and five, including Albert Speer, received reduced sentences.

33. Overy, "The Nuremberg Trials," 16. As article 6(a) states: "Leaders, organizers instigators and accomplices participating in the formulation or execution of a com-

mon plan or conspiracy to commit any of the foregoing crimes are responsible for all acts performed by any persons in execution of such plan."

34. Article 6 of the IMT Charter stipulates the rationale and general elements of each of these crimes. "(a) Crimes against peace: namely, planning, preparation , initiation or waging of a war of aggression, or a war in violation of international treaties, agreements or assurances, or participation in a common plan or conspiracy for the accomplishment of any of the foregoing...

(b) War Crimes: namely, violations of the laws or customs of war. Such violations shall include, but not be limited to, murder, ill-treatment or deportation to slave labour or for any other purpose of civilian population of or in occupied territory, murder or ill-treatment of prisoners of war or persons on the seas, killing of hostages, plunder of public or private property, wanton destruction of towns and or villages or devastation not justified by military necessity;

(c) Crimes against Humanity: namely, murder, extermination, enslavement, deportation and other inhumane acts committed against any civilian population, before or during war, or persecutions on political, racial or religious grounds in execution of or in connection with any crimes within the jurisdiction of the Tribunal, whether or not in violation of the domestic law of the country where perpetrated." See Charter of the International Military Tribunal, in Agreement for the prosecution and punishment of the major war criminals of the European Axis, August 8, 1945, 82 UNTS 279.

35. George A. Finch, "The Nuremberg Trial and International Law," *American Journal of International Law* 41, no. 1 (January 1947): 24.

36. Woetzel, *The Nuremberg Trials in International Law*, 92.

37. Universal Declaration of Human Rights adopted and proclaimed by United Nations General Assembly Resolution 217A(III) of 10 December 1948. United Nations General Assembly Official Records, 3rd Session, A/RES/3/217 (1948); United Nations Convention on the Prevention and Punishment of the Crime of Genocide adopted and opened for signature by General Assembly Resolution 260A (III) of 9 December 1948, United Nations General Assembly Official Records, 3rd Session, 78 U.N.T.S. 277. For a comprehensive discussion of the structure of the Convention and its primary goals, see William Schabas, *Genocide in International Law* (Cambridge: Cambridge University Press, 2000).

38. See *Report of the International Law Commission to the General Assembly*, U.N. GAOR, Supp. No. 10, U.N. Doc. A/1316 (1950).

39. Sadat, *The International Criminal Court: The Transformation of International Law*, 34–35.

40. Roy Lee, ed. *The International Criminal Court: The Making of the Rome Statute* (The Hague: Kluwer Law International, 1999), 5.

41. See *Report of the International Law Commission Covering the Work of its Forty-Third Session*, 29 April–19 July 1991, 46 U.N. GAOR, Supp. No. 10, U.N. Doc. No. A/46/10 (1991).

42. Quoted in James Crawford, "The ILC's Draft Statute for an International Criminal Tribunal," *American Journal of International Law* 88 (1994) (2001): 141.

43. See *Report of the International Law Commission on the Work of its Forty-Sixth Session*, U.N. GAOR, 49th Sess., Supp. No. 10, U.N. Doc. A/49/10 (1994).

44. Ivan Simonovic, "The Role of the ICTY in the Development of International Criminal Adjudication," *Fordham International Law Journal* 23 (1999): 440–459.

45. See, e.g., Rachel Kerr, *The International Criminal Tribunal for the Former Yugoslavia* (Oxford: Oxford University Press, 2004), 6–8.

46. For a discussion of culture of impunity, see Payam Akhaven, "Beyond Impunity: Can International Criminal Justice Prevent Future Atrocities," *American Journal of International Law* 95 (2001): 7–31.

47. It should be noted that it is precisely this claim of bias that has allowed Milosevic to conduct a long drawn-out trial in the Hague, where he stands accused of committing genocide, crimes against humanity, and war crimes.

48. See *Prosecutor v. Plavsic.* Case No. IT-00-39&40/I-S. Sentencing Judgment. www.un.org/icty/ind-e.htm.

49. See the Press Release, AFR/95L/2898. Available at http://www.un.org/News/Press/docs/1998/19980904.12898.html.

50. Michael Mandel, "Politics and Human Rights in International Criminal Law: Our Case Against NATO and the Lessons to be Learned from it," *Fordham International Law Journal* 25 (2001): 95–115.

51. Anne Bodley, "Weakening the Principle of Sovereignty in International Criminal Law: The International Criminal Tribunal for the Former Yugoslavia," *International Law and Politics* 31 (2001): 417–471.

52. Lee, *The International Criminal Court: The Making of the Rome Statute,* 5.

53. John Washburn, "The Negotiation of the Rome Statute for the International Criminal Court and International Lawmaking in the 21st Century," *Pace International Law Review* 11 (1999): 366.

54. *United Nations Diplomatic Conference of Plenipotentiaries on the Establishment of an International Criminal Court,* Rome, 15 June–17 July 1998. Volume II (New York: United Nations Publications, 1998).

55. See *Final Act of the United Nations Diplomatic Conference of Plenipotentiaries on the Establishment of an International Criminal Court,* U.N. Doc. A/CONF.183/10 (July 17, 1998).

56. Nico Kirsch and Ved Oosterveld, "Legality, Morality and the Dilemma of Humanitarian Intervention after Kosovo," *European Journal of International Law* 13, no. 1 (2002): 574.

2
Legal Principles and Political Issues

> As a general rule, enactment of statutes was either entirely norm existent, or where it existed, the absence of any distinction between finding and making law usually prevented the emergence of any idea of the legislative act as a general rule to be "applied by the judge." The doom simply carried the authority of precedent.
>
> —Max Weber, *Economy and Society, Vol. 2*

THIS CHAPTER OFFERS a detailed analysis of the formal application of the ICC's rules of procedure and the structural principles and operations of the ICC, including its internal mechanisms of accountability. The central aim is to lay the legal groundwork for our discussion of the ICC in parts II and III, where I will examine the theoretical and empirical parameters of political legalism. One of the legal issues I address in this chapter is whether the ICC's automatic jurisdiction via the territoriality principle provides a constructive alternative to universal (forms of) jurisdiction. I argue that the complementarity principle and automatic jurisdiction offer an important option to universal jurisdiction, since it resolves the effects arising from the political tensions between universal jurisdiction and state sovereignty.

To support my argument, I first examine the political issues surrounding the application of the complementarity principle and how the retributive justice of the ICC (punishment) will complement restorative forms of justice, or truth commissions. Applying the complementarity principle raises several legal and political concerns, notably the stratification of juridical power and the difficulty of proving the unwillingness of states to investigate and prosecute. Indeed, the complementarity principle, while raising many political concerns, also redresses some of the deeper underlying political issues surrounding the exercise of universal jurisdiction (e.g., the Belgian Statute). In the last section, I assess the structural features of the ICC's procedural legitimacy, including the guidelines for exercising discretionary power, the internal accountability mechanisms of the ICC, and the importance of narrowing the gap between domestic and international law.

Complementarity and Its Limits

In the previous chapter, I discussed the International Law Commission's (ILC) decision to incorporate the complementarity principle in the preamble of its final draft statute. This decision, as we saw, was intended to provide a plausible compromise between national sovereignty and the Court's jurisdiction; for it was agreed that not all states would willingly transfer their sovereignty to the ICC unless assurances were made that the Court would not exercise jurisdiction over crimes committed within their territorial borders.[1] The complementarity principle, it will be recalled, allows nation states *prima facie* to investigate and prosecute the core crimes of the ICC Statute, which have been committed within their territorial borders. When national courts prove unwilling or unable to investigate or prosecute the defendant, the ICC can require the national government to surrender the targeted perpetrator to the ICC in the Hague. Thus, while states retain the right to investigate and prosecute, the ICC's jurisdictional authority can trump [their] state sovereignty when the ICC Prosecutor determines that there is adequate evidence indicating the state's unwillingness to investigate or prosecute in a timely manner.

In many ways, then, the complementarity principle serves as the (functional) heart and soul of the ICC's juridical structure. Procedurally, the scope of the complementarity principle ranges from judicial assistance to the ICC's request of surrender. In particular, Article 17(2) contains the conditions and rules of procedure concerning the Court's powers. It stipulates, *inter alia*, that the ICC can intervene when national courts 1) shield the defendant from investigation and prosecution; 2) there is an undue delay in initiating an investigation and prosecution; and 3) there exists a biasness against the defendant.[2] The purpose of these rules is to "create an incentive for states, and to encourage them to develop and then apply their national criminal justice systems as a way of avoiding the exercise of jurisdiction by the ICC."[3]

But it is also true that political realities will likely complicate the application of such rules. For instance, the six-month period may provide nationalist groups the time necessary to apply additional pressure on the ICC not to intervene. This may also coincide with worsening political conditions, in which the ICC's request of surrender and/or issuance of an international arrest warrant may engender further political instability in the region. In both cases, the Prosecutor may need to defer to national courts for political reasons. Not only will this expose the ICC's reliance on state cooperation, but it may also engender perception of the Court's unwillingness to uphold the rule of law on the national and global levels.

Many legal scholars have been quick to assert that the complementarity principle, while important to advancing substantive criminal law, subjects the Court to the "whims of state cooperation."[4] Some have even suggested that it will stratify the ICC's jurisdiction by creating a rigid, juridical "legal order."[5] Whether the ICC will, in practice, impose a hierarchical juridical order remains to be seen. However, the prospects for such an order suggest that the ICC's ethical commitment will likely trump any decision to defer to national courts (chapter 4). It is this trumping power that reflects one of the most important procedural features of the ICC Statute: namely, the elimination of all political forms of national immunity. Such a procedure is contained in Article 27(2), which eliminates all forms of national amnesty law in respect of the political offense doctrine (justifies the political circumstances of crimes with the determination of the seriousness of the crimes). As Christine Cervasio points out, the political offense doctrine has long served as "an exception to extradition when the crimes of the accused or convicted are incidental to, or somehow connected with, political order in a certain country."[6]

Prosecutorial and Non-Prosecutorial Options

One of the central questions that this doctrine raises is whether the ICC's complementarity principle can supplement non-accountability options of international criminal justice such as truth commissions. Pardons and amnesties of course have become an important feature of restorative justice, which seeks to promote national reconciliation ("healing") by establishing an historical record of guilt.[7] Certainly the most notable case is the South African Truth and Reconciliation Commission (TRC). More than any other commission, the TRC has exposed the complex interrelationship between restorative and retributive justice (punishment). In doing so, this has raised many substantive questions regarding the future effectiveness of international criminal justice. For instance, can the ICC complement the successes of the TRC by trying the very worst perpetrators, thereby meeting the residual needs for vengeance? Or will the ICC's role in this respect undermine the incentive system and limited objectives of truth commissions?

Of course, not all devastated or war-ravaged countries will opt for truth commissions: they may, as the case of the Iraqi Tribunal shows, choose to establish their national tribunal to investigate and prosecute crimes, believing that the best way to deal with national grievances is through their own national criminal court system. Yet, it should be stressed here that where heinous crimes have been committed, national criminal courts will still need to meet the strict evidential standards of the international criminal justice system.

The issue that arises, then, is whether deterrence can resolve the deep underlying tensions of national and civic conflicts. For many, the scars of conflict and the lingering tensions associated with national conflict are best addressed through the national healing provided by truth commissions.[8] However, if the granting of pardons is meant to serve as motivation for suspected perpetrators to confess, then the ICC's use of the commission's investigative record to indict one of the perpetrators may test the willingness of the state to establish the commission. This might have the unfortunate effect of undermining the effectiveness of the commission and eliminating any future motivation on the part of the perpetrators to confess to their crimes. Thus, on the one hand, it could be argued that restorative justice should be allowed to prevail over the wishes of the ICC to investigate and prosecute such perpetrators. On the other hand, if restorative justice replaces retributive justice, it would "eliminate the possibility of revisiting the crime."[9] Such prioritization would result in the loss of faith in the criminal justice system and possibly encourage some would-be perpetrators to acquire a quasi form of immunity.

But can and should the ICC become an instrument for assuming command over domestic laws? And if so, how should it go about complementing national courts in this respect? As Garth Meintjes points out, it may be "more appropriate to use the term ineffective instead of invalid when referring to a domestic amnesty, since validity is determined by natural, not international law."[10] Other legal scholars suggest that amnesties may provide an effective source of evidence that can *only* be used against the worst perpetrators of gross human rights violations, not lesser criminals. From this limited standpoint, the principle aims of the ICC and truth commissions would not necessarily conflict, since truth commissions could gather testimony from subordinates of the worst perpetrators, which could later be used by the ICC to indict the worst perpetrators.

The point that I am trying to make here is that truth commissions do not necessarily need to use a direct means to indict the worst perpetrators. Rather, they must obtain whatever evidence they can to establish the guilt of the worst perpetrators. But as the limited scope of the Guatemala and Argentina Truth Commissions suggest, the gathering of such information is likely to remain a difficult and volatile task. Indeed, the very worst perpetrators may, in certain cases, use their viable political influence to obstruct the investigative work of commissions.[11]

Still, it is possible, as Michael Scharf points out, to see amnesties as providing an important source of evidence, which will, in time, "induce human violators to agree to peace and to relinquish power."[12] In this way, the ICC and truth commissions would work together to establish the guilt of the targeted perpetrators, while also prohibiting any amnesty law to preempt provisions of the ICC Statute. This nonetheless makes the transparency of the ICC all the more important to consider in terms of the complementarity principle. By transparency, I mean the exchange of information which conditions the (growth of) knowledge and awareness of the institution's goals, rules, and tasks. A critical component of transparency is the specificity of rules. The ICC Statute, for instance, can be said to enjoy a relatively high level of transparency in this sense, since it specifies the rules of procedure for requesting the surrender of a perpetrator to the ICC.

Perhaps the most important rule in this regard is the 30-day provision to establish wrongful intent of national courts.[13] Article 18(2), for instance, specifies two conditions under which the ICC may intervene in the affairs of the national judiciary. First, it allows states 30 days to begin their investigation of a case; from the time that they receive a notice from the Prosecutor indicating his or her intent to investigate the international crime. Second, the provision requires the Prosecutor to automatically defer to the state for a period of at least six months. Note that the Pre-Trial chamber can, at any time after the 30-day period (up to the six-month period) authorize a request of surrender, if it deems the investigation to be ineffective or inconsistent with the Court's evidential standards.

But determining the unwillingness of states, as opposed to inability, is certain to be difficult. At minimum, it will require subjective judgments of state intent that may lead to conflicting interpretations of the validity of this intent. Thus, for example, even if the ICC adequately determines that the national court's slow investigative proceedings constitute an unnecessary delay in the process, it is possible that national courts or state leaders will contest this interpretation, especially if it unduly conflicts with their sense of national pride. What this suggests is that the application of the complementarity principle will likely turn on the national government's inability to investigate or prosecute.

The determination of inability, however, should present fewer political obstacles, since it is based on the condition of partial or complete state collapse (see Article 17(3)).[14] Here, it is important to distinguish between political instability and political inability caused by state collapse. The former refers to the civic political stability or internal fighting, as illustrated by the civil war in Turkey pitting the Kurdish rebels and state (military) authorities; while, the latter refers to the conditions of anarchy stemming from severe internal fighting and rebellion (e.g., Somalia). At the PrepCom negotiations, for instance, there emerged considerable disagreement over what should constitute partial collapse.

State delegates addressed this issue by choosing to delete partial collapse, replacing "total" and "significant" with "the unavailability of the national judicial system," and basing the admissibility of a case on whether "the state is unable to obtain the necessary evidence and testimony or otherwise unable to carry out its proceedings."[15] As a result, the latter clause reinforced the transparency of evidence by establishing a concrete threshold of state collapse. Still, this did little to resolve the question of unwillingness, or whether the Court could expect to eliminate the political obstacles associated with the national court's intent to investigate or prosecute.

Complementarity and Its Effects: Stratification or Stricter Transparency?

Another way that the Court seeks to guard against the potential effects of unwillingness is to stipulate the special exceptions to the *Ne Bis In Idem* rule, which prohibits trying a defendant twice for the same crime.[16] But unlike the double jeopardy rule of domestic courts in most developed states, the ICC reserves the right, under certain extenuating conditions, to suspend the application of this principle. This essentially allows the ICC to address the failure of domestic courts to meet the strict evidential standards of the ICC Statute.

The main implication of this rule, however, is that it will facilitate what Madeleine Morris refers to as the stratification of jurisdiction. Morris, for instance, argues that "the Prosecutor will operate within a structure framed by the Treaty that encourages him or her to be attentive to the interests of the majority of States Parties to the ICC treaty and to certain elements of the Court's broader international audience but much less so to the interests of principally affected states or victims of populations."[17] In her view, the ICC's focus on state leaders, and not civilians, may end up biasing the Court toward the national population as a whole. Not only will this narrow focus ignore the crimes committed by civilian perpetrators of gross human rights atrocities, but it will also mean that the Court will be able to target certain state leaders for political reasons.

Here, Morris distinguishes between what she calls "active" and "stratified" concurrent jurisdiction. Whereas stratified concurrent jurisdiction underscores the effects of the imbalance of judicial resources across the international level, active concurrent jurisdiction characterizes the ICC's ability to address effectively the needs and motivations of the affected state.[18] Such effects include the limitation on national plea bargaining arrangements and the national government's ability to develop its judiciary after a long protracted civil war. What these effects suggest is that the ICC will need to induce national courts to cooperate with the Court. As Morris points out: "one motive for exercising jurisdiction concurrently with the ICC would be that while the state has a functioning judiciary, the state cannot obtain extradition of those defendants."[19] Given this factor, she concludes that the ability of the ICC to eliminate the effects of stratified concurrent jurisdiction will depend on its willingness to negotiate an arrangement in which national courts are allowed to try some of the gross offenders of human rights abuses in exchange for developing their criminal judicial system.

But Morris's conclusion faces difficulties in two respects. First, the ambiguous relationship between the Court and the United Nations has yet to be resolved. To the extent that interference between the United Nations and the ICC remains a viable problem, the apprehension of perpetrators also remains unclear. Second, because the Court lacks an effective enforcement mechanism, its arbitrary discretionary power will come under considerable scrutiny, especially if the exercise of its discretionary power results in perceptions of unfairness or possible biasness toward developing states. Indeed, it could be argued that the complementarity principle provides many necessary safeguards for ensuring that the worst perpetrators will be properly punished. For, as already suggested, the success of the complementarity principle will depend on the specification of elements of crimes that comprise its general principles of accountability.

General Principles of Accountability

There are three general principles of the ICC Statute that specify the elements of individual guilt of the perpetrator: 1) the mental element (*mens rea*), or the knowledge and intent to commit a crime,[20] 2) the mitigating elements of the self-defense, and 3) superior orders.[21] The advantage of the specification of these elements of crimes is that they allow us to effectively derive guilt and intent from the widespread character of the execution of the crime. The downside, as Antonio Cassese contends, is the unintended consequences of such specification. Thus, for instance, the exclusion of recklessness from the ICC Statute may necessarily undermine the ability of the prosecutor to investigate war crimes committed unintentionally, but which resulted in serious consequences nonetheless.[22] Here, it should be noted that the issue of recklessness was resolved (at the Rome Conference) when it was agreed that all crimes within the jurisdiction of the ICC would require intent and knowledge.[23]

It is also worthwhile to mention that the mental elements of crimes lack the precision of national domestic law, which stipulates the procedural rules for determining intent/motive, and more importantly, assigns specific codes of penalties. Scholars critical of *mens rea* emphasize that the mental element leaves out provisions for addressing the consequences of non-intent. The issue of whether or not to include recklessness also raises the question of whether mistakes of fact can be linked with a lack of knowledge of the crime.[24] As Roger Clark argues, distinguishing between the accused perpetrator's knowledge of the circumstance (of one's intent) from the circumstances of the crime itself might provide an additional method for validating a criminal's intent.[25] So, for example, if the facts in the case prove that a general was misled, then the circumstances of the accused perpetrator's actions would point to his or her lack of knowledge of the circumstances or intent to commit the crime. This is not to mean that the circumstances will prove that the person *never* intended to commit the crime, but rather that his or her actions were the product of some other person's skillful knowledge of the consequences of a plan.

The ICC Statute provides the grounds for self-defense "when the person acts reasonably to defend himself or herself or another person or, in the case of war crimes, property which is essential for the survival of the person or another person or property which is essential for accomplishing a military mission." Critics of self-defense contend that recognizing one's right to defend the protection of property for accomplishing a military mission ignores the intent or plan of the military mission itself.[26] In other words, allowing for any such conditions would open the door for conflicting and open-ended interpretation of self-defense. For instance, the U.S. mission to apprehend Saddam for past and future serious international crimes (with the ultimate purpose of protecting its homeland) raises the thorny issue of whether the Iraq War was offensive or defensive in nature. At the very least, the principle of preemptive attack appears to blur the line between offensive and defensive intentions. It is precisely this blurring, as we shall see in chapters 6 and 7, that requires that the Court eventually adopt a clear-cut definition of the crime of aggression, one which contains the specific acts and elements to substantiate and validate the exercise of jurisdiction.

Universal Jurisdiction and the Universality Principle

So how does automatic and/or concurrent jurisdiction differ from universal jurisdiction? The automatic jurisdiction of the ICC refers to the ICC's *prima facie* right to exercise jurisdiction over matters (or nationals) concerning crimes that were committed within the territory of a state party.[27] It can therefore offer to adjudicate over these matters since it, in principle, exercises jurisdiction over any of its core crimes. This is how it invokes the universality principle: by deriving its authority from the principle that all core crimes are universally condemned (chapter 1). The United States, as we shall see (chapter 6), has vehemently objected to the ICC's automatic jurisdiction on the grounds that it violates international treaty law. The question that arises, then, is how automatic jurisdiction via the complementarity principle will likely minimize the political tensions caused by the application of universal jurisdiction.

Here, it is important to realize that neither the ICC nor ICTY exercise universal jurisdiction *per se.* Automatic jurisdiction over nationals (in conjunction with concomitant jurisdiction), for example, merely constitutes the validated suspension of certain constraints on international judicial authorities, such as the power to launch its own investigation and the authority to request the surrender of a perpetrator of gross human rights violations. By universal jurisdiction, therefore, we are referring to the unrestricted exercise of discretionary power to investigate and prosecute civilians and non-civilians, regardless of nationality. In this sense, state sovereignty does not, in any way, restrict the application of this jurisdiction. This is because jurisdictional authority, in this case, is predicated on the idea that the necessary implementation of these elements of crimes transcend state sovereignty.

Note that universal jurisdiction, when subsumed under the universality principle, constitutes one of four bases for jurisdiction under international law. The nationality principle, for instance, refers to the jurisdiction over the nationals of one state. By contrast, personal jurisdiction underscores the Court's jurisdiction over nationals of states parties; and territorial jurisdiction provides for the Court's jurisdiction over human rights crimes committed in the territory of a state party. It is this latter principle that, under certain circumstances, may subject nationals from non-states parties to the jurisdiction of the Court (e.g., where there is no extradition treaty between the nonparty and state party). Nevertheless, under the universality principle, every state has a sufficient and overriding interest in exercising jurisdiction over those criminal offenses that states have universally condemned. Whether or not a state consents to a treaty, all states must abide by this overriding interest; for, again, every state has a duty to uphold the basic norms and rules that comprise this overriding interest.[28]

As noted above, the automatic jurisdiction of the ICC is designed to uphold this and the territorial principle by allowing the Court to exercise jurisdiction over nationals of third party states for crimes committed within the territory of the state party. The latter party, or host state in this case, is thus obligated to consult with the ICC on the options available for prosecuting the national from the third party state (see Article 90(2)). Alternatively, if the state party has signed an extradition treaty with the other state, it is obligated to consult the Court concerning the terms of the treaty before agreeing to extradite the criminal to the requesting state.

In this way, the ICC can request the surrender of a national of a non-state party on two conditions: 1) that the crimes perpetrated by the national occurred within the territory of a state party; and 2) if the U.N. Security Council refers a situation to the ICC Prosecutor in which the crimes of perpetrators rise to the level of a threat to international security and peace. As the Darfur crisis illustrates, a U.N. referral can have a dramatic effect on the ICC's decision to investigate. Thus, for instance, when the Security Council referred the situation of the Darfur crisis to the ICC in March of 2005, the ICC Prosecutor, Luis Moreno Ocampo, subsequently announced that the ICC had gathered enough evidence to investigate the heinous crimes committed by various high-ranking authorities of genocide.

To sum up: the difference between universal jurisdiction and the ICC's automatic jurisdiction is that the ICC's automatic jurisdiction refers to its jurisdiction over crimes committed by any national within the territory of a state party. It therefore does not exercise autonomous jurisdiction over the territorial borders of non-states parties; only over those nationals of non-states parties who have committed serious crimes within the territorial borders of a state party. What this suggests, then, is that the political effects and tensions of universal jurisdiction may be more intense than those associated with the exercise of automatic or concurrent forms of jurisdiction (e.g., the ICC or ICTY respectively). In fact, one of the problems with universal jurisdiction is that it typically fails to offer any safeguards against the issuance of indictments against sitting heads of state. The result is that tensions may necessarily arise between state and international authorities.

Consider, for example, the Belgian Statute, which was adopted in 1994 to investigate and prosecute perpetrators of the Rwanda genocide. It was based on the (state) decision to amend the penal laws of the Belgian criminal system, in order to investigate any perpetrator of war crimes and crimes against humanity.[29] In 1999, however, the government amended the statute to include the crime of genocide. This was soon followed by several case referrals by private plaintiffs, alleging that crimes of genocide and crimes against humanity had been committed by various leaders, including the sitting prime minister of the Democratic Republic of Congo, Abduldaye Yerodia, and the Prime Minister of Israel, Ariel Sharon.[30] Although the International Court of Justice (ICJ) determined that the Belgian judges could not indict sitting heads of state, this decision did not eliminate the prospects of investigating and prosecuting these perpetrators as civilians.

Indeed, by the spring of 2001, various complaints by the most powerful states ratcheted up tensions between the Belgian government and these states. For instance, indictments against Dick Cheney, Colin Powell, and General Shwarzikoff, alleging that these leaders had committed war crimes during the Gulf War, prompted the United States to apply coercive pressure on the Belgian government to rescind the statute.[31] There were two prongs to their strategic attack. First, the U.S. Secretary of State, Colin Powell, sent the Belgian government a stern warning that its continued support of the statute would discourage state leaders from attending NATO meetings in Brussels. This was soon followed by U.S. Secretary of Defense, Donald Rumsfeld's threat to withhold the U.S. pledge of 70 million dollars for the construction of a new NATO headquarters. The Belgian government responded to the U.S. threats by withdrawing the indictments against U.S. officials, and restricting the scope of investigations and prosecution (to Belgian citizens only).[32]

The demise of the Belgian Statute signaled the end of one of the most intriguing experiments of universal jurisdiction. More importantly, it exposed the volatile tensions that can arise between and among states when one state exercises universal jurisdiction over other states. In doing so, the Belgian Statute calls attention to the need for political mechanisms that can control the effects of these tensions or competitive pressures. To recall, the Nuremberg Tribunal showed just how formidable these controls could be in terms of victors' justice (chapter 1). What is more, the ICTY, as we saw, demonstrated the important limitations of international jurisdiction and the political tensions that can arise when courts indict sitting state leaders during wars.

This brings us to the strategic advantages of the complementarity principle. Recall that the complementarity principle provided a compromise between those wishing to curtail the ICC's jurisdiction and those wanting to vest the ICC with broad powers of jurisdiction. This reflected the limited expectations at the time that states would be willing to give up their sovereignty. It was also intended to ensure that states would have some protection against an overzealous prosecutor, and that states would retain the *prima facie* right to investigate and prosecute crimes committed within its own territory. In this way, however, the complementarity principle eliminates many of the heated pressures that might arise from the exercise of juridical power, insofar as it provides *prima facie* recognition of state sovereignty.

But the complementarity principle, although promising to stabilize expectations and to control for potential grievances, does not ensure the elimination or complete stabilization of political tensions that might arise between the ICC and non-states parties. As we shall see, not all non-states parties recognize this stabilizing role of the complementarity principle, even though it does offer an important mechanism for mediating between universal jurisdiction and state sovereignty (the shielding of perpetrators from investigation and prosecution). It therefore will be important to distinguish between an active application of the complementarity principle—one that steers the ICC in the direction of an abiding commitment to the ends of global justice—and a passive application of the principle, in which the ICC steers clear of the political overtones of a case by deferring to national courts. Thus far, I have suggested that the ICC needs to pursue an active application of this principle in order to harness its political resources to its ethical commitment to global justice.

Political Resources: Internal Mechanisms of Accountability

In this section, I shall assess the formal basis of these resources by examining the ICC's formal governing structure. The ICC's formal structure in this sense, which some have referred to in terms of a quasi-constitutional structure,[33] consists of several mechanisms of accountability, including: 1) the "cessation of the conflict and thereby the ending of victimization; 2) prevention and deterrence of future conflict; 3) rehabilitation of the society as a whole and of the victims as a group; and 4) the reconciliation of the society as a whole and the victims as a group."[34] Enacting these mechanisms of accountability, therefore, will depend on the functionality of the ICC's system of governance, membership, and hierarchy of norms. Let us therefore assess each one of these governing traits.

The Formal Operations of the ICC

The Office of the Prosecutor, which consists of the Prosecutor and a Deputy Prosecutor, is the only organ of the ICC that can initiate a case (*propio motu*) (see Article 42(1) of the ICC Statute).[35] Despite this power, however, the ICC Statute provides a system of institutional checks and balances that are designed to address the potential abuses of the ICC Prosecutor's discretionary power. The Assembly of States Parties, for instance, can hold the ICC Prosecutor accountable in two principal ways.

First, it can require the Prosecutor to report back to the Assembly with the details of an investigation, especially if the proceedings result in accusations of the abuse of prosecutorial power.[36] At the Rome Conference, for instance, some delegations proposed a plan for enhancing the accountability of the Prosecutor, in which the Prosecutor would be required to file an annual report to the Security Council. But the majority of state delegations at the meeting ultimately voted against the plan, claiming that the information divulged by the Prosecutor would compromise the confidentiality of the Prosecutor's investigation.

Another check on the Prosecutor's power involves the Assembly of States Parties' power to elect the Prosecutor for a single nine-year term. Article 42(4), for instance, calls for the Prosecutor "to be elected by secret ballot by an absolute majority of the members of the Assembly of States Parties"; while Article 42(3) stipulates that the Assembly of States Parties will elect a person of "high moral character, to be highly competent in and have extensive experience in the prosecution or trial of criminal cases." Here it should be stressed that the Assembly of States Parties can vote by secret ballot to terminate the tenure of the Prosecutor, Deputy Prosecutor(s), and judges with a majority vote, on the condition that the Appeals Chamber rules that the Prosecutor committed "serious misconduct or breach of his or her duties under this Statute, or is unable to exercise the functions required by the Statute" (see Article 46(1)a and b).[37] It is this provision that holds important implications for the ICC Prosecutor's willingness to investigate hard cases. For if the Prosecutor decides to launch multiple investigations of individuals belonging to a targeted ethnic group, then its actions may become the source of national protest against the ICC. One of the ways that Ocampo has sought to minimize the political complications arising from this scenario is to devise a set of special prosecutorial guidelines for implementing the rules of procedure in a fair and consistent manner.[38]

The second major internal component of accountability is the Pre-Trial Chamber. If, for instance, the Appeals Chamber determines that there are serious grounds for disqualification, then they can refer the matter to the Assembly of States Parties, which must then be followed by a vote on whether or not to remove the Prosecutor, Deputy Prosecutor, and/or judges.[39] In this context, it could be said that the Pre-Trial Chamber constitutes the most essential mechanism of internal accountability, since it provides a screening test of the Prosecutor's evidence. In other words, if the Pre-Trial Chamber determines that an error has been made, or that the Prosecutor's information does not meet the evidential standards of the Court, the Chamber (the three-judge panel) can authorize the Prosecutor to stop an investigation (see Article 12). Note that the Pre-Trial Chamber will also be responsible for screening out the information provided by non-state actors.[40] Given the influential role played by NGOs in the ICTY, NGOs will, on the one hand, provide an equally, if not more substantial amount of information or eyewitness testimony to the Office of the Prosecutor. On the other hand, much of this evidence provided by NGOs may not meet the strict evidential requirements of the ICC. This is by no means intended to diminish the importance of NGO participation. Rather, it suggests that NGO participation may have the unintended effect of burdening the Office of the Prosecutor with too much evidence and information.

An additional constraint on the Prosecutor's power involves the right of the U.N. Security Council to defer the investigation of a case, as stipulated under Article 16 of the ICC Statute (see chapter 1). Procedurally, the Security Council's right of deferral requires a Security Council resolution to enact and renew the deferral on a yearly basis by a majority vote. While it could be argued that the right of deferral allows the Security Council to intervene in matters involving high security risks, it is fair to say that such power will be used sparingly, if at all. The point here is that the Security Council is not likely to restrict the actions of the ICC, since this would create some degree of antagonism between it and the Court. Instead, there is a strong likelihood that the Security Council will wish to work along side the ICC in promoting international criminal accountability and international peace and security, for that matter.

In short, the procedural constraints placed on the ICC Prosecutor are important to understanding how, at least on a formal level, the ICC will deal with the prospects of an abusive Prosecutor or an imbalance of power that might affect public perception of its fairness and legitimacy. More importantly, these formal constraints suggest that the ICC will operate in a way in which its checks and balances will mitigate the effects of the imposition of outside organizational interests, while also enhancing the chances that the ICC will unite around a set of policies and strategic actions.

State Responsibility and Compliance

Another crucial factor of the ICC's formative development is increasing membership or the growing number of ratifying states. The reason for this should be obvious enough. The more ratifications, the more that the ICC will eliminate the likelihood of non-state party noncompliance. As of the writing of this book, the ICC had received 98 ratifications. It is quite possible that 150 might constitute a potential threshold for solidifying the ICC's moral legitimacy, and strongly discouraging any form of noncompliance. But it is also true that ratification will require significant legal adjustments by some countries.

Under the ICC Statute, a state's obligations to surrender the worst perpetrators to the ICC, will require states to make the following changes to their domestic legal systems: 1) remove any provision of amnesty or special immunity from the constitution, which could be used to unlawfully shield a perpetrator;[41] 2) maintain extradition treaty law consistent with the absolute obligation to surrender a national to the ICC; and 3) eliminate any provision on the death penalty.[42] Such adjustments can either take the form of amendments to the state constitution (e.g., France and Germany), or new domestic legislation to meet the ICC's procedural requirements of surrendering the worst perpetrators to the ICC (e.g., Canada and New Zealand).[43]

As noted earlier, states parties will no longer be able to invoke national laws to shield an accused perpetrator from investigation and prosecution. Even if immunities serve the purpose of establishing the historical record or promoting national reconciliation, they cannot impede the Court's jurisdiction over crimes committed within the territorial borders of states parties. This is why the ICC retains the right to adjudicate on issues of extradition treaty law which might conflict with the ICC's right to request the surrender of a perpetrator to the ICC.

The adjudication of extradition treaty law therefore requires states to recognize its "distinct nature" when surrendering perpetrators to the Court.[44] For some legal scholars, this figures to eliminate many of the procedural requirements and legal wrangling of extraditing one national to another state, thus providing a streamlined process for surrendering persons to the ICC. More concretely, the adaptation of extradition law to the ICC will curtail the amount of time and resources necessary for extraditing a defendant to another country (receiving). On the other hand, the incompatibility between the ICC and state constitutions will likely intensify the issue of ratification in two fundamental ways.

First, the ICC Statute eliminates all reservations contained in Article 120, which might undermine an important negotiating and comprising function of treaty law.[45] Second, there is the difficult and often slow political process of amending a constitution. Constitutional amendments, for instance, often require a two-thirds majority vote in federal assemblies, as well as ratification in local or state assemblies. If politics enters into this process in the form of intense lobbying by interest groups, it is quite possible that the amendment process will be further complicated. Other possible scenarios include the dissolution of the parliament or popular referendum, both of which involve political pressures that can hamper domestic adaptation to ICC law.

However, it is unlikely that the ICC's strict evidential standards will unduly delay ratification. As Helen Duffy states: "in many circumstances there may be strong arguments that, upon ratification, there would be no inconsistency between the constitutional order and the Rome Statute, as the Statute would itself form part of that constitution or take precedence over inconsistent parts of it."[46] Thus, on the one hand, domestic criminal systems that already prohibit the death penalty, and provide most, if not all the basic standards of protection for the defendants, should expect a smooth transition.

On the other hand, domestic criminal systems that offer few standards for protecting the basic rights of defendants will need to significantly adjust their criminal systems to meet (internalize) the ICC's legal standards for a defendant's basic rights.[47] Article 55(2), for example, provides the right to be "informed prior to being questioned," to remain silent, to choose one's legal counsel, and the right to be questioned before a counsel. In addition, the Statute also provides an extensive list of rights for the defendant during the trial, including the rights to be tried without undue delay, to be informed of the charges against him or her, and to not be forced to confess his or her guilt. It should also be mentioned that many state constitutions already contain provisions protecting these basic rights, as we shall see in further detail in chapter 7 when we discuss the role of Arab states in the ICC. In sum, the ICC provides a systematic and novel institutional framework for actualizing its proscriptive norms against genocide, crimes against humanity, and war crimes, and bridging the gap between state and international law.

Conclusion

In this chapter, we examined the parameters of several key legal principles and the political issues surrounding their application and enactment. As we saw, the complementarity principle constitutes the central principle of the ICC's governing structure and its juridical power. Certainly, the increasing number of ratifications will provide an important basis for projecting the ICC's juridical power. But it is also true that the ICC will confront political realities that will require it to administer and enact its rules of procedures in a prudent manner. And while the complementarity principle appears to provide a mechanism capable of stabilizing some of the effects arising from the tensions between its jurisdictional powers and state sovereignty, the question that arises is how the Court will accomplish the task of harnessing its internal politics (or mechanisms) to its role as an effective player in global politics. In the following part, I shall draw on several empirical, ethical, and normative theories to theorize about this issue and the increasing convergence of politics, power, and ethics that it involves.

Notes

1. The importance of this principle can also be characterized by its place in the ICC Statute. The Preamble of the ICC Statute reads: "An international Criminal Court ("The Court") is hereby established. It shall be a permanent institution and shall have the power to exercise its jurisdiction over persons for the most serious crimes of international concern, as referred to in this Statute, and shall be complementary to national criminal jurisdictions. The jurisdiction and functioning of the Court shall be governed by the provisions of this Statute."

2. The article reads: "a) the proceedings were or are being undertaken or the national decision was made for the purpose of shielding the person concerned from criminal responsibility for crimes within the jurisdiction of the Court referred to in article 5; b) there has been an unjustified delay in the proceedings which in the circumstances is inconsistent with an intent to bring the person concerned to justice. c) the proceedings were not or are not being conducted independently or impartially, and they were or are being conducted in a manner which, in the circumstances, is inconsistent with an intent to bring the person concerned to justice."

3. Phillipe Sands, "After Pinochet: The Role of National Courts," in Philippe Sands, ed. *From Nuremburg to the Hague* (Cambridge: Cambridge University Press, 2003), 76.

4. See e.g., Phillipe Sands, "After Pinochet: The Role of National Courts," in Philippe Sands, ed. *From Nuremburg to the Hague* (Cambridge: Cambridge University Press, 2003), 71–72; Cassese, "The Making of the Rome Statute," *European Journal of International Law* 15 (1999): 144.

5. Andrew Clapham, "Issues of Complexity, Complicity and Complementarity: From the Nuremburg Trials to the Dawn of the New International Criminal Court," in Phillipe Sands, ed. *From Nuremburg to the Hague* (Cambridge: Cambridge University Press, 2003), 64.

6. Christine Cervasio, "Extradition and the International Criminal Court: The Future of the Political Offense Doctrine," *Pace International Review* 11 (1991): 420.

7. Priscilla Hayner provides four criteria to characterize a truth commission: "1) it focuses on the past; 2) it does not concentrate on any one specific event, but attempts to paint the overall picture of certain human rights abuses, or violations of international humanitarian law, over a period of time; 3) it usually exists temporarily and for a pre-defined period of time, ceasing to exist with the submission of a report of its findings; and 4) it gains some sort of authority from its sponsor that allows it greater access to information, greater security or greater protection to dig into sensitive issues, and a greater impact with its report." Quoted in Steven R. Ratner and Jason S. Abrams, *Accountability for Human Rights Atrocities in International Law*, Second Edition. (Oxford: Oxford University Press, 2001), 228–229. See also Priscilla Hayner, "Fifteen Truth Commissions—1974 to 1994: A Comparative Study," *Human Rights Quarterly* (1994).

8. See e.g., Mark S. Ellis, "The International Criminal Court and Its Implication for Domestic Law and National Capacity Building," *Florida Journal of International Law* 15, no. 2 (2002): 227; Antonio Cassese, "The Statute of the International Criminal Court," *European Journal of International Law* 10 (1999): 141–171.

9. Benjamin N. Schiff, "The Case of the South African Truth and Reconciliation Commission," in M. Cherif Bassiouni, ed. *Post-Conflict Justice* (Ardsely, NY: Transnational Publishers, 2003), 327. It should be noted that the ICC Statute fails to address the validity of pardons granted to perpetrators that have been tried in national courts. It remains unclear as to whether pardons will fall directly under the procedural safeguard against partiality; or whether, in some cases, a pardon might serve as an effective role in promoting national reconciliation. On this point, see John T. Holmes, "The Principle of Complementarity," in Roy Lee, ed. *The International Criminal Court: The Making of the ICC* (The Hague: Kluwer Publishers, 1999), 76.

10. Garth Meintjes, "Domestic Amnesties and International Accountability," in Dinah Sheldon, ed. *International Crimes, Peace, and Human Rights: The Role of the International Criminal Court* (Ardsley, New York: Transnational Publishers, Inc, 2000), 87–88.

11. For a discussion of the comparative weaknesses and strengths of truth commissions, see Jonathan Tepperman, "Truth or Consequences," *Foreign Affairs* 81, no. 2 (March/April 2002).

12. Michael Scharf, "Justice Versus Peace", in S. Sewall and C. Kaysen, eds. *The United States and the International Criminal Court* (Lanham, MD: Rowman and Littlefield Publishers, 2000), 180.

13. See Holmes, "The Complementarity Principle."

14. Holmes, "The Complementarity Principle," 53.

15. Holmes, "The Complementarity Principle," 54.

16. For a good discussion of the implications of the *Ne bis in idem* rule for the Court, see Ganz Knoops, *Surrendering to International Criminal Courts* (Ardsley, NY: Transnational Publishers, 2002).

17. Madeleine Morris, "Complementarity and Conflict: States, Victims, and the ICC," in S. B. Sewall and Carl Kaysen, eds. *The United States and the International Criminal Court* (Lanham: Rowman & Littlefield Publishers, Inc. 2000,) 201. Morris also points out that the ICC will prove demeaning to the common people by going after only state leaders and not their followers. But the suggestion that the ICC will demean the common people by devaluing the role or responsibility of the state leader remains a moot point; for it could also be argued that most followers may well see it in their interests to claim that they had no choice in whether they followed or disobeyed the orders of their commanders and state leaders.

18. Morris, "Complementarity and Conflict," 204.

19. Morris, "Complementarity and Conflict," 204.

20. The mental element of the crimes validates the liability of the crime. Article 30(2 and 3) states: 2. "For the purposes of this article, a person has intent where:

(a) In relation to conduct, that person means to engage in the conduct;

(b) In relation to a consequence, that person means to cause that consequence or is aware that it will occur in the ordinary course of events.

3. For the purposes of this argument, "knowledge means awareness that a circumstance exists or a consequence will occur in the ordinary course of events. Know and knowingly shall be constructed accordingly."

21. It should be noted that all of these principles represent significant (albeit complex) sources for advancing international substantive law. Cassese, "The Statute of the International Criminal Court," 153.

22. Cassese, "The Statute of the International Criminal Court," 154.

23. Per Saland, "International Criminal Law Principles," in Roy Lee, ed. *The International Criminal Court: The Making of the Rome Statute* (The Hague: Kluwer Publishers, 2001), 205.

24. Article 32 reads: 1) A mistake of fact shall be a ground for excluding criminal responsibility only if it negates the mental element required by the crime. 2) A mistake

of law as to whether a particular type of conduct is a crime within the jurisdiction of the Court shall not be a ground for excluding criminal responsibility. A mistake of law may, however, be a ground for excluding criminal responsibility if it negates the mental element required by such a crime, or as provided for in Article 33.

25. Pierre Prosper and Roger Clark, "Justice Without Borders," *Temple International and Comparative Law Journal* 17 (2003): 87.

26. Cassese, "The Statute of the International Criminal Court," 155.

27. See, e.g., Darren Hawkins, "Universal Jurisdiction for Human Rights," *Global Governance* 9 (2003): 291–299.

28. It could also be argued that the failure to ratify or cooperate with the Court constitutes a breach of international law: a clear-cut violation of rules of the Statute. In this respect, the failure to investigate amounts to a gross negligence to uphold international rules and norms.

29. Steven R. Ratner, "Belgium's War Crimes Statute: A Postmortem," *American Journal of International Law* 97, no. 4 (2004): 887.

30. Ratner, "Belgium's War Crimes Statute," 890.

31. Ratner, "Belgium's War Crimes Statute," 891.

32. Ratner, "Belgium's War Crimes Statute," 895.

33. As John Washburn notes, "the ICC represents a new institution with the responsibilities of governance, administration, structure, financing, and fundamental procedures." See John Washburn, "The Negotiation of the Rome Statute for the International Criminal Court and International Lawmaking in the 21st Century," *Pace International Law Review* 11 (1999): 365.

34. M. Cherif Bassiouni, "A Universal Model," in M. Cherif Bassiouni, ed. *Post Conflict Justice* (Ardsely, NY: Transnational Publishers, 2000), 852.

35. This power ultimately came to be regarded as essential for promoting the Court's effectiveness and independence. For without the Prosecutor's *proprio motu* powers, the Prosecutor would have to rely on states or the United Nations to refer cases which would make its *ex officio* powers largely dependent on the states, and also restrict the scope of its discretionary powers.

36. It should be noted that while the Assembly's powers are designed to eliminate the arbitrariness of the Court, it does not operate like a state legislature, which makes new laws.

37. By comparison, Article 46 (2)(a) calls for a two-thirds majority by the Assembly of States Parties as well as a two-thirds majority by the remaining judges.

38. Allison Marston Danner, "Enhancing the Legitimacy and Accountability of Prosecutorial Discretion at the International Criminal Court," *American Journal of International Law* 97, no. 3 (July 2003): 523.

39. Article 42(8) states: "Any question as to the disqualification of the Prosecutor or a Deputy Prosecutor shall be decided by the Appeals Chamber.

(a) The person being investigated or prosecuted may at any time request the disqualification of the Prosecutor or a Deputy Prosecutor on the grounds set out in this article;

(b) The Prosecutor or the Deputy Prosecutor, as appropriate, shall be entitled to present his or her comments on the matter."

40. Alison Marston Danner refers to the informative role played by NGOs as an informal mode of accountability. As she states: "it is informal because it is implied, rather than explicitly described, in the Rome Statute. It is commonsensical because it rests . . . upon the understanding of how the Prosecutor will actually have to go about his work in order to be effective" ("Enhancing the Legitimacy and Accountability of Prosecutorial Discretion," 525).

41. States will also need to consider a) the penalties of punishment that prohibit the death penalty, b) the extradition of indicted criminals to the ICC (when the ICC requests this in accordance with Article 12) and, c) as already mentioned above, any immunities granted to a head of state.

42. Helen Duffy, "National Constitutional Compatibility and the International Criminal Court," *Duke Journal of Comparative and International Law* 11 (2001): 6.

43. It should be noted that Article 27 of the Vienna Convention prohibits states from using domestic law to justify their "failure to prosecute" (see Vienna convention). In this respect, ratification preempts the use of domestic law to investigate and prosecute crimes.

44. Ellis, "The International Criminal Court and Its Implication for Domestic Law and National Capacity Building," 232.

45. Helen Duffy, "National Constitutional Compatibility and the International Criminal Court," 10.

46. Duffy, "National Constitutional Compatibility," 23.

47. Ellis, "The International Criminal Court and Its Implicaton for Domestic Law and National Capacity Building," 226.

II

THEORY AND ETHICS

3

Legalization, Pragmatic Ethics, and Integration

> Where international law was once the 'law of nations' in their external relations, the residual core of international public law has become increasingly enmeshed within a web of rules and governing the rights of individuals and groups . . .
>
> —Christian Reus-Smit, *The Politics of International Law*

WHAT IS THE ROLE OF ETHICS in determining how the ICC Prosecutor exercises his or her discretionary power? And how will ethics intersect with politics to further legitimize the juridical authority of the ICC? In the previous chapter we saw how the ICTY had moved beyond the politics of victors' justice and exposed the growing complexity of the political dimension of international criminal courts. The ICTY, of course, is an independent legal institution. However, its powers of enforcement cannot be entirely detached from the Security Council's Chapter VII powers, since any difficult case of non-compliance can be seen as an extended breach in international peace and security. The ICC, on the other hand, is an independent and permanent institution established under international treaty law. The different sources of creation in this respect will arguably focus more attention on state compliance in the implementation process of the ICC's decisions. It will also, as I have been proposing, require further analysis of the complexity of the ICC's political dimension, including the evolving link between (the need for) political legitimacy and (enforcing) moral accountability.

The theoretical issue that we need to address here, then, is how the ICC's experience or means of adapting to its global political environment will shape its self-directed application of the rules aimed at realizing the ethical goal of moral accountability. How does the ICC's pragmatic dimension or character in this sense justify the use of practical guidelines for directing the exercise of the Prosecutor's power toward this ethical goal? And how does this reveal the limits of scientific theories which ignore this particular dimension of global institutions by simplifying the institutional dynamics of legitimacy?

In this chapter, I will address these questions by first assessing the limitations of legalization theory and its reductive approach to the interaction between law and politics.[1] As we shall see, scientific approaches to law and politics oversimplify the political impact of legal institutions, by situating the politics of international criminal courts along a narrow spectrum between "pure bargaining and the political considerations of adjudication."[2] The challenge here is to show how the ethics and politics of the ICC diverge and recombine in ways that place us outside or beyond this formal spectrum.[3] This points to an even bigger challenge, which I will address in the following chapter, of understanding the unique political and ethical dynamics of the ICC's juridical power and how this exposes both the limits and possibilities of global juridification.

I will then follow up my discussion of legalization theory by examining the pragmatic dimension of the ICC or its capacity to deal with the political and social effects of its decisions or rulings. Here, I draw on John Dewey's theory of public law to understand how the ICC exhibits certain (character) pragmatic traits that will be crucial to understanding its political development. I argue that Dewey's idea of self reflexivity allows us to understand the prospects and formal limits of a self-directed application of rules aimed at realizing the ethical goal of moral accountability.

Integrating International Law and International Relations

The increasing focus on the politics of law during the post-Cold War era has been accompanied by a growing interest in integrating the disciplines of International Law (IL) and International Relations (IR). Prior to the post-Cold War era, however, these two disciplines tended to remain at odds. While IR scholars employed independent and dependent variables to examine the causal effects of rules, international legal scholars focused on the political substance of laws and rules.[4] The former in this sense focused on the casual impact of rules and functional traits of institutions (e.g., transaction costs and norm transparency, information exchange), and sought to operationalize the above variables through the application of game theory.[5] Nevertheless, the differences, as Stanley Hoffman explains, was one in which "international relations theory has reacted against international law, which it has tried to describe, deconstruct, or demythologize as a mere tool of states and their interests."[6]

Over time, however, it became clear that the two disciplines were not mutually exclusive. In fact, the two shared deep mutual concerns for international cooperation and global stability. For some, this suggested the possibilities for not only further comparative analysis, but potential collaboration.[7] Only recently, however, have the two paths of IL and IR converged methodologically through the collaborative efforts of legal scholars such as Anne-Marie Slaughter, and international relations scholars, including Robert Keohane, Duncan Snidal, Andrew Moravcsik, and Kenneth Abbot.[8] As we shall see, others have sought to square the circle between functionalism and cooperation theory by analyzing the relationship between institutionalism and the practical evolution of regimes, or what they refer to as "rational design."[9]

The aim of this section is to assess the parameters of these empirical or scientific approaches and to address their limitations with respect to understanding the complex interaction of law and politics. My argument here is that these scientific approaches, while important to understanding the effects of legal institutions or their functional traits (i.e., obligation, precision of rules), also limit our understanding of the changing functional parameters of global politics.

Bridging the Divide

One of the first systematic efforts to study the normative and political content of world politics was Myres McDougal's and Harold Lasswell's analysis of world public order in the late 1950s (the two principal scholars of what came to be known as the New Haven School).[10] In their study on world order, McDougal and Lasswell argued that human dignity constituted an essential dynamic of world order: a non-coercive element of international law, whose civil appeal could be distinguished from coercive power. According to McDougal and Lasswell, new methods were needed to assess the content of world order, including, as they note, "various processual modes to clarify the issues 'on which the diverse system of public order could be resolved by peaceable persuasion rather than bellicose coercion.'"[11] Although their study tended to lack empirical and scientific analysis, it did manage to introduce an important distinction between the normative influence of human rights and external coercion. It would be this distinction, in fact, that would exercise considerable influence over many later prominent international scholars, including H. L. A. Hart and Thomas Franck.

Hart, for instance, distinguished between what he referred to as primary and secondary rules. Whereas the former referred to the coercive rule of law of the state, the latter reflected the normative obligations of subjects of international law, or as Hart states "the capability of states of becoming a subject of international obligation or coercion."[12] Following Hart, Franck theorized that states were driven by a deep desire to abide by the rules. He characterized this desire as a normative pull towards compliance with international rules, or a voluntary choice to play by the rules that states perceived as legitimate.[13] In this way, the function of legitimacy, as we shall see in the context of a mutual legitimacy push (chapter 8), reflected the state's wish to be treated with respect and, perhaps more importantly, to maintain its reputation or honor by averting the political and economic costs associated with noncompliance (e.g., U.N. economic sanctions and the suspension of diplomatic ties).[14]

Accordingly, the normative pull towards compliance highlighted the functional difference between the rule of law and the voluntary desire to comply with international rules. Although this normative pull addressed the key question of why states comply with rules that cannot be adequately enforced, it also left open the issue of whether the normative influence of rules could be validated by scientific evidence. In other words, if the perception of the legitimacy of rules determined the normative pull, then what determined this perception? Was there a way of validating or objectifying this perception?

To address these questions, legal scholars and political scientists needed to realize that, while certain methodological differences continued to divide these disciplines, a mutually shared need existed to address the increasing importance of international human rights violations and their causal impact on global politics. In order to bring together these disciplines, it was important that IR and IL seek some common methodological ground. In her seminal essay on IR and IL, Anne-Marie Slaughter argued that the methodological divide between IL and IR represented a false dichotomy of methodological concerns. In fact, both IR and IL, in her view, shared an abiding interest in explaining the influence and function of rules and norms. Moreover, the fact that legal scholars and political theorists have long found common ground in constitutional theory suggested that IR and IL could find similar ground as well: namely, in the legalization of world order (legitimacy and obligation).[15] In this respect, Slaughter's essay helped lay the initial groundwork for methodological convergence and served to inspire other legal scholars to address the topic of integrating IR and IL.

Perhaps the most notable attempt in this latter respect was Robert Beck's, Anthony Arend's, and Robert Vander Lugt's edited volume on international rules.[16] Here, the authors take stock of the overlapping methods and objectives by showing how the convergence between and among different contending interpretations have helped engender an interdisciplinary discourse on the political and legal effects of international rules.[17] This not only applied to Liberal Institutionalism, but also to both Feminism and Postmodernism, which revealed the political dynamics of legal power and legitimacy at the international level—something which mainstream scholars had largely ignored or dismissed.[18] As such, Postmodernism and Feminism exposed the complex influence of politics in law and the attendant need to devise alternative interpretations of law. The radical focus on the interaction of politics and law and legitimacy and politics seemed to play an important role in this respect; for it arguably inspired mainstream IL and IR scholars to devise an objective framework for studying this interaction.

Legalization and World Politics: Theoretical Advance or Methodological Stasis?

A key variable of this objective framework is the decentralization of power at the international level. For many mainstream IR theorists, decentralized enforcement at the international level represents a soft form of rule of law in which the transparency of rules and the fear of punishment represent functional components of the international system.[19] More importantly, it raises the question of whether the functional components of institutions explain the causal effects of norms and rules, or how levels of legitimacy might be measured in terms of obligation and the precision of rules.

In his article on the two optics of IR and IL, Keohane focuses attention on what he referred to as two causal pathways of understanding the dynamics of compliance and the causal effects of state interest and behavior, notably a "normative and instrumentalist optic."[20] As he notes, whereas an instrumentalist optic "focuses on interests" as the cause of compliance and cooperation (exclusively), a normative optic emphasizes the power and legitimacy of norms in "pulling them towards compliance."[21] In his view, the agenda and rule-setting of institutions explain how normative and instrumental factors "work in tandem with each other, not at cross purposes with each other."[22] For Keohane, compliance can and often does lend itself to scientific analysis or the causal effects of norms and rules on cooperative arrangements between and among states. For this reason, the subjective desire to be respected cannot explain the casual patterns of a state's desire to belong to a community. In fact, as Keohane points out, the normative pull in this sense becomes tautological since a shared desire to abide by rules is the same thing as proving one's desire to belong to the community.[23] Thus, a scientific explanation of international norms and legitimacy and obligation must be able to overcome the indeterminacy of this subjective factor (desire). It must, in other words, establish casual patterns in the international environment, which measure the impact of global rules and norms on state and non-state behavior.

In regard to this task, several recent interpretations of decentralized enforcement have revealed the growing complexity of these global patterns. John Ruggie, for instance, states that the shift toward global governance reflects the unbundling of state sovereignty: "whereby states deal with issues they deem to be inescapably transterritorial in scope, and that a key indicator of such a shift would be the emergence of multi-perspectival political practices and doctrines for the governance of those spaces."[24] From this perspective, the pooling of state sovereignty constitutes new forms of institutional norms and decision-making bodies (EU, WTO, and ICC); hence new modes of global governance.

Moreover, Joseph Nye's conception of soft power stresses the multiple channels through which states learn to bargain and negotiate on issues.[25] Soft power in this sense explains why many states are willing to bargain with other states, even though anarchy at the international level conditions the fear of some states or their decision to cheat. In short, bargaining allows states to pursue their long-term economic and social benefits; it shows how imperfect knowledge and lower transaction costs provide the opportunities for relative gains. Accordingly, international rules and norms can be characterized as functional attributes of the international system. Not only do they create tasks for cooperation and integration, but they also demonstrate the important link between organizational growth and the problem-solving capabilities of international criminal courts.

Legalization and Its Limitations

So how does legalization theory seek to integrate IR and IL? Here, legalization refers to "a particular set of characteristics that institutions may possess."[26] It is a process by which the legalizing of authority at the international level reflects the administering and adjudicating of international rules and norms in the form of dispute settlement and decision making [e.g., World Trade Organization (WTO), the Montreal Protocols, and the European Union (EU)].

There are three dimensions of legalization: obligation, precision, and delegation.[27] While obligation is characterized as the duty or commitment to abide by one's responsibilities to implement international norms and rules at the state level, precision refers to the specific terms of a treaty or a set of rules that facilitate the implementation of programs or policies aimed at securing compliance. Delegation, by comparison, represents the capacity of the authorities of the regime to administer the penalties for noncompliance. It is along these dimensions, as the authors note, that the concept of legalization constitutes a multidimensional continuum, ranging from the ideal type of hard legalization to soft legalization.

According to the authors, the decentralization of power at the international level requires us to explain how rules and norms facilitate bargaining and create high levels of transparency or access to information in international institutions (e.g., informational technology). Among the most notable or high profile institutions included in their study are the ICC, WTO, the European Union Court of Justice on Human Rights, and the Vienna Convention. All of these institutions assume a particularly high level of effectiveness, ranging from high to low. Thus, for example, the ICC displays a high level of obligation, precision, and delegation and is therefore considered one of the most effective regimes.

Here, it is important to stress the authors' concession regarding the complex interaction of law and politics, namely, "the difficulty in identifying the causal effects of legalization."[28] In their view, the interaction between law and politics represents a continuum. "At one end of the continuum," they explain, "lies the pure bargaining among states, in which states can freely exchange information and trust fully that the other will comply with the rules; at the other end, are the political considerations involved in the legal adjudication such as the ICC prosecutors or Judges of the Dispute Settlement of the WTO."[29] The latter end signifies the unpredictable, often unwieldy nature of exercising discretionary power in high-intensity political conflicts. But the question that arises here is how the political effects constitute or determine the political considerations involved in adjudicating power.

Clearly, a legal institution such as the International Court of Justice (ICJ) must consider the political nature of each case when adjudicating matters related to border disputes (e.g., the dispute between Eritrea and Ethiopia). On the other hand, the ICJ's rulings are also meant to determine the legality of the case in which states that have consented to the ICJ's authority pledge to abide by the ICJ's ruling. The result is that the ICJ's opinion becomes binding, in much the same manner as a U.S. Supreme Court decision.

What makes the ICC different in this respect is the increased possibilities of non-compliance (by non-states parties) to the ICC's legal rulings. Indeed, unlike the ICJ, the ICC will have to weigh the gravity of the political consequences of intervening in the judicial affairs of non-states parties, especially those that show a strong unwillingness to cooperate. The ICC, of course, can always rely on international pressures to dampen the effects of non-state party noncompliance with its rulings. But in cases where the state has become isolated, or condemned, there is the likelihood for resistance that will challenge the formal capacity of the ICC to enforce the proscriptive norms and rules of its statute. What this means, then, is that the expectations of non-compliance will likely determine which cases the ICC will pursue and at what time, especially if it means avoiding high political and economic costs. This might, as I have suggested earlier, result in the inconsistent exercise of discretionary power (where the ICC pursues one hard case but not another), thereby generating the complex political overtones of a case, or protests against the Court's decision not to investigate or prosecute.

The point I want to stress here is that international criminal courts cannot simply rely on impartial judgment or procedural neutrality to legitimize their power. The complexity of the ICC's political dimension requires a flexible and self-directed application of the rules which can project its juridical power consistent with its rules and standards of fairness. Again, it is this self-directed application that brings together the internal politics of the ICC with its legitimacy, and which presupposes a flexible political form of legalism, as we shall see in further detail in chapters 6–8. What we need to be asking, then, is whether we can mediate between the effects of national resistance and the procedural neutrality of the ICC. How, in other words, will the ICC's determination to pursue the worst perpetrators of gross human rights violations derive from the formulation of political strategies that substantiate its moral commitment to hold accountable such perpetrators?

Now, this is not to mean that ethical considerations do not enter into the ICJ's deliberation process, nor that its rulings fail to hold strong ethical implications for those parties involved in the dispute. Rather, it suggests that, in the case of the ICC, the pursuit of moral accountability will entail a complex intersection of politics, ethics, and power, one in which carefully crafted political strategies and policies—which are designed to counter the effects of non-state party resistance—will facilitate the pursuit of this moral goal (to hold accountable all of the very worst perpetrators of gross human rights abuses). In this way, the political effects of its case selection can be seen as constitutive of its ethical and political development, since, again, it will require political strategies that direct and move it toward the realization of its moral goal.

The problem with legalization theory, therefore, is that it ignores the constitutive dimension of an institution's internal politics. This raises several questions including: How, or in what plausible way, should we understand the causal link between the ICC's ethical commitment and the political connotations of its role in promoting international security and peace? How do the ICC's ethical commitments presuppose the need for a self-directed application of its rules and a pragmatic approach? Does this provide a source for substantiating high levels of obligation and legitimizing the ICC's discretionary power for that matter?

In the following section, I shall attempt to link the ICC's ethical commitment(s) with its pragmatic, evolutionary character by showing the similarities between a self-directed application of its rules and the self-reflexivity of law and institutions. Thus, by evolutionary, I am referring to the possibilities of linking the evolution of a regime with its political and ethical development. Scientific formulations of the evolutionary growth of institutions tend to ignore this ethical dimension of evolution. A "rational design" approach, for instance, assumes that institutional growth is a product of the problem-solving capacity of the institution.[30] It focuses on three dimensions of institutionalism: centralized task building, membership rules, and rules for controlling the institution.[31] As such, it treats cooperation among states "as forward looking, as states use diplomacy and conferences to select institutional features to further their individual and collective goals, both by creating new institutions and modifying existing ones."[32] Thus, as institutions learn to resolve problems through the modification of rules, they also evolve as institutions capable of further promoting the collective interests and goals of states. As the authors of rational design theory assert: "Continuing calls for change remind us that most institutions evolve as members learn, new problems arise, and international structures shift."[33]

Within this context, the ICC, it could be said, will evolve in relation to efforts by the Assembly of States Parties (the ICC's legislative organ) to debate, vote on, and potentially resolve issues such as the role of the Security Council in determining acts of the crime of aggression.[34] Given this, it is important to delve into the evolving political implications of the ICC's legislative functions, rather than simply treating the ICC as a mechanism of accountability "without any participatory element."[35]

In short, while legalization and rational design theory help to explain the effects of regimes, they fail to show how these effects are also constitutive of the power shaping the landscape of global politics or the operations of global institutions. The exclusion of ethics in this respect limits our understanding of how the ICC will evolve in the coming years, or rather, how its ethical commitment will intersect with its politics and power to hold accountable the very worst perpetrators of gross human rights abuses.

Pragmatic Ethics and the Limits of Juridical Power

Thus far, I have stressed how ethics cannot be separated from the problem-solving strategies of global institutions. Much of this has to do with the practical design of ethics, which is to link action with the promotion of some common good, whether this involves the general social welfare or political freedom. If we exclude the ethical traits of power from our analysis of the operations of that power, we also lose an important component for explaining the limits of power on a case by case basis. The ICC's juridical power, as we have seen, will turn on its own experience and intelligence to strategically administer and enact its rules of procedures in the pursuit of its moral objective of holding accountable the very worst perpetrators of gross human rights violations. In this section, I turn attention to John Dewey's theory of value and public law, in order to shed light on the pragmatism of the ICC, or the link between the experience (situation) of the Court and its practical strategies for containing the effects of (the exercise) its own power. But before we do this, let us analyze how pragmatism has merged as an important form of social and ethical critique of international society, beginning with Richard Rorty's critique of the mirror of nature.

Pragmatism: Relevance and Application

One of the reasons why the pragmatism of Richard Rorty continues to interest many IR theorists is that it addresses the problem of uncertainty or the relativity of our knowledge/truth claims.[36] How, in other words, do we justify our knowledge of ethics when the basis of these claims to knowledge reflect (or mirror) our impression of or ideas about the essence of nature? The problem of justification in this sense returns us to the writings of Kant, who theorized that the foundations of knowledge presupposed the possibilities of regulative moral principles that were derivative of our experience (phenomena). Kant's well-known thesis of cosmopolitan right was that practical or moral reason transcended our experience by allowing us to live in accordance with universal maxims or the categorical imperative (see also chapter 5).

For Rorty, however, Kant's moral foundations reflect false or privileged representations of our experience. As he states: "It is pictures rather propositions, metaphors than statements, which determine most of our philosophical convictions."[37] According to Rorty, then, the formal and regulative rules guiding our moral actions need to be questioned in terms of the changing social circumstances of society. The reason for this is that the paradoxical detachment from our experience (with nature) is what problematizes our justification of universal ethics. In other words, our living in accordance with our moral ideals (maxims) does not presuppose the transcendence of nature; it simply represents a form of experience or a mirror of nature. In the end, our universal moral foundations are anything but actual. Rather, they underscore the relativity or plurality of truth (claims).

The problem with Rorty's critique, however, is that it relativizes the cognitive meaning of even the strongest natural desires, such as the passion for moral justice. But the desire for justice or accountability, as I have been arguing, is not some cognitive picture *per se*, but an intrinsic and objective element of our moral experience. As moral beings, we assert this objectivity through the institutional mechanisms that embody our fundamental conceptions of justice or the common good. It is in this respect that, as rational human beings, we universally condemn the crime of genocide and crimes against humanity. It is also in this manner that the principles and rules of the ICC cannot be conceived as simply formalistic or hallow statements of moral accountability.

The question that arises, therefore, is whether we can begin to understand more fully the ICC's evolution in terms of the structural features of the ICC's political experience or its internal politicization in this case. Answers to these questions will invariably turn on notions of self-reflexivity, that is, the ICC's capacity to deal with the effects of its (discretionary) power and the consequent ability to adapt to the political and social aspects of its global environment. With Dewey's insights into the evolutionary character of public and private institutions we are able to gain some appreciation of the complexity of the ethical and political dynamics of the ICC.

Unlike Habermas's discursive ethics (chapter 4), which is predicated on the evolving systemic changes associated with societal rationalization (the decoupling of systems and lifeworld), Dewey's theory of value and public law is concerned with explaining the practical and evolving ability of institutions to govern the consequences of their actions. For Dewey, it is fair to say, an institution's particular enactment of law or calculated adoption of policies reflects the natural (evolutionary) traits of that institution's pragmatic character. As Molly Cochran states, his [Dewey's] theory of value is "an inquiry into the character of the ethical agent . . . integral to finding the right course of action."[38] In the context of the ICC, then, the ethical traits of intelligence and experience can be linked to the policies and actions associated with the consistent case *selection* process of the ICC. The flexible enactment of the rules and law in this sense presupposes the (political) guidelines and policies needed to deal with the effects of the exercise of juridical power.

There are three basic dimensions of Dewey's theory of public law. First, Dewey theorizes that the indeterminacy of public acts constitutes a problematic dimension of the application of law. Here, Dewey theorizes that the causality of legitimate forms of government, while a necessary source for explaining the practices and policies of states or other institutions, cannot be detached from the observational methods for determining the consequences of policy decisions.[39] For Dewey, it was important to distinguish between public and private transactions. For while public transactions involve an exchange between two or more parties that generates consequences for the public as a whole, the latter concerns the consequences of a private transaction that remains confined to the private domain, that is to say, between the two private actors involved.[40] The former suggests that the consequences of a public transaction entails responsive governmental controls or decisions to ensure that the social circumstances are taken into account by state authorities. The ethical reasoning of political deliberation therefore, needs to be adapted to this demand, since no predetermined principle can effectively regulate the consequences of governmental action.

Second, human fallibility contradicts the effectiveness of scientific methods. The general fallibility of judgments, in Dewey's view, exposes the conceptual flaws of relying on scientific causal factors to explain public/state affairs. Again, pragmatism's main purpose is to show that human errors inhere in governmental practices. To assume otherwise is to embrace a policymaking process that leads to an arbitrary exercise of power and the underestimation of the human capacity to correct these errors. As Dewey notes, "the main facts of political action, while the phenomena vary immensely with diversity of time and place, are not hidden events when they are complex . . . they are facts of human behavior accessible to human observation."[41]

These two dimensions culminate in a third dimension of Dewey's theory: institutional self-reflexivity. Such self-reflexivity depends on one's capacity to detect the consequences of error or moral judgment; it "involves," as Dewey explains, "the selection of persons to serve as representatives of the interests created by these perceived consequences and to define the functions which they shall possess and employ."[42] Dewey is careful not to adopt a linear perspective on progress, since "retrogression is what makes it necessary to correct for the defects in decisionmaking."[43] His emphasis on retrogression is meant to convey an immanent, albeit open-ended process of accumulating political knowledge; not a linear trajectory of progress.

Given these three dimensions, it is important to stress the close link between a self-directed application of the rules and the dimension of self-reflexivity. Again, a self-directed application of the rules refers to a flexible adherence of these rules; it reflects the autonomous capacity of the ICC to draw on its own institutional resources to further engage and shape the circumstances of its environment. This is how I have sought to link the ICC's formative development with its internal politicization. In this respect, Dewey's formulation of the dimension of self-reflexivity reveals the importance of fallibility as a (evolutionary) source of the flexible application of rules. On the one hand, it shows how the rule of law or the strict application of the law (by extension) can make it impossible to address these imperfections of judgment, or to advance society, for that matter.

On the other hand, Dewey's theory demonstrates how the flexible application of the law will involve a far more complex set of policy arrangements for managing the social consequences of one's actions. In many respects, then, a self-directed application of the rules, as understood in this book, takes us beyond Dewey's principle of self-reflexivity. For it underscores the need for structural policy arrangements on the international level, which provide a range of sub-structural contexts for extending effective strategic action or the flexible adherence to the rules. Thus, for instance, a new cooperative arrangement between the ICC and the U.N. Security Council, (which will involve institutional reengineering) will allow the ICC to address social concerns that might typically remain beyond the scope of its influence. In this sense, political legalism may be viewed, in part, as a structural pragmatic approach on the international level, since the ICC, as an international institution, must adapt to a far more complex set of (global) situations than those found on the state societal level (Dewey's focus).

In another sense, Dewey's formulation of a pragmatic character might enable us to further understand the self-directed application of the ICC's rules in terms of a consistent case selection process. Case selection in this respect will need to be derived from the observed patterns of state resistance or noncompliance in order to provide the basis for strategically overcoming these effects through diplomatic negotiations or direct bargaining between the Prosecutor and state officials. A pragmatic criteria of case selection, therefore, will allow the ICC to organize its experience and intelligence around a set of guidelines for directing its actions toward the ethic of moral accountability. Steven Ratner, for instance, proposes several pragmatic guidelines for justifying the exercise of discretionary power of international criminal courts. These include a) the severity of the atrocities with which the defendant is associated (e.g., heinous prosecution); b) strength of evidence; c) the political powerlessness of the state; and d) the absence of opposition from any state to their prosecutions ("foreign policy repercussion").[44]

Such guidelines might also address the practical effect of the ICC's geographical focus. The problem, of course, with targeting individuals according to regions (even if this is where much of the gross human rights abuses have occurred) is that it may serve as the grounds for hotly contesting the ICC's fairness. Certain lessons, therefore, might be learned from the establishment of the ICTY as an independent, self-functioning court (chapter 1). Critics of the ICTY's involvement in the Kosovo War, for instance, argue that such an effect disguises the government's control over the media in the United States and other liberal societies. Edward Herman and David Peterson, for instance, suggest that the Kosovo War exposed NATO's "destructive" control over the media and reflected the strong partnership between the U.S.-led NATO alliance and the media (CNN's role in selling and packaging NATO's war).[45] Whether this confirms the politicization (NATO's) of the ICTY is not altogether clear, however. But perception of political bias is almost certain to arise in connection with the inconsistent exercise of discretionary power in high-intensity political conflicts.

It is this perception that also reflects the tension between state sovereignty and the ICC's global juridical power. On a practical level, I have tried to show how a fuller understanding of the ICC's pragmatic character allows us to steer, albeit in a limited way, in the direction of moral accountability. Yet, as we shall see, a self-directed application of the ICC's rules also involves discursive and cosmopolitan considerations of the ICC's formative evolution.

Conclusion: Implications of Pragmatic Ethics

In this chapter, I showed how pragmatism allows us to explain the role of experience and intelligence in the Court's formative evolution, particularly in the context of a consistent and reliable case selection process. Thus, Dewey's theory is relevant to consider here, since it demonstrates the importance of linking a self-directed application of the rules with the self-reflexivity of institutions. In this way, the imperfections of institutions will require more complex formulas of policymaking that can further direct the ICC toward the ethical goal of moral accountability.

A growing number of theorists have suggested that the intelligibility of the ethics of accountability will depend on our ability to articulate the policy influence of overlooked sources of international law (non-state actors or private actors).[46] As Claire Cutler points out, "the movement away from the hierarchical model of rule and analyzing the tensions and counter-trends in contemporary legal regulation provides a clearer analytical understanding of the multiplicity of legal subjects and sources constituting international law."[47] If conventional IR theory is to work in this direction, however, it will need to develop a pragmatic and ethical focus on global politics. More than that, it will need to work within a global perspective to explain the needed policy structures for *flexing* the global juridical power of the ICC. This calls attention to the topic of world society and the role of the ICC in shaping world society as a whole. In the next chapter, I will explore this topic and how the increasing need for political legitimacy constitutes a form of world societal rationalization or global juridification.

Notes

1. The concept of legalization was the specific theme of a recent issue of *International Organization*, entitled "Legalization and Global Politics." See Kenneth W. Abbot, Robert Keohane, Andrew Moravcsik, Anne-Marie Slaughter, and Duncan Snidal, "The Concept of Legalization," *International Organization* 54, no. 3 (2000): 401–419.

2. Abbot et. al., "The Concept of Legalization," 419.

3. As Caroline Fehl has demonstrated in a recent article, the ICC may even provide an important test case for bridging IR approaches. See Caroline Fehl, "Explaining the International Criminal Court: A 'Practice Test' for Rationalist and Constructivist Approaches," *European Journal of International Relations* 10, no. 3 (2004): 359–360.

4. See, e.g., Oscar Shachter, "General Course in Public International Law," *Recueil des Cours* 5 (1982): 1–395; H.L.A. Hart, "International Law," in Robert J. Beck, Anthony Clark Arend, and Robert D. Vander Lugt, eds. *International Rules: Approaches from International Law and International Relations* (Oxford: Oxford University Press, 1996), 75–93.

5. The strand of IR theory to which I am referring here is liberal institutionalism. See, e.g., Robert Keohane, *After Hegemony* (Princeton: Princeton University Press, 1983); op. cit., International Institutions: Two Approaches, *International Studies Quarterly* 32 (1998): 379–96; Robert Axelrod, *The Evolution of Cooperation* (New York: Basic Books, 1984). For an overview of regime theory and its liberal variants, see Stephen D. Krasner, "Structural Cause and Regime Consequences," in Stephen D. Krasner, ed. *International Regimes* (Ithaca, NY: Cornell University Press, 1983).

6. Stanley Hoffmann, "The Political Ethics of International Relations," in Joel H. Rosenthal, ed. *Ethics & International Affairs* (Washington D.C.: Georgetown University Press, 1999), 27–48.

7. See Anne-Marie Slaughter, "International Law and International Relations Theory: A Dual Agenda," *American Journal of International Law* 87 (1993).

8. See Kenneth W. Abbot, Robert Keohane, Andrew Moravcsik, Anne-Marie Slaughter, and Duncan Snidal, "The Concept of Legalization," *International Organization* 54, no. 3 (2000): 401–419.

9. See Barbara Koremenos, Charles Lipson, and Duncan Snidal, "The Rational Design of International Institutions," *International Organization* 55, no.4 (2001): 761–799.

10. See Myres McDougal and Harold Lasswell, "The Identification and Appraisal of Diverse Systems of Public Order," *American Journal of International Law* 53 (1959).

11. McDougal and Lasswell, "The Identification and Appraisal of Diverse Systems," 3.

12. Hart, "International Law," 77.

13. Thomas Franck, *The Power of Legitimacy Among Nations* (New York: Oxford University Press), 38.

14. See Abram Chayes and Antonio Chayes, *The New Sovereignty: Compliance with International Regulatory Agreements* (Cambridge, MA: Harvard University Press, 1995).

15. See Slaughter, "International Law and International Relations Theory."

16. Robert J. Beck, Robert J. and Anthony Arend and Robert Vander Lugt, eds. *International Rules: Approaches from International Law and International Relations.* (Oxford: Oxford University Press, 1996).

17. Robert J. Beck, "International Law and International Relations: The Prospects for Interdisciplinary Collaboration," in Robert J. Beck, Anthony Clark Arend, and Robert D. Vander Lugt, eds. *International Rules: Approaches from International Law and International Relations* (Oxford: Oxford University Press, 1996), 7.

18. David Kennedy, "A New Stream of International Law Scholarship," in Robert J. Beck, Anthony Clark Arend, and Robert D. Vander Lugt, eds. *International Rules:*

Approaches from International Law and International Relations (Oxford: Oxford University Press, 1996), 230–252; see also Nigel Purvis, "Critical Legal Studies in International Law," *Harvard International Law Journal* 392 (1991): 81–127; Hilary Charlesworth, C. Chinkin, S. Wright, "Feminist Approaches to International Law," *American Journal of International Law* 85 (1991): 613–645.

19. As Andrew Hurrell notes: "bargaining outcomes do not depend on the achievement of some notion of optimum allocative efficiency, but rather on the perceptions that the outcome meets some criterion of justice and equality." See Andrew Hurrell, "International Society and the Study of Regimes: A Reflective Approach," in Robert J. Beck, Anthony Clark Arend, Robert D Vander Lugt, eds. *International Rules.* (Oxford: Oxford University Press, 1996), 219.

20. Robert Keohane, "International Relations and International Law: Two Optics," *Harvard Journal of International Law* 38, no. 2 (1997): 491. Keohane defines institutions as "persistent and connected set of rules (formal and informal) that prescribe behavior." See Keohane, "International Institutions: Two Approaches," 387.

21. Keohane, "International Relations and International Law," 491.

22. Keohane, "International Relations and International Law," 501.

23. Franck, *The Power of Legitimacy Among Nations,* 38.

24. John G. Ruggie, *Constructing a New World Polity* (New York: Routledge Press, 1999), 167.

25. Joseph S. Nye, *Power in the Global Information Age: From Realism to Globalization* (New York: Routledge, 2004); op. cit., *Soft Power* (New York: Public Affairs, 2004).

26. Abbot, Keohane, Moravcsik, Slaughter, and Snidal, *Legalization and Global Politics*; op. cit., Judith Goldstein, Miles Kahler, Robert Keohane, and Anne-Marie Slaughter, "Introduction: Legalization and World Politics," *International Organization* 54(3)(2000): 385–399.

27. Abbot, Keohane, Moravcsik, Slaughter, and Snidal, *Legalization and Global Politics,* 402–403.

28. Abbot, Keohane, Moravcsik, Slaughter, and Snidal, *Legalization and Global Politics,* 419.

29. Abbot, Keohane, Moravcsik, Slaughter, and Snidal, *Legalization and Global Politics,* 419.

30. Barbara Koremenos, Charles Lipson, and Duncan Snidal, "The Rational Design of International Institutions," *International Organization* 55, no.4 (2001): 761–799.

31. Koremenos, Lipson, and Snidal, "The Rational Design of International Institutions," 763.

32. Koremenos, Lipson, and Snidal, "The Rational Design of International Institutions," 766.

33. Koremenos, Lipson, and Snidal, "The Rational Design of International Institutions," 767.

34. It should be noted again that while the Assembly's powers are designed to eliminate the arbitrariness of the Court by serving as a quasi constitutional body, the Assembly does not make laws *per se*; it can only amend the ICC Statute (see ICC Statute,

Article 121). Assembly of States Parties. (2003) *Draft Paper on the Definition and Elements of the Crime of Aggression*. ICC-ASP/2/10.

35. Ruth Grant and Robert Keohane, "Accountability and the Abuses of Power in World Politics," *American Political Science Review* 99, no. 1 (2005): 29–44.

36. See Richard Rorty, *Philosophy and the Mirror of Nature* (Princeton: Princeton University Press, 1979).

37. Rorty, *Philosophy and the Mirror of Nature*, 12.

38. Molly Cochran, *Normative Theory in International Relations* (Cambridge: Cambridge University, 1999), 178.

39. John Dewey, "Search for the Public," in Larry A. Hickman and Thomas M. Alexander, eds. *The Essential Dewey: Pragmatism, Education, Democracy*, Vol. 1 (Bloomington: Indiana University Press, 1998), 281–307.

40. Dewey, "Search for the Public," 285.

41. Dewey, "Search for the Public," 286.

42. Dewey, "Search for the Public," 291.

43. Dewey, "Search for the Public," 290.

44. Steven R. Ratner, "Belgium's War Crimes Statute: A Postmortem," *American Journal of International Law* 97, no. 4 (2004): 888–897.

45. Edward S. Herman and David Peterson, "CNN: Selling Nato's War Globally," in P. Hammond and E. S. Herman, eds. *Degraded Capability: The Media and the Kosovo Crisis* (London: Pluto Press, 2001), 111–122. See also Edward S. Herman, "Propaganda System One: From Diem and Arbenz to Milosevic," in Raju G.C. Thomas, ed. *Yugoslavia Unraveled* (Lanham, MD: Lexington Books, 2000), 243–258.

46. See Andrew Linklater, "The Problem of Harm in World Politics: Implications for the Sociology of States-System," *International Affairs* 78 (2002): 319–338; Claire Cutler, "Law in the Global Polity," in Morten Ougaard and Philipp Higgot, eds. *Towards a Global Polity* (London: Routledge Press, 2002), 58–77.

47. Cutler, 73.

4

Constructing World Society: The Ethics and Politics of Global Juridification

> But, so far, we have not got any rules finding definitions, and, as we cannot set forth such rules without a previous knowledge of nature, that is without a definition of the understanding and its power, it follows that either that the definition of the understanding must be clear in itself, or that we can understand nothing.
>
> —Spinoza, *Ethics*

THIS CHAPTER ADDRESSES the relationship between the ICC's juridical structure and the construction of world society. As we saw earlier, the ICC enacts and administers the rules of procedures when states fail to uphold their obligation to investigate and/or prosecute gross human rights offenses. It is this procedural power that allows the ICC to function independently of state juridical power and to assert its jurisdictional authority over non-compliant states. One of the aims of this chapter is to examine the relationship between the nature of the ICC's juridical power and the new moral order of world society. How, in other words, does the ICC constitute a flexible mechanism for administering the elements of a new critical world order?

Anyone who is familiar with Max Weber's writings, for instance, will recall how Weber conceptualized the evolution of modern society in terms of the dialectical interaction of instrumental rationality and the disenchantment with worldviews. Weber, as we shall see, believed that legal domination, or the macro-structure of legal authority, had emerged out of the ethical conviction of worldviews, or the value rationalization of modern society. Because the enactment of rules and laws operated independently of moral and ethical considerations (neutrality), citizens learned to obey or strictly abide by the judgment and rulings of criminal and civil courts. The unethical elements of the social order therefore, were manifested by the dominant rule of legitimate authority or societal rationalization (bureaucratical rule).

What makes the ICC unique in this sense, is that it lacks the key component of this rule, namely, a citizenry to obey the rules and laws of the ICC. The ICC of course, is an international legal institution, whose legal authority is derived from state consent. In this way, its juridical structure represents a displaced model of traditional legitimacy, that is, a decentralized or decentered form of juridical authority, which relies principally on state consent to validate its political and moral legitimacy.

Given this transformation of juridical authority, the first part of this chapter analyzes the transition from an international to world society in which human rights, financial institutions, and NGOs have, in certain respects, transcended state sovereignty. Here, I focus on Barry Buzan's recent efforts to systematize English School Theory (EST) to explain the limitations and possibilities of understanding the global nature of the ICC's juridical authority and the tensions between universalism and particularism. The second part of the chapter focuses in greater depth on the conceptual components of world society and how the ICC fits into this schema or evolving societal rationalization. I claim that the complementarity principle provides an important rational link between the ICC's juridical power and legal domination, since it validates and encourages further rational discussion of the (global) need to justify and enact certain norms at the international level.

Again, the assertion of the ICC's global juridical authority can and should be understood as an increasingly complex form of functional differentiation. In this way, it is possible to identify two aspects of the ICC's functional role as a global form of legal juridification. First, the ICC provides the substantive context for projecting this legal authority; and second, it encourages the very rational discussion of justifying and enacting norms that will strengthen this context. In this way, global juridification, as understood in this book, refers to the adoption of global procedures and rules for administering and projecting legal authority at the interstate level. The process of rationalizing this upward projection of decentralized authority is what constitutes a flexible and decentered model of juridical power. Such decentering, as we shall see, presupposes the discursive dimension of this new juridical authority and the importance of Habermas's conception of discursive ethics.

From International to World Society

There have been many recent theories of world society that have revealed the complex and changing dynamics in the world order. As we shall see, many of these theories help us to understand the role of the ICC in shaping this society. The purpose of beginning with Buzan's analysis of international and world society is that it exposes some of the key tensions between a society of states and world society, including the role of collective enforcement. We will therefore examine some of these tensions and the importance of social constructivism for advancing a systematic analysis of world politics. In doing so, we will assess the limitations of Buzan's and Wendt's social theory, before moving on to engage various political sociological theories to investigate the global juridical power of the ICC.

Problems and Limitations

In his recent book, *From International to World Society?* Buzan argues that the English School has failed to develop a systematic distinction between international and world society. What he proposes here is a new approach for EST: a scientific theory of international politics that draws on, and in many ways rivals the scientific or grand theories of IR (i.e., Wendt's social theory of international politics). Whether or not Buzan succeeds in developing the basis for a grand EST, it is important to examine some of his insights into the problems of EST and how they allow us to situate the ICC's global juridical power in the emergence of world society. Let us therefore begin with Buzan's primary focus on the distinction between international and world society.

International society is typically defined in terms of a community of states sharing a common fate and adhering to a mutually agreed upon set of values aimed at promoting and maintaining international peace and security. What regulates the behavior of states belonging to this society are the moral constraints of international order.[1] Earlier theorists (realists) of the English school, such as Martin Wight, theorized that international society could be defined principally in terms of a balance of power and the moral constraints of the international system. Concerning this idea, he states that

> International society is a society unlike any other, for it is the most comprehensive form of society on earth. It has four peculiarities: It is a unique society composed of the other, more fully organized societies which we call states. States are its prime and immediate members, even if there is a sense in which its ultimate members are men.[2]

In this respect, international society constitutes an evolving society whose dynamics and dimensions have been shaped by years of conflict, competition, and bargaining. In this manner, Wight theorized that international society represented a competitive realm of interests, values, and ideas, in which the intellectual struggle to understand the interstices of power, order, and civility in the international system explained the preferences for different theoretical approaches to international politics.[3]

But if the need for an international order explains why states mutually agree to protect the basic norms and principles governing relations among states, then what is the precise distinction between an international system and international society? Hedley Bull (and Wight) addressed this broad question by focusing on the transnational implications of the coordination of EC policy. Here, he proposed that the constitutionalization of the EC (through treaty law) represented a growing trend toward stronger international enforcement, or a new world order in which states had become more willing to give up their sovereignty in return for stronger forms of international enforcement.

But Bull failed to arrive at a concrete working definition of world society. For him, world society remained an abstract concept or what he referred to as "the totality of global social interaction." As he states:

> By a world society we understand not merely a degree of interaction linking all parts of the human community to one another, but a sense of common interest and common values, on the basis of which common rules and institutions may be built. The concept of world society, in this sense, stands to the totality of global social interaction, as our concept of international society stands to the concept of the international system.[4]

For Bull, more observational methods will need to be employed to analyze the formal and informal operations of world society. Following Bull, then, Buzan contends that contemporary English School theorists have failed to develop or employ such methods to analyze the role of economic integration and other sociological developments of international society.

Where, then, did EST go wrong in terms of developing a systematic theory of world society? According to Buzan, the answer lies in the English School's somewhat narrow focus on human rights issues. While the works of John Vincent, Nicholas Wheeler, and Tim Dunne offer important analyses of the shared obligations of the international community to intervene in humanitarian crises, they have not, in Buzan's view, provided a systematic conception of world society.[5] In fact, the crucial distinction between solidarism, or a "wide-ranging set of norms, rules, and institutions, covering both coexistence issues and cooperation in pursuit of shared interests, including some scope for collective enforcement,"[6] and pluralism (the particular goals of equal sovereign states pursued in terms of self-interest) has proved largely restrictive of EST as a systematic theory.[7]

For Buzan, however, it is the need for coercion that ultimately exposes and problematizes the limitations of solidarism. As he states: "observance of human rights has to be imposed on those who do not share belief in the value and or does not calculate observance of it as being to their advantage, then one faces the problem that this prohibition can, in the short term only be expanded by coercion."[8] In this manner, protecting universal human rights becomes the source of an ineluctable tension between the ideals of the interhuman domain or global civil society (e.g., universal reason, tolerance, equality, and inclusivity) and state coercion.

The question that arises, then, is how do we prevent coercion from becoming the prevailing norm. Buzan's answer is that "the essence of the matter is whether individual rights/world society necessarily conflict with state's rights/international society, or can be in harmony with them . . . whether solidarism can progress to the point where it calls into question the state system."[9] In short, the concept of world society, while providing what Buzan calls "incipient ontological foundations,"[10] still remains a vague concept, or, as he puts it, "the dustbin of theories and ideas . . . an incoherent mix of cosmopolitan morality and universalist values."[11]

Now, this may be misrepresenting the state of the art of world society studies, especially since other sociological theories of world society, such as the Stanford School, have studied the transformative impact of social and environmental movements and NGOs on state behavior.[12] But Buzan's argument here is not that we should downplay the evidence of these studies, but rather that we should incorporate them into a systematic, normative IR theory. In this manner, EST needs to begin examining the emergence of universal morality within a sociological and economic framework that uses the evidence and rigorous analysis of NGOs to validate the internalization of norms.

Buzan refers to this validating process in terms of the how and why of internalizing norms and social expectations (that other states will enforce these norms). Here, he distinguishes between "thin" and "thick" forms of solidarism to identify the varying degrees of shared values and norms, and the types of moral constraints imposed by the interstate system. John Vincent's later writings on humanitarian intervention can, for instance, be classified in terms of a "thin" form of solidarism, since they focus on the violability of non-intervention under various circumstances, while at the same time stopping short of endorsing a universal principle of collective intervention. Thick solidarism, by contrast, places greater emphasis on the moral violability of state sovereignty, by stressing how severe violations of humanitarian norms constitute a breach in international law and the problem of legitimizing collective humanitarian (U.N.) action.

If the distinction between thick and thin solidarism exposes the underlying internal tensions of the concept of world society, then moving beyond these tensions, as Buzan suggests, will require an expanded focus on the sociological and economic factors of international society. More specifically, it will entail the use of general scientific variables to explain why actors internalize norms. For Buzan, as we shall see, Alexander Wendt's constructivist theory of international politics provides an important basis for developing a systematic EST. But the issue that this raises is whether constructivism that is centered in state sovereignity allows us to understand the constitutive, yet problematic tensions between enforcement and human rights.

Indeed, we need to be especially wary of this issue of legitimizing the authority of global institutions, since Buzan seems to underemphasize the issue of political legitimacy at the global level. Indeed, the main reason why enforcement becomes problematic in this sense is that global institutions require strong forms of political legitimacy to compensate for the lack of enforcement at the global level. It is of course true that Wendt stresses the importance of legitimacy in terms of the Kantian culture. But in doing so, he also raises the important issue of whether the historical emergence of new standards of legitimacy validates the primacy of global actors, or whether it alters the content of the intersubjective structure of international society.

Constructivism: Scope and Limits

Social Theory of International Politics

Constructivism in IR theory posits that the international system represents an intersubjective network of values, norms, beliefs, and interests, and that the interaction of these phenomena shapes the institutional practices and norms that govern relations between and among states and international organizations. In this sense, constructivism in IR theory explains how norms and rules both constitute and regulate the behavior or expectations of states; and why the formation of state identity can be understood in terms of this interactive process. In *Social Theory of International Politics*, Wendt is able to build on his earlier work on constructivism by formulating the scientific or general variables for analyzing the constitutive nature of state identity and cooperation in the international system. As noted earlier, Buzan adopts Wendt's theory as a working framework of analysis for developing a systematic EST.[13] Therefore, let us briefly assess Wendt's social theory of international politics.

Wendt distinguishes between three cultures of anarchy: Hobbesian, Lockean, and Kantian. Each one of these cultures (of anarchy) refers to three degrees of internalization, or corresponding analytical variables: coercion, calculation, and belief. As one might expect, the most pronounced type and degree of coercion derives from the Hobbesian tradition, in which state behavior is driven by enmity and fear of international violence, or a state's need to maximize their security to defend itself against external attack.[14]

Lockean culture, by contrast, refers to the regulative function of liberal ideas, such as autonomy and tolerance, or rather, the implementation of civil and political rights embodied in the natural rights of freedom, property, and life. In this cultural realm, autonomy, tolerance, and respect serve as the basis for voluntary self-restraint in an anarchic world. It is upon the basis that states tend to pursue relative and absolute gains to secure peace, freedom, and property.[15] Coercion in this sense can be explained by reference to rational calculation which constitutes the prevailing mode through which states internalize the values of peace and cooperation.

The Kantian culture of anarchy derives from Kant's ideas on the international solidarity among states. Kant, for instance, emphasizes how moral maxims exert a self-regulating influence over political affairs. To this end, Kantian culture suggests a third degree of internalization: the role of legitimacy in which "states identify with each other, seeing each other's security not just as instrumentally related to their own, but as literally being their own."[16]

For Buzan, Wendt's three cultures of anarchy provide a consistent analysis of the intersubjective framework of international society, even though it offers a somewhat questionable justification of states as the essential, primary agents of this framework. In effect, it takes into account not just the "type of social structure, but also its mode or depth of internalization."[17] As such, Wendt's theory explains the how and why of the internalization of shared norms, by linking together the social structure of international system with the what, or the particular shared value(s).

Still, Wendt's social theory of international politics is not without its limits. Indeed, according to Buzan, Wendt's theory blurs the distinction between community (*Gemeinshaft*) and society (*Gesellschaft*), by failing to explain the depth of "internalization of identity" (third mode), or, to show how the degree of internalization of norms and values corresponds with the distinctive properties of community and society on the international level. The task of linking state identity with systemic variables requires further analysis of the distinctive properties of international society and community. Thus, whereas international society can be characterized by the constraints imposed by the rules of the system (Grotian), a community underscores an arguably deeper sense of identity, that is, a stronger set of attachments to the common good that can, over time, be revised by the states and actors belonging to that community.

A deeper sense of what it means to belong to a community, therefore, is what encourages us to contribute to the general welfare and well-being of society. It forces us, in fact, to engage the how/why dimension of Wendt's scheme in ways that reveal the inclusivity of other identity formations or agents; and not just states.[18] To this end, Wendt's desire to establish "clear patterns of social interactions" among the three domains, although important for achieving parsimony and analytic clarity in his theory, also, as Buzan insists, "borders on heroic simplification."[19] Buzan's argument, then, is that the English School can enrich Wendt's social theory, by incorporating non-state actors of international society into the mix or interaction of the three general variables across the three domains. Put differently, it will entail analysis of the growing homogenization of domestic structures via the convergence of state expectations around an increasing range of norms and institutions. As he states:

> The issue of community and belief emerge more strongly for solidarist international societies, where an ever-changing range of cooperative norms, rules, and institutions is likely both to reflect, and encourage, a move towards increasing similarity in the domestic structures and values of the state concerned.[20]

Solidarism, as suggested earlier, is predicated on liberalist assumptions; the most important being that certain constitutional or basic human rights serve to mediate between civility and uncivility. The active intervention of these rights through (international) institutions is what allows us to stabilize the expectations of civil society; it ensures individuals that their civil rights are secure and protected. In the past several years, what we have seen is the emergence of global institutions that now actively mediate between transnational civil and uncivil society. The ICC is perhaps the most visible institution in this respect. And like other global civil institutions such as NGOs, its civilizing function motivates us to understand the limits and possibilities of establishing cooperative arrangements, or the enforcement of the governing norms of transnational civil society. This is why we distinguish between transnational civil and uncivil society; for it allows us to have some concrete sense as to how we are advancing beyond uncivil forms of conduct.

But the question that this raises is whether we can expect the ICC to induce all state leaders to refrain from gross human rights abuses, or rather, to act in accordance with their rational interests of maintaining and promoting their reputation (status) within the global civil society. Buzan, however, remains skeptical of the certainty of state refrain. In his view, "should human rights and democracy be accepted as primary institutions of global international society, that would not entirely remove their tension with sovereignty and non-intervention (not to mention war), so creating pressure for adaptation and reinterpretation in both directions."[21]

Still, this does not mean that such tension should be interpreted as unduly restrictive. In fact, it is precisely this tension, as I have argued, that allows us to understand the political development of the ICC or its ability to adapt to its global political environment. Buzan, therefore, is correct to believe that "coercion is never very far from clarification and the belief in international politics."[22] But he remains unclear as to how this reinterpretation and adaptation can and should occur. Much of this has to do with his failure to develop a globally (de)-centered analysis of institutions, or to work from a world society perspective which, as Martin Shaw insists "requires recognition in the institutions and culture of the state system of the demands of society for accountability."[23]

Indeed, analyzing the global operations of institutions is what allows us to understand the outcome of the power transference from the state to global level. By operating within state-centered perspective, Buzan must necessarily limit himself to the restrictive nature of global civil society institutions. In the end, he must leave it up to critical theorists such as Andrew Linklater to engage the possibilities of the emergence of world society and the conceptual and concrete operations of this society.

Buzan is not alone in this respect, however. Conventional analysis of prohibition regimes, for instance, continues to work within a state-centered perspective to analyze the emerging global dimensions of power. As one of the most influential scholars of prohibition regimes, Ethan Nadelman argues that "the ultimate success of global prohibition regimes depends primarily on the vulnerability of an activity to the global that suppresses efforts by states."[24] Other IR scholars focus on the impact of prohibition regimes by examining the functional attributes of the global common good, namely, a "shared sense that all members have a positive stake in building and maintaining long-term cooperative relationships."[25] This, however, steers us away from the more pressing normative and sociological issue of whether state sovereignty will restrict the ICC's juridical power, or whether the application of the ICC' s new standards of legitimacy (and its attendant ability to promote its political legitimacy) will allow it to overcome the tensions between state sovereignty and its global juridical power.

In short, the limits of realism, institutionalism, and constructivism leave many questions unanswered concerning the "obligatory force of legal rules, the uniqueness of the modern institution of international law, the role of law in legitimation struggles and the progressive cosmopolitanization of international law."[26] Christian Reus-Smit, for instance, argues that the complexity of the politics of law requires a more critical engagement with social constructivism to understand both the positive and negative implications of the cosmopolitanization of law. In his view, the main limitation of social constructivism is that it treats norms, interests, and identities as natural, or given features of an intersubjective framework. In this way, it fails to address the question of why states or other actors identify with certain norms during a certain time period; or alternatively why these agents learn to identify with evolving moral standards of legitimacy.[27]

How we address this issue will depend on our ability to theorize about two topics: the ICC's role in cosmopolitanizing international law and its mediating function within the fluid division between universalism and particularism.[28] I will address the former topic in the following chapter where I theorize about the political cosmopolitanism of the ICC. The latter, as I have suggested, forces us to consider the implications of the ICC for an emerging world society. As Jason Ralph insists, the ICC will continue to push us further in the direction of a world society governed by universal morality, requiring more sophisticated theoretical analysis of the ICC and its role in shaping state identity.[29] The theoretical task, then, is this: to focus on the evolution of the ICC's political legitimacy, and more importantly, to link this evolution with world society as a whole. As we shall see in the next section, we will need to conceptualize its juridical structure as a new political space for imagining and even concretizing the possibilities of a flexible form of global juridical power.

Global Juridification: A Novel Flexible Institutional Macro-Structure?

Turning to the notion of global juridification, it is important that we understand how or in what ways the ICC can and should be conceptualized as a legal representation of world societal rationalization. There are two ways in which I will approach this task. First, I shall briefly outline Weber's and Habermas's social theory of societal rationalization, and show how their social critiques of society allow us to grasp the concept of global juridification and the attendant role of legitimacy in promoting social integration and consensus formation (mutual understanding as a precondition for legitimizing and validating the legal and moral norms of the ICC). Here, I will work from Weber's conceptualization of legal domination to Habermas's theory of discursive ethics to investigate the meaning and significance of the flexible nature of the ICC's juridical authority. I will then discuss the implications of the ICC's global juridical power for understanding and advancing world society.

Juridical Authority and Its Evolution into the Global Realm

As noted earlier, Weber's conception of juridical authority is based on the idea that the juridical structure of modern society evolved from the disenchantment of world views with modern capitalist society. Disenchantment, in this sense, reflects the contradiction between one's ethical world views (religion) and the capitalist system (the power of money exchange). Weber theorized that capitalist modern society arose out of the moral calling of Calvinists; more specifically, the doctrine of predestination which resulted in new tensions between the individual and society and encouraged the believer to rationalize the objectivity of his belief (his or her productive contribution to the accumulation of capital).[30] As Weber states: "[But] since Calvin viewed all pure feelings and emotions . . . with suspicion, faith had to be proved by its objective results in order to provide a firm foundation for the *certitudo salutis*."[31]

The objectivization of one's beliefs was predicated on the distinction between instrumental rationality (the actual enactment and application of the prevailing norms and rules of society), and value rationality (how moral beliefs and values define the meaning and scope of these rules and laws). The growth of modern society, in this sense, referred to the creation of large bureaucracies, police forces, and legislative bodies: all autonomous rational structures of the state and modern capitalist society embodying the effects and ends of instrumental rationality. The legitimacy of these institutions thus reflected the dominant function assumed by these institutions in maintaining and administering societal order. This was how Weber derived the well-known term of the state's monopoly on the use of violence.[32] In sum, Weber theorized that individuals and groups learned to orient their religious motivations, intent, and actions to modern society. The result of this evolving orientation was that citizens learned to obey societal laws which, in turn, served as the basis of dominant and legitimate types of authority in society.

Accordingly, Weber understood juridical power, or the application and enactment of rules and laws, as reflecting a rigid manifestation of instrumental rationality (the iron cage). In this sense, instrumental rationality tended to turn its back on the Enlightenment ideals of reason and freedom by undermining individual freedom via the domination of juridical authority. The problem, however, with this scenario is that it leaves open the question of whether the institutional effects of instrumental rationality (e.g., legal domination, bureaucratization of the state that detaches the values and beliefs from the administrative function of legitimate authority) can be overcome by the flexible application of rules and laws.

In his critique of Weber's theory of the rationalization of society, Habermas theorizes that Weber's analysis of legal domination arises out of his failure to grasp the complexity of societal rationalization.[33] For Habermas, the normative possibilities and complexity of capitalist modern society reflects the divergence between higher levels of social differentiation and the lifeworld, or the background/horizon of human experience in society. It is the rationalization of the lifeworld that produces higher levels of social differentiation, such as social movements and classes, and instantiates the reification of structures of consciousness, including the media's reporting of events, global consumerism, and money.

Thus, on the one hand, Weber, according to Habermas, was correct to theorize that the rationalization of modern society had resulted in reified forms of consciousness. On the other hand, he was wrong to believe that such rationalization resulted in permanent pathological effects, such as the loss of individual freedom, inflexibility of reason and rational public consensus on issues. Bureaucracy, in other words, is not the logical corollary and petrified ethical result of legal domination. As Habermas states: "the bureaucratization that sets in when ethics is replaced by law is, in the first instance, only an indication that the institutionalization of a steering medium is coming to its conclusion."[34]

For Habermas, what is important to recognize is that modern society is not evolving along a narrow teleological or deterministic path. Rather, it is increasing in complexity, which has raised the linguistic stakes of reaching mutual consensus and understanding, and the issue of how best to govern the moral and practical defects of society, namely, "the delinguistication of the media."[35] Thus, one of the main tasks in overcoming the effects of this uncoupling of a socially differentiated system and lifeworld is to realize how the discursive dimension of ethics (moral consciousness) can and should be linked to politically legitimate institutions *qua* modern argumentation and justification.[36] By this, Habermas means to say that any notion of legal domination, especially at the international level, comes into conflict with the norms of inclusion and equal participation in those liberal modern societies that validate one's claims as free and moral citizens and subjects of the law.

Discursive ethics, therefore, refers to moral duties and obligations embedded in linguistic actions, or the struggle to reach mutual understanding. It is, as Habermas theorizes, rooted in the following moral principle: "For a norm to be valid, the consequences and side effects that its general observance can be expected to have for the satisfaction of the particular interests of each person affected must be such that all affected can accept them freely."[37] In this sense, the discursive and ethical dimension of juridical authority is intricately connected to the shared objective of overcoming the chronic deficit in political legitimacy; that is to say, the process in which the demands for social and political inclusion validate the actions and convictions of citizens and entities alike (valorize diversity or multiculturalism).

Thus, for Habermas, it is the constitutionalization of law that provides the flexible processual framework for validating these actions and for operating within what he calls a decentered understanding of the world.[38] As he states: "The basic sociocognitive concepts of the social world and of norm-governed interaction thus evolve within the framework of a decentered understanding of the world, which in turn stems from a differentiation of speaker and world views."[39] From this standpoint, discursive ethics offers us a basis for understanding the decentered nature of global juridical power. More concretely, in terms of the ICC, this decentered and flexible form of power can be characterized by the qualitative distinction between the "citizens" of a state and the subjects of international law. For unlike state juridical authority, the ICC is comprised of sources and subjects (states) that cannot be counted on to comply with the demands of the ICC.

Yet it is precisely this decentered notion of juridical power that also presupposes a flexible consensus formation among the organs or players involved in the ICC's application of the rules of procedure and norms. From this vantage point, global juridical authority can be conceptualized in terms of the functional differentiation of juridical power at the global level, or what was referred to earlier as the unbundling of state sovereignty: a new set of political practices for administering power.

Another way we can understand this spatial idea of the ICC's power is through the diffusion of proscriptive norms. Here, it is possible to view the ICC's global juridical power as providing a minimal threshold of norm-governed interaction, in which states and individuals have come to internalize these norms, by actively discussing and shaping the moral universality of the ICC in regard to promoting international peace and security. Lothar Brock, for instance, argues that the emergence of institutional networks of NGOs, judicial institutions, human rights conventions, and charters symbolizes the increasing norm-governed interaction between local and global institutions/levels.[40] For Brock, constitutional building of human rights norms represents a functionally differentiated form of the people exercising their popular will: namely, the internalization of the ICC's proscriptive norms from the bottom up. The problem, however, with this normative assessment of world society is that it fails to balance the internalization of norms against the realities of increasing concentrations of juridical power at the global level.

This is perhaps why Dietrich Jung states that the "formal rationalization of norms and values . . ." remains the task of theorists to explain "the contemporeignity of non-contemporaneous society."[41] What he means here is that the evolution of the rationalization of world society reflects the qualitative and functional difference between world and modern state societies. Thus, while today's world society has increased in size, it still remains a "fragmented social whole or totality."[42] For Jung, world society seems to reproduce the very distinction between primitive and modern society that Weber and Habermas employed to theorize about the limitations and possibilities of instrumental rationality, or the reification of structural consciousness via the media and money.

In the context of the ICC, such a division is characterized by the uneven development of criminal codes or the gap between national domestic laws and the high standards of international criminal justice. It is this difference that explains the possibilities of what was earlier referred to as the stratification of the complementarity principle (chapter 2). Jung's conclusion, however, is that far from demonstrating a stratified global arrangement, global legal institutions reflect the growing trend toward the ethical force of self-restraint, that is, the erosion of external state coercion as the exclusive form of enforcement. In short, the global authority of the ICC invests the peoples with a desire and motivation to see the institutionalization and enactment of proscriptive norms against genocide. In this manner, it is possible to see the ICC's global authority as structuring the desire and motivation of individuals, states, and societies to uphold human rights norms.

But the question that arises here is whether this new ethical force of restraint will evolve into a potentially rigid form of juridical power; hence, the basis of a new conformity to international law. If, for instance, the legalism of the ICC is not accompanied by substantive political strategies that embody its discursive and communicative dimension, or struggle to reach a flexible consensus on issues concerning threats to its own role in promoting peace and security, then the ICC may well follow the path of a strict form of legalism. Or alternatively, it may become vulnerable to an unmediated projection of power or external politicization. This may necessarily expose the repressive effects of global governance. For, as Michael Dillon argues, "global liberal governance not only institutes certain forms of subjectification, discipline, and compliance . . . it also tends to reduce politics to policing."[43] Thus, the ICC, although it might be considered a decentered and flexible form of global authority, also requires us to understand its dynamic form of political legitimacy.

One way of doing this, as I have stressed in this book, is to distinguish between internal and external politicization. The purpose, again, is to show how the former provides a constructive and inclusive dimension of the politics of criminalizing international law, and how the distinction serves to concretize the discursive dimension of juridical authority in world society: namely, by reference to the active participation of states, NGOs, and individuals, all of which need to contribute to the Court's political dimension.

Conclusion

This chapter began with a discussion of the limits of a state centric conception of world society in order to reveal the possibilities of understanding the ICC's role in constituting world society. It also theorized about the ICC's global juridical power in two ways. First, it conceptualized the meaning and significance of this power by analyzing the works of Weber and Habermas; second, it examined how the ICC formed an important structural component of an emerging world society. Here I drew on various contemporary IR theories of world society to argue my case for understanding the complex political dynamics of the ICC's juridical power.

As we saw, the ICC's new global juridical power represents a flexible value structure or discursive framework of norms and rules: whereby its political legitimacy derives from the normative and ethical considerations of enacting and applying its rules of procedure. To guard against the potential rigidity of its legalism at the global level, however, it will be important to address the evolving link between the ICC's universal morality and its political dimension. The following chapter explores this link in terms of political cosmopolitanism.

Notes

1. Chris Brown, "World Society and the English School: An International Society Perspective on World Society," *European Journal of International Relations* 7, no. 4 (2001): 432.

2. Martin Wight, *Power Politics*, Second Edition (London: Pelican Books and the Royal Institute of International Affairs, 1978), 106.

3. Martin Wight, *International Theory: The Three Traditions* (London: Leicester University Press/Royal Institute of International Affairs, 1991).

4. Hedley Bull, *The Anarchical Society: Study of Order in World Politics* (New York: Columbia University Press, 1977), 279.

5. See, e.g., Nicholas J. Wheeler, "Pluralist or Solidarist Conceptions of International Society: Bull and Vincent on Humanitarian Intervention," *Millennium: Journal of International Studies* 21, no. 3 (1992): 463–487; op. cit., *Saving Strangers* (Oxford: Oxford University Press, 2000); Tim Dunne, "Sociological Interpretations: Instrumental, Legitimist and Coercive Interpretations of International Society," *Millennium: Journal of International Studies* 30, no. 1 (2001): 67–91; Tim Dunne, *Inventing International Society* (Basingstoke: Macmillan, 1998).

6. Buzan, *From International to World Society*, 8.

7. It should be noted that John Vincent was a pluralist in this sense, even though he did suggest the need to suspend state sovereignty under certain conditions. See, e.g., R.J. Vincent, *Human Rights and International Relations* (Cambridge: Cambridge University Press, 1986).

8. Vincent, *Human Rights and International Relations*, 150.
9. Vincent, *Human Rights and International Relations*, 121.
10. Buzan, *From International to World Society*, 149.
11. Buzan, *From International to World Society*, 9.
12. The Stanford School refers to the collective work of various Stanford University sociology professors. It should be emphasized that these scholars see world culture as constituting an independent ontological realm of IR. For a discussion of the main ideas of this school, see John Meyer, John Boli, George M. Thomas, and Francisco Ramirez, "World Society and the Nation-State," *American Journal of Sociology* 103, no. 1 (July 1997): 144–81.
13. See also Barry Buzan, Charles Jones, and Richard Little, *The Logic of Anarchy: Neorealism to Structural Realism* (New York: Columbia University Press, 1993), 165; Barry Buzan and Richard Little, "Reconceptualizing Anarchy: Structural Realism Meets World History," *European Journal of International Relations* 2, no. 4 (1996): 403–434. Buzan's earlier analysis of constructivism or in this case, "deep structure" reveals the importance bringing to the surface the distinction between the actions that "reproduce the deep structure of the state and those that reproduce the deep structure of the international system." Distinguishing between these two actions also entails differentiating between the logic associated with the state and the logic associated with cooperative sovereign states operating in an anarchic structure. However, both constructivism and neo-realism, according to Buzan, fail to show how the international system came into existence. It is this failure to theorize about change in the international system that suggests the limitations of both theories, especially regarding the emergence of global or world society.
14. Wendt, *Social Theory of International Politics*, 260.
15. Wendt, *Social Theory of International Politics*, 285.
16. Wendt, *Social Theory of International Politics*, 305.
17. Buzan, *From International to World Society*, 108.
18. Buzan, *From International to World Society*, 130.
19. Buzan, *From International to World Society*, 130.
20. Buzan, *From International to World Society*, 131.
21. Buzan, *From International to World Society*, 196, 251.
22. Buzan, *From International to World Society*, 196, 251.
23. Martin Shaw, "Global Society and Global Responsibility: The Theoretical, Historical Political Limits of 'International Society,'" *Millennium: Journal of International Relations* 21, no. 3 (1992): 433. For a more recent discussion of the evolving relationship between globalization and the state, see Martin Shaw, *Theory of the Global State: Globality as an Unfinished Revolution* (Cambridge: Cambridge University Press, 2000).
24. Ethan A. Nadelman, "Global Prohibition Regimes: The Evolution of Norms in International Society," *International Organization* 44, no. 4 (1990): 525.
25. Bruce Cronin, *Institutions for the Common Good: International Protection Regimes in International Society* (Cambridge: Cambridge University Press, 2003), 14.
26. Christian Reus-Smit, "Politics of International Law," in Christian Reus-Smit, ed. *The Politics of International Law* (Cambridge: Cambridge University Press, 2004), 29.

27. Reus-Smit, "Politics of International Law," 29.

28. For an excellent discussion of this problem and how it plays into the hands of state dictators, see Ruti Teitel, "The Universal and the Particular in International Criminal Justice," *Columbia Human Rights Law Review* 30, no. 2 (1999): 285–303.

29. See Jason Ralph, "International Society, the International Criminal Court, and American Foreign Policy," *Review on International Studies* 31: 27–44; see also Antonio Franceschat, "The Rule of Law, Inequality, and the International Criminal Court," *Alternatives* 29, no. 3 (2004): 23–42.

30. Weber, *The Protestant Ethic and the Spirit of Capitalism* (New York: Routledge), 109–110.

31. Weber, *The Protestant Ethic*, 114.

32. Max Weber, *Economy and Society*, Vol. 2, edited by Guenther Roth and Claus Wittich (Berkeley: University of California Press, 1978), 952, 980.

33. Jürgen Habermas, *The Theory of Communicative Action*, Vol. One, translated by Thomas McCarthy (Boston: Beacon Press, 1983).

34. Jürgen Habermas, *The Theory of Communicative Action*, Vol. Two, translated by Thomas McCarthy (Boston: Beacon Press, 1987), 318.

35. Habermas, *The Theory of Communicative Action*, 184.

36. Jürgen Habermas, *Moral Consciousness and Communicative Action*, translated by Christian Lenhardt and Shierry Weber Nicholsen. (Cambridge, MA: The MIT Press, 1990), 56–58.

37. Habermas, *Moral Consciousness*, 120.

38. Habermas, *Moral Consciousness*, 141.

39. Habermas, *Moral Consciousness*, 143.

40. Lothar Brock, "World Society From the Bottom Up," in Mathias Albert and Lena Hilkermeier, eds. *Observing International Relations: Niklas Luhman and World Poliics* (London: Routledge, 2004), 99–100.

41. Dietrich Jung, "World Society, Systems Theory and the Classical Sociology of Modernity," in Mathias Albert and Lena Hilkermeier, eds. *Observing International Relations: Niklas Luhman and World Politics* (London: Routledge, 2004), 117.

42. Jung, "World Society, Systems Theory and the Classical Sociology of Modernity," 117.

43. Michael Dillon, "Criminalising Social and Political Violence Internationally," *Millennium: Journal of International Studies* 27(3): 545.

5

Value Pluralism and Political Cosmopolitanism

> Ethical thought consists of the systematic examination of the relations of human beings to each other, the conceptions, interests and ideals from which human ways of treating on another spring, and the systems of value on which such ends of life are based.
>
> —Isaiah Berlin, *The Crooked Timber of Humanity*

ONE OF THE ISSUES discussed in the previous chapter was whether the political dimension of the ICC could be reconciled with its universal morality. In other words, would the combination of its universal morality and the formalization of its juridical power lead to an inflexible and rigid form of juridical power or even the inability to investigate and prosecute the worst perpetrators of violence? And if so, how should we justify its political dimension as a necessary and viable source of its enduring flexibility? This chapter addresses these questions by theorizing about the relationship between the universalism and the particularism of the ICC.

As we saw earlier, the ICC provides a framework of universal morality by encoding the elements of universally condemned crimes. However, the distinction between universal moral condemnation—which has served as the basis for the universality principle—and the motivation to investigate and prosecute these crimes, underscores a crucial tension between universal morality and state politics. Understanding how to overcome this tension requires us to analyze the ICC from a cosmopolitan perspective. As Kimberly Hutchings points out, cosmopolitanism involves not only a commonly moral identity, but also concerns moral communality that is arguably embodied in global political institutions.[1] Cosmopolitanism, she goes on to state, is "the presumption of human moral commonality and the rational accessibility of the moral law" out of which emerges a "common universal or cosmopolitan standard of judgement by which to assess actual political arrangements."[2]

This chapter addresses the question of whether there is a cosmopolitan standard by which to assess the link between the ICC's internal politics and the universal morality of the ICC. In doing so, I examine the following conceptual challenges. How does the ICC's political cosmopolitanism derive from the division between particularism and universalism and develop a distinction between the negative and positive elements of its morality? And how should we maintain the negative freedom of peoples in order to understand the moral boundaries between the state (or individual groups) and the ICC?

Here, I draw on value pluralist theory, which focuses on negative group rights, or the freedom from coercion to promote the idea of diversity. Value pluralism, as we shall see, holds that goods, such as justice, liberality, and equality constitute incommensurable values, and that such incommensurability can lead to conflict, in which hard choices or tradeoffs will be needed to resolve the conflict.[3] As this would suggest, I am drawing on value pluralism to study the claims of three differing entities, namely groups, states, and international organizations. In doing so, I will seek to contrast the meta-ethical claims of pluralism and cosmopolitanism, while at the same time showing how some of the universal strands of pluralism presuppose the tensions between the positive moral duties of the ICC and negative freedoms embodied in the religious customs of certain state societies.

The case of the crime of enforced pregnancy illustrates this point rather nicely. For if the ICC Judiciary decides to intervene on the grounds that the national court must investigate the crime of forced pregnancy, then the Court's actions will likely create the perception of its partiality toward Western culture or women's rights. And yet, if it elects to honor the state party's decision not to investigate the crime, pursuant to the second clause of the provision on enforced pregnancy, then it will expose the Court's unwillingness, or perceived inability, to uphold this new legitimate standard of moral harm. In this way, the ethical dilemma of the Court becomes a challenge of understanding the interlocking roles of ethics and politics and how both serve to constrain and legitimize the ICC's global juridical power.

But it is also true, as I will argue, to see the ICC's universal morality as an emergent context of political cosmopolitanism (the establishment of institutions and mechanisms that would provide a framework of regulation and enforcement throughout the world). Thus, while I do not theorize about the relationship between the ICC and a global *democratic* order per se, short of elaborating upon some of the civil rights encoded in the ICC Statute, I do propose that the ICC represents an important form of political cosmopolitanism. Accordingly, the second part of the chapter draws on various cosmopolitan theories to discuss the interlocking dimensions of universal morality and the ICC's internal politicization.

Understanding the Limits of Particularism and Negative Freedom

Above I mentioned how the ICC Statute contains various civil rights.[4] As we saw in chapter 2, all the relevant provisions in this case conform to the rules embodied in International Covenant on Civil and Political Rights (ICCPR). This should present little, if any, problem for those states with legislation or constitutional provisions that stipulate the conditions for upholding these rights. On the other hand, states that have not signed the ICCPR may have to make significant changes to their respective domestic law, such as the introduction of new legislation, or amendments to the Constitution (chapter 2). Nevertheless, the above civil rights are important elements of the ICC's international legal standards of fairness and civility, which allow the defendants ample opportunity to contest the evidence brought by the Court. Such standards also vest the defendant with the right to act as his or her own attorney which can, as we have seen in the Milosevic trial, lead to delaying tactics and even verbal accusations of the Court's illegitimacy.

What this suggests is that the cost of prosecution will likely be high in some cases, which only reinforces the notion that the ICC will only go after the very worst perpetrators. The question that arises, then, is whether there will be acceptable cases in which the ICC Prosecutor should defer to national courts as a means of resolving the political tensions between the ICC and national courts. Will such cases reveal the inconsistent exercise of discretionary power, and unduly minimize its ethical convictions for holding accountable the worst perpetrators?

As the complementarity principle suggests, the political complications of exercising discretionary power is likely to stem from cases involving unwillingness rather than inability. This is because while inability might refer to objective indicators such as partial collapse of the national judiciary, unwillingness is more likely to reflect a subjective assessment of the situation. Thus, when hard pressed, the Prosecutor may end up asserting his or her own subjective desire to prosecute against the national leader's denial that they are unwilling to investigate or prosecute. This might be helpful in encouraging and guiding national courts to uphold the ICC's evidential standards. But it might also become intertwined with the political complications and realities of investigating and prosecuting hard cases (see chapter 2).

Thus, one of the reasons for engaging value pluralism is to show how certain national societies might justify the particular claims against the universal morality of the ICC.[5] Below, I shall draw on various theories of value pluralism to explain some of the moral implications of relativizing the harm principle. Two theoretical questions addressed in this section are as follows: Can we reasonably justify a national society's or state's cultural freedom vis-à-vis the universal moral authority of the ICC? And lastly, does value pluralism explain and validate the need for the Court role in accommodating particular differences of conceptions of the Court, even if these conceptions conflict with the Court's moral authority?

Theories of Value Pluralism

Isaiah Berlin, the well-known political philosopher of the latter half of the twentieth century, is credited with inventing the modern theory of value pluralism. One of the main tenets of his theory is that values have and will always remain incommensurable since there is no single good to measure all other goods. The incommensurability of values in Berlin's view is a fact of life. Concerning this point, Berlin states that

> Pluralism entails that since, it is possible that no final answers can be given to moral and political questions about value and more than that, that some answers that people give, and are entitled to give, are not compatible with each other, room must be made for a life in which some values may turn out to be incompatible, so that if destructive conflict is to be avoided compromises have be effected, and minimum degree of toleration, however reluctant, becomes indispensable.[6]

As this passage suggests, moral conflicts tend to arise when different groups and classes of people formulate differing conceptions of the truth, and then seek to defend these truths at all costs. For Berlin, monist theories, which, in his view, call on individuals to sacrifice their lives in pursuit of a single conception of justice, breeds intolerance towards alternative forms of the truth. As a result, monism tends necessarily toward oppression and brutal forms of dictatorship.[7] Avoiding this fate nonetheless requires a deeper appreciation of not just the incommensurability of values, but also the inevitability of conflict between these values, which may in turn, require difficult choices or trade-offs to resolve the conflict.

The fact that values are incommensurable does not diminish the capacity to understand and appreciate the differences of other peoples.[8] It simply suggests, in Berlin's view, that there is a minimal awareness of a liberty that all humans possess.[9] It is out of this minimal awareness that one learns to develop socially; that is, to respect each other's cultural and religious differences within an institutional setting. In this sense, moral progress, as Claude Galipeau notes, is where "most moral rules and practices, such as tolerance can only be understood fully in the context of institutional development or the moral progress in resolving major ethical conflicts."[10] The question that arises, however, is whether we can formulate prescriptive, rational measures to resolve this conflict. In other words, does a pluralistic interpretation of liberalism permit us to formulate a set of rules or principles for regulating this conflict? Unfortunately, Berlin offers few answers as to how liberalism prescribes certain constitutional rules to resolve the conflict between the plurality of goods.[11]

Given this lack in Berlin's theory, John Gray argues that Berlin's value pluralism tends to render liberalism "indefensible," by failing to elaborate the rational basis for a morally objective theory of value pluralism.[12] The solution Gray proposes is a *modus vivendi* agreement: "a settlement that finds terms of coexistence on the basis of any interests and values regarding divergent values."[13]A *modus vivendi* agreement in Gray's view is an example of what he calls strong pluralism, which stresses that the liberal principle of neutrality fails to determine the interests of agents. This is the main reason why Gray insists that liberal theories of basic liberties and equality "must still appeal to conceptions of human interests to give their principles a definite content."[14] Gray's point, then, is that any liberal theory that assumes a detached *a priori* position to resolve ethical conflicts oversimplifies the complexity of sociological and cultural circumstances.

What is interesting to note here is Gray's critique of the harm principle. Here, he argues that the type of liberties the harm principle protects will vary with circumstances, and that the principle will involve "making judgement of comparable harm."[15] It is, of course, true that those societies that lack a developed criminal system reveal the difficulties of criminalizing all forms of serious harm (e.g., Libya, Yemen, and Saudi Arabia; see chapter 7). But this holds little weight in respect of the ICC, where all crimes are universally condemned as grave crimes. Indeed, while it may be argued that genocide constitutes a crime of virtual incomparable gravity, all the elements of crimes specified in the ICC Statute are of equal gravity. This, as we shall see in the next section, becomes an important condition for determining the universalization of the harm principle in the context of the ICC.

Still, not all theorists concur that a *modus vivendi* agreement "salvages" the rationality of Berlin's value pluralism. Jonathan Riley, for example, contends that Berlin's theory reflects a minimal core of liberal rationality, in which diversity remains coterminous with the universal protection of basic human rights.[16] Perhaps the best way to describe Berlin's liberal minimalism in this respect is to call him an "ethical naturalist." As Galipeau writes: "Berlin is an ethical naturalist: he holds to a minimum content theory of natural law, one that includes liberty as a fundamental view."[17] Again, this raises the question as to whether this minimum content of theory can be articulated in a way that allows us to embrace certain liberal principles, as fixed, non-negotiable moral standards.

As already noted, value pluralists do not reject universal principles and constitutional rules. Rather, they are interested in explaining the flexibility of these principles: namely, the responsiveness of this principle to a plurality of needs, beliefs, and interests. Thus, if democratic societies are to be considered truly tolerant and respectful of cultural differences, then they must allow cultural/national differences to flourish. For William Galston, curbing the imposition of liberal ideals is one way of understanding the need for improving the self-awareness of one's freedom to choose in liberal societies.[18] As he states:

> a politics of self-aware pluralism will be a different kind of liberalism, however. The value pluralist liberal state will respect self-aware autonomous lives but will not insist on promoting Socratic or Milian ideals (or any others) as valid for all citizens. It will limit the agreement on principles and practices required of all citizens to constitutional essentials, parsimoniously understood.[19]

In other words, Galston believes that autonomy is one possible mode of existence in liberal societies. This is not to say that he advocates an "anything goes" approach that would subordinate liberal ideals to the changing and intolerant demands of groups. Rather, it means that state intervention into the civil affairs of peoples should be strictly limited. In Galston's view, the Constitution cannot adequately resolve the question of how best to secure a viable and diverse political community, since it only expresses the basic, most fundamental principle(s) for regulating the peoples' freedoms.

Given this need for minimal state intervention, Galston proposes two essential constitutional prescriptions: "a basic level of social provision, and a system of education sufficient to promote not only economic competence but also law-abidingness and civic attachment."[20] Both prescriptions reflect minimal constitutional standards of protection to which all individuals are entitled, and it is this minimal public ordering, according to Galston, that ensures human flourishing in liberal societies. But the question that this raises in respect to the ICC is whether the protection of a state party's national customs is coterminous with unintended forms of serious harm deemed to be morally undesirable.

As noted earlier, provisions that allow national customs to take precedence over the Court's authority may provide a desirable tradeoff at the negotiating table, but their legacy is certain to leave some women defenseless against the state's repressive laws. One might even argue that the permissibility of harm in this respect challenges the woman's entitlement to equal protection under the law by denying her the same protection as men. Thus, while Galston's approach mirrors one element of the Court's seeming liberal order, it requires a stronger moral commitment to uphold the new standards of moral concern.

One of the principal ways that George Crowder theorizes about this stronger commitment is to rethink the implications of Berlin's ethical naturalism. For Crowder, Berlin's emphasis on human dignity and freedom of conscience suggests a strong tendency toward prioritizing human virtue in his theory of value pluralism.[21] More specifically, it stresses a strong tendency toward perfection, as opposed to neutrality. The difference, then, between perfection and neutrality goes as follows: while neutrality assumes that certain basic liberal principles and procedures can and should remain impartial to the politics and views of illiberal groups, perfectionism encourages individuals to liberate themselves in accordance with liberal principles such as personal autonomy, which is something that Crowder insists is crucial to liberalism. As Crowder notes, to the extent that a choice must be made between neutrality and perfectionist forms of liberalism, pluralism "pushes us towards perfectionism or a virtues based approach."[22]

What this suggests is that the liberal virtues of human conscience and dignity will always remain intrinsic to the protection of an individual's negative rights against state intervention that restricts his or her freedom of conscience, or what Crowder refers to as "pluralist liberalism." Preserving and protecting these virtues provides the basis for what might aptly be called a weak form of pluralism, in which constitutional prescriptions and standards can be seen as a manifestation of Berlin's idea of moral progress. The issue that Crowder's pluralist liberalism raises is whether the negative rights of states parties should necessarily constrain the universalization of the harm principle. In other words, if it is true that the ICC will have to respect the negative rights of states parties, or the freedom against the Court's enforcement of provisions, then should it also expect to encounter cases that will warrant some special consideration or accommodation of the repressive effects of national customs. Perhaps more important, does Crowder's virtues-based assessment of Berlin's ethical naturalism suggest a normative link between the Court's ethical and moral growth and the active pursuit of global justice or cosmopolitan ends? The next section critically investigates this implicit link by theorizing about the analogous relationship between the universalization of the harm principle and the Court's ethical growth.

Cosmopolitanism and the Universalization of the Harm Principle

Another way of addressing the question of the Court's moral universality is to determine how the ICC provides a form of mediation between radical interpretations of the universalization of the harm principle and meta-ethical conceptions of negative rights. As noted earlier, value pluralism underscores a strong commitment to the particular conceptions of justice or the societal good. In the case of the ICC, this reflects the need to accommodate deeply rooted customs (in order to secure compliance) and to defend the negative liberties of all defendants (chapter 7). Yet, what the Court intends to do in the way of upholding the basic rights of all defendants, and what it should do to promote its universal morality are two very different moral concerns. Whereas the former refers to the formal implementation of its civil standards or rules of procedure, the latter reflects the political calculations or strategies needed for achieving its ethical objectives of investigating the very worst perpetrators and upholding new moral standards of legitimacy (e.g., proscriptive norms against gender violence). Such a distinction also presupposes the tension between the strict application of its ethical objectives and the particular political realities of violence and noncompliance that may negate the application of these objectives.

One of the issues that we need to address, then, is whether we can treat the Court's universal morality as an incipient form of political cosmopolitanism. In other words, can we conceive the Court's politics or political legalism as a precondition for exercising and advancing its moral universality? In this section, I will address this question by showing how the ethical application of its juridical power reflects an emergent context of political cosmopolitanism—that is, a transformative process of a global political order in which political rights, universal ideals of reason and freedom (the right to self-determination and autonomy), and political power have been increasingly institutionalized at the global level. Although the nation state still remains, at least for now, the primary organizing principle of international relations, globalization does, as David Held states, underscore a "deeper and shared common understanding of humanity that can unite all individuals across states and culture."[23] As a particular case of this emerging order, the ICC's complementarity principle (function) does point to what Simon Caney refers to as a weak form of cosmopolitanism.

Here, Caney distinguishes between radical and weak cosmopolitanism. Those considered more radical, for instance, tend to focus on the universal moral foundations of international society and the overlapping properties of national and international law. Weaker or milder versions of cosmopolitanism, on the other hand, consider only the positive claim of cosmopolitanism, namely the adherence of states to the global principles of justice.[24] By this definition, a liberal rights approach to global and distributive justice characterizes a weak form of cosmopolitanism, even though a weak liberal universalist such as Rawls rejects the extension of the distributive principle to the global level, where the greatest benefit of wealth creations would fall to the least advantaged states.[25]

In his essay on *Law of the Peoples*, for instance, Rawls theorizes that the global distributive principle ignores the basic and self sufficient requirement of society of states: namely, that states need only be politically decent in order to meet the fundamental criteria of a society of peoples and/or social cooperation. For Rawls, the decency of peoples is what constitutes the prescriptive force of the law of peoples; it reflects the application of tolerance and respect, a fundamental requirement for promoting and sustaining social cooperation.

It is also worthwhile to mention the extension of this principle to the global realm (from weak to strong cosmopolitan). Charles Beitz, for instance, argues that states can and should agree to a set of principles aimed at promoting global justice. As he explains, the natural distribution of resources is a principle to which all states are capable of agreeing, and that state leaders who do not know "the resource endowment of their own societies" can and should agree to the principle of fair and equal distribution of resources across states.[26] Certainly, this presents an interesting case for understanding the ICC's weak cosmopolitanism via a global schema of distributive justice (in the form of redressing the effects of or even eliminating sources of the even development among national judiciaries); however, it is a topic that remains beyond the scope of this book.

The conceptual issue that I deal with below is how the interlocking features of the ICC's moral universality and its politics reflect a weak form of cosmopolitanism. To do this, I will first explain more fully what I mean by the evolving synthesis of universal morality and politics, before moving on to discuss how the universalization of the harm principle constitutes an important mode of analysis of the ICC's universal morality. The ICC's political legalism, I shall argue, cannot be detached from this mode of analysis, since it underscores the political tensions between the particular objections to the ICC and its universal morality.

Bridging Ethical and Political Cosmopolitanism

The distinction between ethical and political cosmopolitanism is an important feature of Kant's writings on cosmopolitan right (see chapter 4). As is well-known, Kant argued that the passions and desires belonged to the natural realm as phenomena (experience), and that such attributes conditioned our rational actions or obligations to act according to universal maxims and imperatives. In this manner, reason allows us to rationalize our orientation to society; the passions provide the motivation to do so.[27] Kant, in this respect, conceptualized politics as the corollary of experience, or as the progressive development of institutional arrangements that would secure the moral foundations of society. Politics embodied the tensions between nature and morality by demonstrating how the pursuit of universal morality required external coercion (state military/police, and non-moral order legal institutions) to harmonize the wills of citizens and leaders. As Hutchings states: "[Kant's] Politics is conceived as being both based on and directed towards moral universality, yet nature dictates that precisely because we are men our identity and actions as citizens must be framed within a coercive and therefore non-moral order, the juridical realm of the state."[28] Kant thus distinguished between universal morality and nature by demonstrating how politics, while providing the avenue toward universal morality, presupposed the tensions between ethics and nature. To the extent that politics could not be equated with universal morality in this sense, Kant's conception of universal morality underscores the crucial distinction between ethical and political cosmopolitanism.

Conceptions of nation-state models of cosmopolitan citizenship have traditionally adopted this distinction to the show the interlocking relationship between national identity and the universal ideals of self-determination.[29] Global conceptions of cosmopolitan citizenship, on the other hand, emphasize a different governing arrangement rooted in the transformation of the international system. As noted above, Held argues that the erosion of state sovereignty represents an upward projection of power and legitimacy; hence, the emerging spatiality of global institutions and their attendant capacity to draw on their legitimacy to implement, and, in a certain sense, enforce the universal ideals of self-determination and autonomy. For Held, the juridical authority of international criminal institutions will play an increasingly important role within this emerging global network.

> Certain standards are specified for the treatment of all, which no political regime or association can legitimately violate. . . . to allow the expansion of the influence of regional and international courts to monitor and check political and social authority of a global order consisting for multiple and overlapping networks of power involving the body welfare, culture, civic associations, and the economy.[30]

What this suggests is that the ICC can and should complement certain forms of restorative justice, while also helping to integrate the civic values of society. But it is also important that we not overlook the autonomous juridicial structure of the ICC (chapter 4). The autonomous function of the ICC's juridical power, in other words, underscores the importance of dealing with the political realities that will shape its juridical authority; or more concretely, determine which cases to pursue. It is thus important that we realize that the ICC is a unique political institution, whose political legitimacy is not directly tied to the promotion of democratic values per se (although it may, in an indirect fashion, in the context of enforcing the norms of a global civil society); but rather, to the performance of its democratic and constitutional set of governing mechanisms (chapter 2). These are, of course, internal governing mechanisms, which, as we shall see in chapters 6–8, provide the framework for devising political strategies that promote the ICC's political legitimacy: its ability to advance the goal of international peace and security in a fair and efficacious manner.

Thus, it is important that we not separate the ICC's internal polticization from its ethical or moral development. In fact, as I have been suggesting, its political and ethical development are mutually inclusive. This means that we need to maintain a dual focus on its universal morality and political legalism by examining how the universalization of the harm principle offers a framework for understanding its cosmopolitan nature of political legalism.

Between Weak and Strong Cosmopolitanism

The harm principle holds that the safety against violence and cruelty shall restrict the liberties of state leaders "to do as they please" while creating responsibilities to others."[31] As one of the foremost IR theorists conducting research on the universalization of the harm principle, Andrew Linklater contends that "the universalization of the harm principle obliges us to avoid harming others unnecessarily and that it is the development of this principle that reflects an evolving global dimension of the post–Westphalian global order."[32] According to Linklater, the universalization of the harm principle refers to two ongoing trends in global politics during the post–Cold War: the geographical scope of moral concern and the depth of moral concern or global morality. His point here is that both premises explain how the increasing number of ratifying states will substantiate new standards of legitimacy of moral concern (e.g., for women's and children's rights against grave harm).

Linklater also contends that the new legitimate standards of moral concern will require more human rights conventions "to address the unspeakable conditions of squalor and extreme vulnerability to global market forces, and to bolster the legitimacy of these conventions in the eyes of the less fortunate peoples."[33] To this end, the serious harm associated with social deprivation may eventually undermine these new standards of legitimacy, since the deeply affected peoples of the developing world may eventually doubt the fairness of international law.[34] At the very least, it will eventually test these new standards of legitimacy by encouraging socially disaffected peoples to doubt the legitimacy of international law. As I have suggested, this will depend on the ICC's ability to actively investigate all serious gender crimes, regardless of national circumstances.

So, how should we understand the evolving universalization of the ICC's morality in terms of the acceptance of the universality of certain crimes against humanity? Again, not all of the ICC's crimes against humanity enjoy universal consensus *per se*, including, most notably, forced pregnancy and enforced sterilization (see chapter 7). Yet it is precisely this difference that presupposes the complex process of universalizing the ICC's morality. Jeremy Waldron, for instance, theorizes that we need to see a particularist challenge to a universal claim as a challenge that affects and shapes the very content of the universal claim. In other words, as he argues, "any resistance to our universalization of human rights doctrine should be read charitably as a direct challenge to the substance of the doctrine . . . it has to be addressed as substance."[35] In this way, it could be said that the evolving cosmopolitan intent of the ICC derives from these moral challenges posed by our deeply embedded ethical convictions. This, however, suggests that state non-compliance will be fundamental to substantiating the universal meaning of the elements of these crimes. But Waldron's interpretation, while revealing the complexity of the process of universalization, leaves open the question as to how we should concretize the actions and rights directed toward a cosmopolitan purpose or end (e.g., equal respect and freedom).

In other words, does the ICC's global obligation(s) to investigate and prosecute the worst perpetrators signify the political responsibility to resolve local problems that can only be resolved by global institutions? Many recent attempts to address this issue have resulted in intriguing, albeit unclear analyses of a common framework of universal morality, including Amitai Etzioni's theory of an emerging normative synthesis between the social values of Eastern authoritarian states (e.g., social order) and the liberal values of Western liberal societies (e.g., liberal autonomy).[36] Etzioni, for instance, argues that the ICC constitutes a key component of an emerging global safety network, in which increased levels of accountability will help to spur the growth of what he refers to as a global nation. Admittedly, this seems a bit overreaching, since the ICC remains a formative institution. What is more, the ICC's universal morality is contestable in terms of the gap, or political tensions between domestic and international law, which arguably limits its range of influence. More importantly, narrowing this gap on an aggregate level (ratification), will not eliminate these tensions. In short, we cannot effectively deduce the practical application of the ICC's universal morality from the complete erosion of these tensions.

The point that I am arguing here is that state politics or the above political tensions will always exist on some level, thereby validating Kant's thesis of the intrinsic link between nature and politics in a global civil society. This, however, does not mean that the ICC's weak cosmopolitanism will remain weak or strictly formalistic. Rather, it signifies how the practical application of the ICC's universal morality will derive from its political legalism or its self-directed application of its rules of procedures. This, as I have been arguing is where its moral authority or autonomy will converge with its political actions and goals in the direction of a cosmopolitan end (to hold all of the worst perpetrators accountable). It is this suggestive model of political cosmopolitanism that underscores the important distinction between state and global juridicial power.

Thus, it should be clear by now that the ICC will need to direct itself toward the ethical cosmopolitan ideal of the elimination and prevention of gross human rights atrocities; and that by focusing on its internal politicization, it may begin to evolve into a strong model of political cosmopolitanism. Only in this way can it begin to concretize its cosmopolitan intent and to advance the universalization of the harm principle.

Conclusion

This chapter drew on political theory and international relations theory to assess the political cosmopolitanism of the ICC. It argued that the ICC, while constituting a weak form of cosmopolitanism, signifies an evolving form of political cosmopolitanism, in which the ICC's political legalism figures to bring together its moral autonomy with its political actions directed towards a cosmopolitan end. This is one of the ways of concretizing and validating the universalization of the harm principle and the ICC's morality for that matter. Again, the ICC's political legalism can and should be seen as a formative concept of the ICC's development. Accordingly, this will require us to look at some of the political and moral challenges that will serve as the basis for formulating the concrete approaches of the ICC's internal politicization. The next part explores three of these challenges, including U.S. opposition to the ICC, the role of Arab states, and the relationship between the ICC and the United Nations.

Notes

1. Kimberly Hutchings, "Political Theory and Cosmopolitan Citizenship," in Kimberly Hutchings and Roland Dannreuther, eds. *Cosmopolitan Citizenship* (London: St. Martin's Press, 1999), 12.

2. Hutchings, "Political Theory and Cosmopolitan Citizenship."

3. Isaiah Berlin, *The Crooked Timber of Humanity* (Princeton: Princeton University Press, 1990); op. cit., Isaiah Berlin and Raja Jahanbegloo, *Conversations with Isaiah Berlin* (New York: Charles Scribner's Sons, 1991); William Galston, *Liberal Pluralism* (Cambridge: Cambridge University Press, 2002); John J. Gray, "Where Pluralists and Liberals Part Company," in M. Baghramanian and A. Ingram, eds. *Pluralism: the Philosophy and Politics of Diversity* (London: Routledge Press, 2000), 85–102. Here, it should be mentioned that while value pluralists concede that ethics can be universal, (e.g., tolerance and the respect for differences), they also insist that the freedom from coercion can and should always be balanced against homogenizing liberal values, such as liberal autonomy and neutrality.

4. It is worth re-emphasizing the contents of Article 55(1), which provides a list of rights for the defendant during and after the investigation, including "the right not to incriminate himself or herself or to confess to guilt; and the right not to be subject to any form of coercion, duress or threat, to torture or any form of cruel, inhuman or degrading treatment or punishment. Further, defendants put on trial will be informed of their rights, that prior to questioning there will be grounds to believe that he or she has committed a crime within the jurisdiction of the court, and to have legal assistance at the person's choosing."

5. It should be noted that several scholars have attempted to advance a *modus vivendi* to the international level. For a discussion of the international dimension of the *modus vivendi* principle, see John Charvet, "Epilogue: Further Reflections on Value Pluralism in International Relations," in M. Lensu and J. Fritz, eds. *Value Pluralism, Normative Theory and International Relations* (London: St. Martin's Press, 2000), 196–204; Stephen Chan, "Aspirations and Absent Methodologies in Universalism: Towards a Multicultural Normative Theory," in M. Lensu and J. Fritz, eds. *Value Pluralism, Normative Theory, and International Relations* (London: St. Martin's Press, 2000), 59–75. As Charvet (202) notes: "a *modus vivendi* is one that is mutually advantageous for the participants in relations to an actual distribution of power and interests . . . and should bind Fascist and communists societies to liberal international law: to the extent that it secures them the provisional means to pursue their conception of the good in their own territory without intervention by other societies. The parties to the agreement must hold conceptions of the good that are compatible with the public acknowledgement of liberalism."

6. Berlin and Jahanbegloo, *Conversations with Isaiah Berlin*, 44.

7. Berlin, *The Crooked Timber of Humanity*, 79.

8. This idea may be viewed as the modern equivalent of Aristotle's eudaemonism: the notion that all humans contribute some proportion of their awareness of the good through the activities that they engage in.

9. Berlin, *The Crooked Timber of Humanity*, 80.

10. Claude Galipeau, *Isaiah Berlin's Liberalism* (Oxford: Clarendon Press, 1994), 117.

11. Michael Kenny, "Isaiah Berlin's Contribution to Modern Political Theory," *Political Studies* 48 (2000): 1028.

12. Gray, "Where Pluralists and Liberals Part Company", 86.

13. Mary Baghramian and Alice Ingram, eds. *Pluralism: The Philosophy and Politics of Diversity* (London: Routledge Press, 2000), 7.

14. Gray, "Where Pluralists and Liberals Part Company," 97.

15. Gray, "Where Pluralists and Liberals Part Company."

16. John Riley, "Crooked Timber and Liberal Culture," in M. Baghramian and A. Ingram, eds. *Pluralism: The Philosophy and Politics of Diversity* (London: Routledge Press, 2000), 122.

17. Galipeau, *Isaiah Berlin's Liberalism*, 119.

18. Kymlicka argues that cultural diversity is a public good intrinsic to liberalism. In this way, he argues that liberal autonomy is a fundamental core value of diversity, which prescribes liberal solutions to conflicts between and among cultural groups. The main criticism of Kymlicka's argument, however, is that it requires illiberal groups to abide by their group-differentiated rights (i.e., autonomy, polyethnic rights, and special representation rights, within liberal and democratic institutions). The result is that those groups not willing to exercise their rights in the context of liberal and democratic institutions will remain marginalized; their rights invalidated along liberal lines. See Will Kymlicka, *Multicultural Citizenship: A Liberal Theory of Minority Rights* (Oxford: Oxford University Press, 1995).

19. Galston, *Liberal Pluralism*, 62.

20. Galston, *Liberal Pluralism*, 66.

21. George Crowder, *Liberalism and Value Pluralism* (London: Continuum Publishing, 2002), 62.

22. Crowder, *Liberalism and Value Pluralism*, 223–224.

23. David Held, *Democracy and the Global Order* (Palo Alto, CA: Stanford University Press, 1995), 283.

24. See, e.g., Simon Caney, "International Distributive Justice," *Political Studies* 49 (2001): 974–997.

25. Rawls's original position, which holds that in a veiled state of ignorance, one can determine a set of principles that allows each person the opportunity to develop his or her political institutions, and which confers the greatest benefit to the least advantaged. Justice as fairness, then, means that people will choose fundamental principles of justice, such as tolerance and equality of opportunity, behind what he refers to as a veil of ignorance. See John Rawls, *A Theory of Justice* (Cambridge: Harvard University Press, 1971); op. cit., Rawls, *Political Liberalism* (New York: Columbia

University Press, 1993). For a good discussion of Rawls's false cosmopolitanism, see Leif Wenar, "The Legitimacy of Peoples," in Pablo De Greiff and Ciaran Cronin, eds., *Global Justice and Transnational Politics: Essays on the Moral and Political Challenges of Globalization* (Cambridge: MIT Press, 2002), 65–67.

26. Charles Beitz, "Justice and International Relations," in Charles R. Beitz, Marshall Cohen, Thomas Scanlon, and A. John Simmons, eds. *International Ethics* (Princeton: Princeton University Press, 1983), 292, 294.

27. See Immanuel Kant, "Perpetual Peace: A Philosophical Sketch," and "Idea for a Universal History with a Cosmopolitan Purpose," in Hans Reiss, ed. *Kant's Political Writings* (Cambridge: Cambridge University Press, 1970), 41–53, 116–130.

28. Hutchings, *Political Theory and Cosmopolitan Citizenship*, p. 16.

29. See David Miller, *On Nationality* (Oxford: Clarendon Press, 1995).

30. David Held, *Democracy and the Global Order* (Palo Alto, CA: Stanford University Press, 1995), 271.

31. Held, *Democracy and the Global Order.*

32. Andrew Linklater, "The Problem of Harm in World Politics: Implications for the Sociology of States-System," *International Affairs* 78 (2001): 326.

33. Linklater, "The Problem of Harm in World Politics," 337. Linklater points to various categories of harm, including the deliberate harm in the relations between independent political communities, deliberate harm caused by governments to their own citizenry, unintended harm, negligence, and stresses the failure of international law to address treatable diseases and starvation in the developing world.

34. Linklater, "The Problem of Harm in World Politics," 327.

35. Jeremy Waldron, "Arguing a Universal Claim," *Columbia Human Rights Law Review* 30 (1999): 313.

36. See Amitai Etzioni, *From Empire to Community* (New York: Palgrave Macmillan, 2004), 51–52. For Bhikhu Parekh, such a task will reflect a global-oriented national citizenship. As he explains, a "globally oriented national citizenship is based upon a delicate balance between several complementary, but also potentially conflicting virtues, such as the appreciation of our common humanity and of our deep differences, etc." Parekh, "Cosmopolitan and Global Citizenship," *Review of International Studies* 30 (January 2004).

III

POLITICAL LEGALISM: POLITICAL STRATEGIES AND POLICY ARRANGEMENTS

6

U.S. Opposition and Strategic Accommodation

> One must be sufficiently prudent to know how to avoid becoming notorious for those vices that would destroy one's power and seek to avoid those vices that are not politically dangerous; but if one cannot bring oneself to do this, they can be indulged in with fewer misgivings.
>
> —Machiavelli

IN THIS CHAPTER, I assess the sources of U.S. opposition to the ICC and the strategic relationship between the ICC and U.S. opposition. In doing so, I contextualize one of the central claims of Dewey's pragmatism discussed in chapter 3: namely, the capacity of the ICC to govern the consequences of its own rules and imperfections. I propose that the ICC's self-governing capacity (or autonomous and quasi-constitutional structure) needs to be viewed as a basis for formulating a counter-strategy to U.S. opposition. The counter strategy proposed here derives from political legalism and is intended to serve as a policy framework for promoting the ICC's internal politicization.

In developing this strategy, I will focus on two U.S. core objections: the contention that the Court's jurisdiction violates customary international law, since it requires that states parties surrender nationals of non-states parties to the ICC;[1] and the claim that the ICC's jurisdiction over its military personnel will allow the ICC to pass legal judgment on matters related to national security decisions, thus bypassing the U.N. Security Council where the U.S. holds a veto.[2] Together these objections raise a troubling issue: whether the ICC can and should proceed without the United States. Or alternatively, if the ICC should heed U.S. demands for special protection of their military personnel overseas. As this would suggest, the tensions between the advocates of the ICC and the proponents of the U.S. position have become increasingly polarized. In effect, one is either opposed to the ICC on the grounds that it poses a threat to U.S. national security and that its Statute must be revised accordingly,[3] or one is staunchly opposed to the U.S. position on the basis that its core objections are rooted in false legal and political pretenses.[4]

But is there a constructive middle ground to explore here, one that might shed light on the ICC's political development? In this chapter, I argue that a constructive middle ground is needed in order to move us beyond this debate. Here, I draw the distinction between the political reality of U.S. special responsibilities overseas and the abuse of this political reality, either in the form of special exemptions or political and military coercive tactics to seek immunity. A third way, I claim, would build constructively on this distinction by revealing how amendments to the ICC Statute would serve as an effective source of accommodation of U.S. legal concerns.

The objective of this chapter, then, is to assess the validity of these (U.S.) concerns against the moral imperative for international criminal accountability. In doing so, I will claim that at some point, the Assembly of States Parties, the United Nations, and EU will need to deal or negotiate with the United States (e.g., the strain it has placed on U.S.-European relations),[5] and that a willingness to adopt provisions such as a balanced crime of aggression will not undermine the influence of NGO pressures on the U.S. Senate. Again, the point of all this is not to yield to U.S. hegemony, but to find ways of asserting the ICC's juridical authority against the United States, or rather to develop the political substance of its rules. As we saw in chapter 2, the United States has, up until now, been a strong supporter of international criminal justice, including, most notably, the International Military Charter (IMT), the ICTY, and the ICTR. Moreover, future U.S. cooperation or compliance could become an important (albeit controversial) factor of the Court's credibility in enforcing the rules of the Statute against noncompliance.

It is worth re-emphasizing that I am not assuming that the role of U.S. military personnel overseas (its disproportionate share of military personnel in military and peacekeeping operations) justifies the basis for special exemption status. Rather, this role reflects an important political reality of hegemonic power that can and often does conflict with the application of moral principles and rules. The need to address this conflict should warrant provisions that address the general context of this conflict, and not satisfy U.S. (special) national interests.

Accordingly, the first section of this chapter discusses the problems of what has become an either/or approach. It then goes on to analyze the effects of the current tactics used by the United States to seek immunity of all U.S. nationals, and how these effects run counter to the ICC Statute. The last part of the chapter explores the parameters and key objectives of a third way of strategic accommodation containing certain amendments to the ICC Statute that would serve as structured incentives for the United States to re-sign and possibly ratify the ICC Treaty.

Dichotomous Views: Sources and Parameters

In order to understand the current divide between proponents and opponents of the U.S. position, let us briefly address the recent events that have marked the shift in the U.S. position from formal opposition to an aggressive campaign to exempt all U.S. citizens from the Court's jurisdiction. Once I have provided this descriptive overview, I will go on to address the three principal issues dividing the proponents of U.S. opposition and the advocates of the ICC.

The U.S. virtual war on the ICC is rooted in the provisions of the American Servicemembers' Protection Act (ASPA), an anti-ICC legislative bill passed in the Senate in December of 2001.[6] Not only did the bill signal U.S. resolve to protect its own servicepersons from unlawful detainment overseas, but it also suggested U.S. determination to eliminate any perceived obstacles to the global war on terrorism. Thus, when the United Nations announced in April of 2002 that the ICC would enter into force on July 1, 2002, the Bush Administration began to take immediate action to disengage the United States from the ICC. This included the decision to withdraw the U.S. signature from the Rome Treaty on May 6, 2002, and its subsequent pledge to veto the U.N. mandate that would extend the date of maintaining peace-keeping operations in Bosnia.[7] The U.S. announcement to veto the Bosnia peacekeeping mission on June 29, 2002 prompted the U.N. Security Council to convene an emergency meeting.

The result was the adoption of U.N. Security Council Resolutions 1422 and 1487 (that renewed 1422), which granted a special 12-month exemption to all U.S. military personnel overseas in U.N.-mandated operations, or rather, to all state personnel of non-states parties. The criticism leveled at resolutions 1422 and 1487, as well as the U.S. text on Article 98 Bilateral Immunity Agreements, which seeks to prevent the ICC from assuming automatic jurisdiction over any of its nationals detained in a foreign state, has exposed the troublesome issues of immunity of U.N. peacekeepers (from non-party states) and whether the ICC's jurisdiction over U.S. citizens necessarily interferes with extradition law.[8]

As already noted, the debate over the issue of U.S. opposition to the ICC tends to be divided along two lines of reasoning: one that contends that the ICC Statute, in its current form, presents a threat to U.S. national security interests and its military responsibilities overseas; and the other that contends that the ICC poses no threat, and that U.S. opposition, and not the ICC, constitutes the real threat to international peace and security. Within this framework, it is possible to locate three issues dividing these two sides. The first concerns the status of non-state parties within the ICC. Some legal proponents of the U.S. position argue that the Court's jurisdiction violates customary international law.[9]

In particular, U.S. authorities have objected that the Court's automatic jurisdiction over crimes committed by nationals of non-states parties runs counter to the principle of state consent and state sovereignty accorded under international law (see chapter 2).[10] For them, state consent represents the legal means by which states validate the specific international rules of a treaty, and for that matter, exercise their sovereignty to implement and enforce international rules. Madeleine Morris, for instance, notes that "the development of international criminal law, like the development of other areas of international law, is a process of state consent, agreement, and acquiescence. Its development is, in that respect, a series of more or less directly negotiated outcomes in an incremental process."[11]For Morris, to ignore this evolutionary aspect of international law is to ignore the constitutive role played by state consent in the development of international criminal law.

But advocates of the ICC point to the fact that the U.S. has "exercised treaty-based universal jurisdiction over the nationals of non-party states even in cases in which the crime was not previously recognized as subject to universal jurisdiction under customary international law."[12] By refusing to recognize the ICC's jurisdiction over non-nationals, the United States is necessarily contradicting the spirit of the ICC Statute and the justifiability of its action in relation to other conventions that invoke the universality principle, including the Conventions on Airplane High-Jacking, Torture, and Hostage Taking. As Michael Scharf points out, the U.S. position might "affect negatively existing U.S. law enforcement authority with respect to terrorists and drug-traffickers."[13]

U.S. authorities also object that the ICC's authority is based on a loose and often vague definition of constitutional order on the international level. For instance, John R. Bolton, the U.S. Under Secretary of State for Arms Control and International Security, maintains that the ICC's authority is "vague and excessively elastic," since it does not fit into a coherent "constitutional design that delineates clearly how laws are made, adjudicated and enforced."[14] Similarly, in a *Foreign Affairs* article on the tyranny of universal jurisdiction, Henry Kissinger points out that "the danger lies in pushing the effort to extremes that risk substituting the tyranny of judges for that of governments."[15] From this perspective, the Court fails to measure up to the constitutional legal standards of the U.S. legal system, including, most notably a trial by jury. What this seems to imply is that the absence of a trial by jury will result in a *partial* panel of judges or Prosecutor. But as M. Cherif Bassiouni points out, "the Court's statute contains all of the due process guarantees available in the U.S. legal system, and even goes beyond that. . . ."[16]

A second issue dividing these two camps is the role of U.S. military personnel overseas. It is argued by many supporters of the U.S. position that additional provisions will be needed to grant special protection to U.S. personnel stationed overseas. More than anything, this constitutes the main sticking point in the relationship between the U.S. position and opponents of this position.[17] For it is believed that vengeful states may use the right to refer bogus cases to the Office of the Prosecutor, thus biasing investigations against U.S. military personnel. This concern, however, remains both dubious and quite curious, for the very reason that it dismisses the important legal constraints placed on the Prosecutor's power by the judiciary, the Pre-Trial Chamber's duty to screen the information of a case and, where necessary, to authorize that the Prosecutor stop an investigation.

Given the rather dubious nature of this second concern, many legal scholars and political scientists remain strongly opposed to any provision granting special exemptions to U.S. military personnel.[18] The main line of reasoning here is that any special exemption status will contradict the spirit of the Statute, which expressly prohibits any special immunities of any kind. What is more, the ICC's automatic jurisdiction, as we saw in chapter 2, was never intended to block extradition law, but rather, to offer a framework for adjudicating between the receiving state (the state in which the crime occurred) and the requesting home state. This is how the Court expects to operate as an option of last resort: to provide a mechanism that can further ensure that all states will uphold their international obligations to investigate and/or prosecute. Such a mechanism also reflects the need for some form of systematic universal jurisdiction.[19] Here it should be stressed that the ICTY, which has prosecuted and put on trial many of the worst international criminals, establishes an important precedent for "trying nationals of states that did not consent to its establishment."[20] Accordingly, to the extent that the ICC reduces the transaction costs of international criminal tribunals, it also aims to ensure that all states live up to their international obligations.

A third issue dividing opponents and proponents of U.S. opposition involves the crime of aggression. At the Rome Conference, held between June 15 and July 17, state delegations focused on two important international precedents of aggression: the International Military Tribunal (IMT) at Nuremburg and the U.N. General Assembly Resolution 3314.[21] The IMT, for instance, refers to the crime of aggression as a supreme crime or harm committed against humanity. Meanwhile, the General Assembly Resolution "condemns the use of armed force by a State against the sovereignty, territorial integrity or political independence of another State . . . and called on relevant authorities to consider whether a crime of aggression had been committed with regard to all the circumstances of a particular case."[22] Heated debate over the two precedents revealed many differences regarding the need for a specific definition of the crime of aggression and the role of the Security Council. Generally, state delegates remained divided over the issue of including a comprehensive provision of aggression that would enumerate the acts of aggression, and whether the Security Council, the ICC, and/or the General Assembly should determine when the crime of aggression had occurred.[23]

For its part, the U.S. delegation reasoned that the inclusion of a comprehensive crime of aggression would unduly conflict with the role of the Security Council's Chapter VII powers. At the 6th meeting of the Rome Conference, the U.S. delegation summed up its position, by stating that "including the crime of aggression raised the problem of definition and the problem of the role of the Security Council and the General Assembly Resolution 3314 (XXIX) did not attempt to define aggression as an individual crime, and merely repeated a formula from the IMT." The U.S. delegation contended that the General Assembly Resolution had failed to expose the individual elements of a crime of aggression. For this reason, the crime could *not* be included in the ICC Statute since the Statute's power did not cover crimes committed by the state, but only crimes of individual state leaders and military personnel.

Many of the strongest opponents to the U.S. position on the crime of aggression belonged to the Non-Aligned Movement (NAM).[24] The movement maintained, among other things, that any determination of the definition and occurrence of aggression by the Security Council would politicize the Court, since it would allow the Security Council permanent members to exercise their veto power to block the investigation and prosecution of crimes of aggression. It was, therefore, only logical, in their view, that the General Assembly or Prosecutor be charged with the duties of determining when an act of a crime of aggression had occurred.

In sum, the issues dividing the proponents and opponents of the U.S. position underscores a stark dichotomy between U.S. national security and the ICC's jurisdictional authority. In the next section, I will examine in greater detail the U.S. coercive tactics that have intensified this division.

U.S. Coercive Tactics: Intensifying the Division

The war on terrorism will almost certainly involve more active combat duty overseas, especially in Afghanistan and Iraq. To this end, when we address the concrete realities of U.S. concern for its military overseas, we are also assessing the validity of its measures for special protection. As argued above, such measures are not only inconsistent with the Court's mission to investigate and prosecute the worst perpetrators of gross human rights violations regardless of nationality, but also indicative of U.S. determination to disengage itself from the Court altogether. Even if the United States expects to bear a disproportionate share of the burden in the war on terrorism, it must realize that its special responsibilities in no way validates its demands for special exemption. What this suggests is that we need to distinguish between calls for special protectionist measures and the internalization of these special responsibilities through a strategic framework.

As noted earlier, one of the centerpieces of the U.S. policy of disengagement from the ICC has been the American Servicemembers' Protection Act (ASPA).[25] Not only did the bill signal U.S. resolve to protect its own servicepersons from unlawful detainment overseas, but it also suggested U.S. determination to eliminate any perceived obstacles to the global war on terrorism. The bill, in its original form, called for cutting off military assistance to any country that pledged support for the Rome Treaty, and sought, among other things, to preclude the participation of U.S. military personnel in peacekeeping operations, unless exemption was granted to U.S. military personnel. Although the U.S. Senate initially failed to pass the ASPA in September 2000, it would later vote to enact the bill on December 7, 2001, by a 78-21 vote. The new law formed part of the 2002 Supplemental Appropriations Act for the "Further Recovery from and Response to Terrorist Attacks on the United States."[26]

It should be noted that a key amendment to the new bill, the Hague Invasion Act (sponsored by Jesse Helms), effectively authorized the president to use whatever means necessary to free American military personnel detained in the Hague by the ICC. Not surprisingly, the Hague Invasion Act raised deep concern in several E.U. member states, in particular the Netherlands, where the Court is located.[27] The act also prompted Human Rights Watch to adopt its own agenda known as a "call for action," which was aimed at pressuring the U.S. Congress to repeal the act.[28] However, while providing an important counter-pressure to U.S. opposition, the agenda has had little, if any demonstrable impact on U.S. foreign policy, particularly given the U.S. determination to enforce its text of the Article 98 Agreements.

Another key component of the Bush Administration's virtual war on the Court has been its determination to pressure the U.N. Security Council to adopt Resolution 1422, which grants immunity to all military personnel of non-states parties engaged in peace-keeping missions or special policing operations overseas.[29] Here, one encounters two levels of coercion: the U.S. use of military power to coerce the Security Council to grant immunity to its military personnel; and U.S. pressure placed on the Security Council permanent members to renew Resolution 1422.

As noted earlier, the United States announced in mid June 2002 that it would veto the mandate (on June 30) to extend the Bosnian peacekeeping mission, unless it received assurances that its troops would be immune from ICC investigation. Despite several meetings between the United States and other U.N. diplomats, the two sides failed to reach an agreement on the terms of exemption. Just days before the vote to extend the two mandates that would extend the peacekeeping mission in Bosnia, the United States pledged to veto the mandate. In summing up the U.S. position, John D. Negroponte, the U.S. ambassador to the United Nations, stated the following: "Having accepted these risks, by exposing people to dangerous and difficult situations in the service of promoting peace stability, we will not ask them to accept the additional risk of politicized prosecutions before a court whose jurisdiction over our people the government of the United States does not accept." [30]

Nevertheless, U.N. Security Council Resolution 1422 granted a special 12-month exemption to all U.S. military personnel overseas in U.N. mandated operations, or rather, to all state personnel of non-states parties. Although the provision circumvented the problem of granting exemption status, it enabled the United States to use the Security Council as a means of preempting the ICC's jurisdiction over U.S. military personnel. This was illustrated by the pressure imposed by the United States on the Security Council members to vote to renew the resolution on July 13, 2003. Not surprisingly, U.S. pressure prevailed in a 12-0 vote to renew the 12-month exemption status, which established Security Council resolution 1487 (France, Germany, and Syria abstained).[31]

But did the threat of a U.S. veto end up promoting international security? Or, did the threat exaggerate the security risks of the ICC's jurisdiction over U.S. military personnel? Here, it could be argued that the U.S. perception of the ICC's threat confuses the need for criminal accountability oversight and the ICC's obstruction of military missions overseas. At the very least, it suggests that such immunity violates the automatic jurisdiction of the ICC, which is intended to provide broad and systematic jurisdiction over the most serious crimes. Perhaps it is this need for systematic and impartial jurisdiction that explains the sudden reversal of opinion or the Security Council member's subsequent vote not to renew the resolution in the following year.

Article 98 Agreements: Political and Economic Effects

On another front, the United States has sought to secure the immunity of all American citizens through the text of the Article 98 agreements. The principal intention of the text, as noted earlier, is to prevent the ICC from exercising automatic jurisdiction over one of its nationals in a foreign state. This is based on the U.S. interpretation of Article 98(2), which states that

> The Court may not proceed with a request for surrender which would require the requested state to act inconsistently with its obligations under international agreements pursuant to which the consent of a sending state is required to surrender a person of that state to the Court, unless the Court can first obtain the cooperation of the sending state for the giving of consent for the surrender.

The aim of Article 98(2), it should be stressed, is to resolve any inconsistencies that might arise when a state has simultaneously obliged to surrender a national to the ICC and to extradite the national to the home state. Curiously, the Bush Administration's interpretation runs directly counter to this purpose.

In the text of Article 98 Agreements, the United States calls for the immunity of all American citizens from ICC jurisdiction, and considers U.S. sovereignty over its nationals to be absolute.[32] In this respect, the text is controversial precisely because it seeks to trump the ICC's power to adjudicate on international legal matters. However, the ICC's main function, as noted earlier, is to ensure that states parties abide by their international obligations to investigate and prosecute perpetrators of gross human rights violations. In the case that the home state elects not to prosecute, it would have to submit an explanation to the state party detailing why it chose not to prosecute. This could, under certain circumstances, require the ICC to grant permission to the receiving state to surrender the national to the home state. But the text of Article 98 Agreements clearly aims to exclude the ICC from interstate disputes involving the United States and other (signed) states.[33] In fact, the wording of the text suggests that the United States retains an exclusive right not only over the ICC, but also over states where there is no extradition treaty.

From this standpoint, it could be argued that the text of the Article 98 Agreements violates key elements of customary international law. For in the absence of an extradition treaty, such agreements would invalidate the state's territorial jurisdiction over the crime. Again, it is worth stressing that the aim of the ICC is to set aside any such immunities that might complicate efforts to investigate and prosecute accused perpetrators of gross human rights abuses, and which "bars the Court from exercising its jurisdiction over such a person."[34] Thus, the main effect of the Article 98 Agreements is that they tend to limit the scope of the ICC's jurisdictional authority by removing the institutional constraints designed to facilitate the investigation and prosecution of the worst perpetrators of human rights abuses.

The Article 98 Agreements have also, in conjunction with the ASPA, negatively impacted U.S. relations with other states. In June 2003, for instance, the United States suspended millions of dollars of economic and military aid to 35 countries for not having signed an agreement with the United States. It is estimated that more than $47.6 million in aid and $613,000 in military education programs will be cut off to these countries.[35] Paradoxically, such coercive tactics threaten the stability in these certain regions, including Ecuador, which relies heavily on military aid to fight local insurgencies within its borders.[36]

In sum, U.S. coercive tactics have arguably affected the Court's credibility by preventing the Court from exercising automatic jurisdiction over individual perpetrators of gross human rights violations, regardless of nationality. Such tactics and their attendant effects imply that U.S. opposition will continue to polarize supporters of the U.S. position and the advocates of the ICC.

A Third Way: Formulating a Strategic Accommodative Approach

In order to address the effects of United States opposition, it is important to see these effects as the product of not just U.S. hostility, but also of ICC inaction. One of the ways to address this problem is to ask the question of whether the ICC can preempt these effects by inducing the United States to re-engage with the ICC. The main idea here is that the ICC can draw on its own legal and political resources, with the aim of exposing and moving beyond the present dichotomy via a "third way" strategic approach. Such a strategic, accommodative approach would require amendments to the Statute that would collectivize the political will of the Assembly of States Parties. It would also need to rise above U.S. demands for provisions stipulating special exemptions for its military personnel in that it would entail amendments that would recognize the legal validity of its core concerns. In short, such an approach would be based on the adoption of substantive provisions that would internalize U.S. concerns without stipulating special exemption measures that would violate the integrity of the ICC Statute. As such, it would constitute a strategic, "good will" attempt to induce the United States and other major non-state parties to reconsider the need for a strong and independent juridical authority whose moral and legal mission would address, in certain respects, the political and military interests of hegemonic powers.

As suggested above, a third way will also address the need for a broad consensus among the key players in the Assembly of States Parties, including the Bureau, States Parties attending the meetings, and other invited participants, such as NGOs and inter-regional organizations. Such a consensus will be needed if the ICC is to meet the strict procedural requirements of Article

121(3, 4, and 5) of the Statute, which provides that a two-thirds majority vote is needed to pass an amendment; and that seven-eighths of ratifying parties is necessary to enter the amendment into force. Here, it should be stressed that the use of statutory amendments to accommodate the great powers is by no means novel. One can point to the recent amendments adopted by several signatory states to the Montreal Protocol on Substances that Deplete the Ozone Layer (1987), which sought new time schedules to phase out ozone depleting elements. In particular, the London amendment (1996) stipulated the easing of restrictions on China and India and called for increased technological investment in these countries. But while the amendment targeted these emerging great powers, it had little effect on the other key great power states (e.g., the United States, Britain, France, Germany, and Russia), all of which had adopted alternative technologies to minimize resistance to any further proposed phase-outs.

In this respect, a third way is intended to demonstrate how amendments to the ICC Statute can and should serve as incentives or inducements for hegemonic powers to join the ICC. What this suggests is that a strategic, third way approach, one that brings together the political realities of hegemonic power with the moral legitimacy of the ICC, will likely involve difficult tradeoffs between an assertive ICC and U.S. compliance. Yet, it will be precisely these trade-offs that will offer a plausible strategic framework for internalizing hegemonic interests and values.

Indeed, what makes the ICC unique in this respect is that it is composed of a governing branch (Assembly of States Parties) that is vested with the power to check the authority of the Prosecutor and to adopt the policies needed for enhancing the Court's legal and strategic character.[37] Again, this is not to say that international pressures will play an insignificant role in inducing the United States to ultimately change its position. Rather, it implies that such pressures need to be accompanied by a strategic approach that is based on substantive (elements of crimes and the value of enforcing the law) and procedural law. A third way, then, would strategically target U.S. negative perceptions in two respects: first, by exposing the validity and illegitimacy of U.S. demands; and second, by minimizing the political and legal effects of the U.S. campaign on the legitimacy of the ICC. Unlike the Security Council Resolution 1422, which provides a short-term concession to non-states parties, the framework adopted here does not distinguish states parties from non-states parties. Instead, it provides an additional set of rules and provisions to substantiate the concerns of all states parties involved.

The two policy measures listed below are intended to promote this aim. They include 1) a balanced provision stipulating a level playing field between non-states parties and a definition of the crime of aggression; and 2) a closer relationship between the United States and the United Nations, one that works within the framework of the existing and additional provisions. It should be stressed here that such proposals remain grounded in the opinions and views expressed at the Rome Conference; they provide the resources from which the institutional dynamics of the ICC will likely evolve. As such, the proposals seek to reduce the interference between the Security Council and the ICC, a goal that is especially important with respect to formulating a working and acceptable definition of aggression.

A Balanced Approach to the Rules and Elements of Crimes

Earlier, I had mentioned how the United States had objected to the ICC's automatic jurisdiction over nationals of non-states parties. There, I argued that the need for a systematic form of jurisdiction over universally condemned crimes more than outweighed the U.S. objection. Still, it is important to note the single exception to the ICC's automatic jurisdiction: the transitional provision that allows states that have become party to the Statute to not accept the jurisdiction of the Court with respect to war crimes for up to one year (see ICC Article 124). Paradoxically, the United States, whose opposition to some of the elements of war crimes at the Rome Conference led to the adoption of the provision, has viewed the provision as an unfair advantage of states parties over non-states parties, since nationals of non-states parties could be prosecuted for war crimes in states whose nationals would be immune to ICC jurisdiction over (the same) war crimes. What is curious to note here is how this provision was designed to induce states to ratify the Rome Treaty. In this context, such a provision could be subsumed under the third way, since it provides a counterbalancing inducement to (unintended effect of) Article 124.

Yet, a far more pressing issue in this respect is whether the Assembly of States Parties can adopt a comprehensive crime of aggression. As noted earlier, while the crime of aggression is enumerated in the ICC Statute, there are no specific elements that would allow the ICC to implement this crime. This was one of the main reasons why a special working committee of the Assembly of States Parties was needed to establish a consensus on the definition and elements of the crime of aggression. At the first meeting of the Assembly of States Parties, for instance, the committee adopted the PrepCom's draft paper on the definition and elements of the crime of aggression.[38] The paper stipulated, among other things, that "Where the Prosecutor intends to proceed with an investigation in respect of a crime of aggression, the Court shall first ascertain whether the Security Council has made a determination of an act of aggression committed by the state concerned . . . If no Security Council determination exists, the Court shall notify the Security Council of the situation before the Court so that the Security Council may take action, as appropriate (see article 4)."

With respect to the elements of the crime, the draft paper also focuses attention on the elements contained in the proposal submitted by Somoa, which asserts that the act of aggression should reflect the perpetrator's knowledge of the state military action or the consequence of this action. As Article 1 of the draft paper states:

> a person commits a "crime of aggression" when, being in a position effectively to exercise control over or to direct the political or military action of a State, that person intentionally and knowingly orders or participates actively in the planning, preparation, initiation or execution of an act of aggression.

Despite these stipulations, the elements of the perpetrator's knowledge remain largely unclear, since they do not spell out the constitutive aspects of the perpetrator's motives. Moreover, it remains uncertain, based on these conditional elements, whether the ICC will be able to properly determine when an act of aggression has occurred. Clearly, the Security Council will have to play some role in the determination of when acts of aggression have occurred. But whether this will require an amendment to the U.N. Charter is an issue that the working group and Assembly of States Parties will need to study and resolve.

Given these challenges, the Assembly of States Parties will need to address the issues of whether it can begin to effectively formulate, in an objective manner, the elements of the crime of aggression. This will require that the Court investigate not only the detailed circumstances and elements of the crime itself (a state's act of aggression), but also the circumstances of the crime. On an individual level, then, the challenge becomes one of determining a perpetrator's knowledge, or his or her knowledge that a circumstance of his intent will occur, and the circumstances that prove the absence of such knowledge. Accordingly, the Assembly will need to re-evaluate and clarify the meaning of Articles 30 and 32 of the Rome Statute, which stipulate the mental elements and mistakes of law respectively (see chapter 2). Thus, to reemphasize, if the facts in the case prove that a general was misled, then the circumstances of the accused perpetrator's actions should point to his or her lack of knowledge of the circumstance. Again, this is not to say that the circumstances will prove that the person *never* intended to commit the crime, but rather to stipulate that his or her actions were the product of some other person's skillful knowledge of the consequences of the plan.

The Assembly will also need to stipulate not only the Court's competence over the crime, but also how it will determine the act in relation to the Security Council's Chapter VII powers. What this suggests is that either the General Assembly or some other U.N. body, most notably the Commission on Human Rights (an organ of ECOSOC), will need to be vested with the authority to override a veto of the Security Council (through a two-thirds majority vote), which interferes with the investigation and prosecution of a perpetrator of the crime of aggression. For instance, at the 9th meeting of the Rome Conference held on June 22, 1998, it was suggested that the Commission on Human Rights be conferred the right of referral. In their summary statement, the New Zealand delegation stated that "it might be used to consider creating a nexus between the United Nations human rights machinery and the International Criminal Court."[39]

It should be mentioned that other states supported this idea, including the Afghanistan delegation. Two of the possible reasons for this was that it would allow *other* states parties to have a say on the situation, while also providing more active expertise to the Security Council and the ICC. Here, it is worthwhile to note that a participatory role of the commission on aggression might affect the commission in two ways. First it would complement the commission's work on reporting on gross human rights violations by allowing the commission to investigate a new type of serious international crime. Second, and perhaps more important, it might reduce the current political fiction between North and South countries on the commission (e.g., the increasing focus on southern states for gross human rights violations and the social and political consequences of the North's financial controls over many southern states) by allowing southern states on the commission to play a more influential role in the Court's determination of a core crime. Clearly, this would deflect some attention away from southern concerns: namely, that most of the core crimes will likely occur in developing states, or disaffected regions. In short, the addition of an authoritative organ, such as the commission on human rights, would necessarily preempt the need for an amendment to the U.N. Charter.

An Informative Role of the U.N. Security Council

The Assembly of States Parties might also wish to consider the U.N. Security Council's informative role in the enforcement of prosecutorial judgments. In the context of a third way, this would either entail working more vigorously with existing provisions or adopting additional provisions that would have the effect of increasing cooperation between the Security Council and the United States *via* the ICC. With respect to the former, for instance, the expansion of Security Council Chapter VII powers via Article 54(3c), might provide a framework within which the ICC Prosecutor and Security Council can dutifully share information with one another regarding the criminal responsibility of commanders, as stipulated in Article 28 of the Statute. Such a provision might also encourage the United States to make information available to the Prosecutor, revealing the activities of its servicemen and women and the risks and dangers they face in certain missions.

The Security Council could also share more information with the Prosecutor concerning its involvement in U.N.-sponsored national courts. Such additional input would focus attention on the issue of whether the Court should assist or complement *ad hoc* national tribunals. Note that national courts are important in this respect since they focus attention exclusively on designated nationals, as opposed to the peacekeepers in charge of the maintaining order in the region. Perhaps the most well-known case in this respect is the Special Court for Sierra Leone: a hybrid national criminal court (with a truth commission) that has been established to investigate gross human rights violations.[40] However, the problem with the Special Court for Sierra Leone is that poor social conditions and under-funding threaten to curtail the court's ability to prosecute the worst offenders of human rights.[41] Under these circumstances, the Security Council will need to work more closely with the Secretary General to determine which gross offenders may need to be brought to the Hague. On the issue of immunity for non-state party military personnel, the Security Council will need to minimize the effects of the U.S. peacekeeping threat, by delegating responsibility to regional peacekeepers in an effective and judicious manner.[42]

In short, the informative role of the United Nations coupled with a balanced crime of aggression would provide two important components of strategic accommodation, or what I have been referring to as a third way. In essence, it would address a key, ongoing challenge of international law: namely, the need to internalize the political interests and legal concerns of hegemonic states, or, in this case, the political and economic effects of U.S. opposition to the ICC.

Conclusion

Having analyzed the parameters of U.S. opposition to the ICC, it is important that we continue to reveal the polarizing tension between the advocates of the ICC and the proponents of the U.S. position. Given these tensions, I formulated a strategic approach aimed at moving beyond this polarizing division and advancing the practical implications of political legalism. Such an approach reflected a flexible adherence to the rules of the ICC, or a self-directed and engaged application of the rules and provisions of the ICC Statute. The key criteria was the adoption of certain amendments that would require an extensive, broad-based consensus in the Assembly of States Parties, capable of bringing together the legislative will of the Assembly of States Parties with the reality of hegemonic concerns.

Again, the aim of this political strategy was not simply to understand the potential compatibility between U.S. hegemony and the power of the Rome

Statute, but to articulate the ICC's capacity to draw on its own political resources to confront the hegemonic interests of states in general. In this way, such strategic accommodation, while deviating from a strict adherence to the rules, offered a flexible application of the ICC's juridical power. However, as we shall see in the next chapter, mutual accommodation and assimilation may turn out to be limited, albeit important short-term political options.

Notes

1. See David Scheffer, "The United States and the ICC," in Dinah Shelton, ed. *International Crimes, Peace, and Human Rights: The Role of the International Criminal Court* (Ardsley, NY: Transnational Publishers, Inc, 2000), 203–206; op. cit., Ruth Wedgwood, "The International Criminal Court: An American View." *European Journal of International Law* 10 (1999): 93–107.

2. John Washburn, the co-chairman of the Washington Working Group on the International Criminal Court, maintains that U.S. interests were largely ignored at the meetings of the Preparatory Committee on the Establishment of the International Criminal Court. See John Washburn, "The Negotiation of the Rome Statute for the International Criminal Court and International Lawmaking in the 21st Century," *Pace International Law Review* 11 (1999): 361–377.

3. Wedgwood, "The Constitution and the ICC,"in *The United States and the International Criminal Court*, eds. Sarah B. Sewall and Carl Kaysen (Lanham, MD: Rowman & Littlefield Publishers, 2000); Pierre Prosper and Roger Clark, "Justice Without Borders: The International Criminal Court," *Temple International & Comparative Law Journal* 17 (2003): 85–96.

4. See, e.g., Marc Weller, "Undoing the Global Constitution: UN Security Council Action on the International Criminal Court," *International Affairs* 78, no. 4 (October 2002): 693–711; Carsten Stahn, "The Ambiguities of Security Council Resolution 1422 (2002)," *European Journal of International Law* 14 (2002): 85–104; Michael Leigh, "The United States and the Statute of Rome," *The American Journal of International Law* 95: 124–131.

5. In June of 2001, against U.S. pressure, the European Council adopted a "Common Position" on the ICC that laid out the principles for promoting the ICC. Article 3 of the Common Position states: "the European Union and its Member States shall make every effort to further this process by raising the issue of the widest possible ratification, acceptance, approval or accession to the Rome Statute." The text of the Common Position is available at http://www.scoop.co.nz/mason/stories/WO0210/S0009.htm.

6. See 106 Congress, 2nd Session, H.R. 4654; S 2726, 14 June 2000; U.S. Congress (2002) Supplemental Appropriations Bill. HR 4775, presented for signature by the U.S. President on 26 July 2002 and signed on 2 August 2002.

7. United Nations Security Res. 1422 (2002), 12 July 2002. UN Documents S/PV. 4567; SC/7445/Rev. 1

8. See, e.g., Salvatore Zappala, "The Reaction of the US to the Entry into Force of the ICC Statute: Comments on UN SC Resolution 1422 (2002) and Article 98 Agreements," *Journal of International Criminal Justice* 1, no. 1 (June 2003): 114–134.

9. This contention is discussed in depth in Madeleine Morris "High Crimes and Misconceptions: The ICC and Non-Party States," in Dinah Shelton, ed. *International Crimes, Peace, and Human Rights: The Role of the International Criminal Court* (Ardsley, NY: Transnational Publishers, Inc, 2000), 203–206; see also John Bolton, "The Risks and the Weaknesses of the International Criminal Court from America's Perspective," *Virginia Journal of International Law* 41 (2000).

10. In an address at the *Annual Meeting of the American Society of International Law* on March 26, 1999, Scheffer declared that the ICC's automatic jurisdiction reflected "the single most fundamental flaw in the Rome Treaty that makes it impossible for the United States to sign the present text."

11. Morris, "High Crimes and Misconceptions: The ICC and Non-Party States," 241.

12. Michael Scharf, "The ICC's Jurisdiction over the Nationals of Non-Party States," in Sarah B. Sewall and Carl Kaysen, eds. *The United States and the International Criminal Court* (Lanham, MD: Rowman & Littlefield Publishers, Inc, 2000), 221.

13. Scharf, "The ICC's Jurisdiction."

14. Bolton, "The Risks and Weaknesses of the International Criminal Court from America's Perspective," 218

15. Henry Kissinger, "The Pitfalls of Universal Jurisdiction," *Foreign Affairs* 80, no. 3 (2001): 86.

16. Quoted fromThom Shanker and James Dao, "US Might Refuse New Peace Duties Without Immunity," *The New York Times*, 3 July 2001, 8A. Bassiouni has also assembled several documents that indicate the development of several concepts of international criminal law; see M. Cherif Bassiouni, ed. *The Statute of the International Criminal Court* (New York: Transnational Publishers, 1998). However, it is important to note that full compliance with the ICC treaty may, in some cases, require ratifying states to amend their constitutions. For an in-depth discussion of the compatibility between the ICC Statute and state constitutions, see Helen Duffy, "National Constitutional Compatibility and the International Criminal Court," *Duke Journal of Comparative and International Law* 11 (1999): 5–38.

17. See Ruth Wedgwood, "The International Criminal Court: An American View," *European Journal of International Law* 10 (1999): 100.

18. See M. Cherif Bassiouni, "The Universal Model: The International Criminal Court," in M. Cherif Bassiouni, ed. *Post-Conflict Justice* (Ardsley, NY: Transnational Publishers, 2003), 813–828; Marc Weller, "Undoing the Global Constitution: UN Security Council Action on the International Criminal Court," *International Affairs* 78, no. 5 (October 2002): 693–711; Salvatore Zappala, "The Reaction of the US to the Entry into Force of the ICC Statute: Comments on UN SC Resolution 1422 (2002) and Article 98 Agreements," *Journal of International Criminal Justice* 1 (2003): 114–134.

19. For a detailed analysis of the issues regarding the ICC's jurisdiction, see Menno Kamminga, "Lessons Learned from the Exercise of Universal Jurisdiction in Respect of Gross Human Rights Offences," *Human Rights Quarterly* 23 (2001): 941–944.

20. Steven Ratner and Jason Abrams, *Accountability for Human Rights Atrocities in International Law,* 2nd ed. (Oxford: Oxford University Press, 2001), 217.

21. United Nations G.A. Res. 3314 (XXIX). U.N. GAOR, 29th Sess., Annex para. 10, Supp. No. 31, U.N. A/9631 (1974).

22. United Nations. G.A. Res. 3314 (XXIX). U.N. GAOR, 29th Sess., Annex para. 10, Supp. No. 31, U.N. A/9631 (1974).

23. For a reflective account of the historical and political issues surrounding the adoption of the crime of aggression, see Benjamin Ferencz "Can Aggression Be Deterred by Law?" *Pace International Law* 11 (1999): 341–361.

24. The Non-Aligned Movement (NAM) is a loosely-knit, non-hierarchical organization whose origins can be traced to the founding of the United Nations. NAM is based on five working principles: "respect for territorial integrity, mutual non-aggression, noninterference in each other's internal affairs, equality and mutual benefit and peaceful co-existence." See http://www.Icbl.org/resources/namreportmain.htmloriginofnam.

25. U.S. Congress Supplemental Appropriations Bill. HR 4775, presented for signature by the U.S. President on 26 July 2002 and signed on 2 August.

26. U.S. Congress Supplemental Appropriations Bill. HR 4775.

27. Human Rights Watch, "U.S.: Hague Invasion Act Becomes Law." http://www.hrw.org/campaigns/icc/docs/aspa0202.htm.

28. Human Right Watch, Report on International Justice: "Europe Should Oppose U.S. Law on War Crimes Court." http://www.hrw.org/press/2001/12/ASPAeu1210.htm

29. U.N. Security Res. 1422, 12 July 2002. U.N. Documents S/PV. 4567; SC/7445/Rev. 1; for a good discussion of the issues and implications of this resolution, see Carsten Stahn, "The Ambiguities of Security Council Resolution 1422," 85–104.

30. Quoted in Serge Schmemann, "U.S. Vetoes Bosnia Mission, Then Allows 3-day Reprieve," *The New York Times* (July 1, 2002): 3A.

31. Felicity Barringer, "U.N. Renews U.S. Peacekeeper's Exemption from Prosecution," *New York Times* (June 13, 2003): 18A.

32. Article 4 of the text of the Article 98 Agreements reads: "When the Government of X extradites, surrenders, or otherwise transfers a person of the United States of America to a third country, the Government X will not agree to the surrender or transfer of that person to the International Criminal Court by a third country. Absent the expressed consent of Government of the United States."

33. See Zappala, "The Reaction of the US to the Entry into Force of the ICC Statute: Comments on UN SC Resolution 1422 (2002) and Article 98 Agreements," 129.

34. Christine Cervasio, "Extradition and the International Criminal Court: The Future of the Political Offense Doctrine," *Pace International Review* 1, no. 2 (2001): 438.

35. Elizabeth Becker, "U.S. Suspends Aid to 35 Countries Over New International Court," *New York Times* (July 2, 2003): 16A.

36. It is also worthwhile to note that the European Council has since moved away from its common position of active collective opposition to the U.S. position, by "accepting" the legitimacy of the Article 98 Agreements. However, the EU's "cool" acceptance of the agreements has also forced the Commission to continually reassure certain

states, especially those provisional EU member states, that its decision to sign an Article 98 Agreement with the U.S. will not jeopardize its ties with the EU (e.g., Macedonia's signature in June of 2003).

37. By strategic character, I am referring to the instrumental value of the ICC's rules and procedures and how this value can be brought to bear on U.S. coercion consistent with the legitimacy of the Court or the perception of its fairness.

38. See Assembly of States Parties, "Continuity of work in respect of the crime of aggression resolution ICC-ASP.1/Res.1.2002; and Assembly of States Parties, Draft Paper on the Definition and Elements of the Crime of Aggression. ICC-ASP/2/10 2003.

39. United Nations, *United Nations Diplomatic Conference of Plenipotentiaries on the Establishment of an International Criminal Court*, Rome, 15 June–17 July 1998. Volume II (New York: United Nations Publications, 1998).

40. United Nations, "Fifth Report of Secretary General on the United Nations Mission in Sierra Leone." S/2000/751, July 31, 2000.

41. For a good discussion of the weaknesses and limiting circumstances of the establishment of a special Court for Sierra Leone, see Nicole Fritz and Alison Smith, "Current Apathy for the Coming Anarchy: Building the Special Court for Sierra Leone," *Fordham International Law Journal* 25 (2001): 105–145.

42. Michael Hirsh, "Peacekeeping's Hybrid Future," *Foreign Affairs* 79 (2000): 8–9.

7

Religion and Politics: Arab States and the Role of Islamic Ethics

> Those who say they have got the better of their vindictive passion or of some other kind of painful passion often tell the truth as things are, but not as they are. They speak to us when the causes of their error have been fostered and developed by themselves. But go back further, call these causes back to their beginning; there you will take them unprovided.
>
> —Montaigne

ARAB STATES HAVE PLAYED a largely positive (albeit controversial) role in the establishment of the International Criminal Court (ICC). For instance, at the Rome Conference held between June 15 and July 17, 1998, many Arab state delegations agreed to include the crime of aggression (see Article 5(d) of the ICC Statute), even though some attempted to downplay the role of the U.N. Security Council's powers in determining when an act of aggression had occurred. Furthermore, several Arab state delegations supported the Prosecutor's right to initiate a case (*proprio motu*) on the grounds that this right would affirm the Court's independence and empower the Court's judiciary to investigate the worst perpetrators of gross human rights abuses.

However, as discussed earlier (chapter 5), several Arab state delegations attempted to exclude various elements of crimes of gender violence (forced pregnancy). Not only did the disagreement over forced pregnancy expose Arab state concerns over the jurisdictional overreach of the Court, but it also highlighted the conflict between Islamic and international law. This is not to say that the conflict between Arab states and ICC provisions stemmed from Islam *per se*, but rather that the conflict between Arab states and the ICC constituted a particular example of the general conflict between domestic and international law.

In this chapter, I focus on various political or negotiating strategies adopted at the Rome Conference to induce Arab states to sign the ICC Treaty. I discuss the limitations of the politics of negotiating and bargaining while also raising the political possibilities of cultural adaptation. In particular, I assess the strategies of mutual accommodation and assimilation and examine how these strategies can provide the grounds for some degree of cultural adaptation. In this way, I shall characterize the political nature of the general conflict between international and domestic law as the discrepancy between the state's monopoly on the legitimate use of force and international law (see chapter 2). It should be stressed here that the state's monopoly on the use of violence remains somewhat problematic. This is because international (normative) sanctions or pressures can now, more than ever, influence whether or not a state complies with treaty rules.

Notwithstanding the complex effects of Political Islam or Pan Islamic movements on Arab state politics, I analyze the compatibility between *Shariah* and ICC Statute provisions in order to demonstrate how the state's monopoly on the legitimate use of violence has hindered the political strategies subsumed under political legalism. Here, I assume that the issue of Israel's immunity from the ICC remains an important concern for many, if not all Arab states, even though it is unclear as to how the Israeli factor in this case will continue to shape Arab state resistance to the ICC.

Nevertheless, I will argue two main points in the chapter: that more mutual accommodation will be needed to help resolve future conflicts between Islamic and international law; and that such conflicts between the ICC and Arab states expose the need for adaptation that will facilitate political legalism. It is out of this process of cultural adaptation, I contend, that the relationship between the Islamic ethics of international law and serious international crimes will evolve. The first and second sections of the chapter, therefore, discuss the characteristics of Arab state sovereignty and how these differing types correlate with the differing role played by *shariah*. The third moves on to assess the conflict between the views of Arab states and ICC provisions that surfaced at the Preparatory Commission meetings and Rome Conference, in particular forced pregnancy and the crime of aggression. And finally, the last section analyzes the conflict between Islamic and international law and the concomitant need to further develop the criminal systems in Arab Islamic states *vis-à-vis* the ICC Statute.

Mutual Accommodation and Adaptation: Between Islamic and International Law

What is mutual accommodation? And how does it differ from cultural adaptation? Mutual accommodation and cultural adaptation, as understood here, refer to two different (albeit loosely connected) processes. Whereas mutual accommodation constitutes the ongoing practice of appealing to the interests of all states parties involved, cultural adaptation reflects the willingness of states to reconcile their national customs to international law. By cultural adaptation, therefore, I am not referring to assimilation (e.g., the gradual secularization of Islamic societies), but to (*permanent*) concessions to the rule of law in international relations, which, as Abdullah Ahmed An-Na'im explains, allow Islamic states to resolve the political tensions between secular and Islamic law "with reference to resources within their own traditions."[1]

It is true that Islamic criminal law (*siyar*) and international criminal law share many overlapping functions for the suitable prevention and prohibition of international criminal violations, including prohibition against torture, slavery, and war crimes.[2] However, the lego-political issue explored here is not whether they share the same principles, but how the absence of specific elements of crimes in the penal codes of domestic law in Arab states relates to the repressive use of *shariah* by the Arab state. As this would suggest, *shariah* has never provided a comprehensive system of codes; only a path for striving towards God's will.[3] And even in those cases where *shariah* has been codified, the state may decide to subordinate "progress" to Islam by using its monopoly on the use of force to severely restrict many basic political and civil rights in the name of God's will. The question that arises, then, is how does Islamic law, particularly in Arab states, relate to ICC provisions?

Most legal scholars and political scientists tend to ignore the issue of cultural adaptation by claiming that international rules and norms will ultimately be assimilated into state practice. As we saw earlier, many assume that the Court's legitimacy, or the perception of its impartiality, will foster an environment of mutual respect and the tacit desire to adapt domestic law to the ICC's strict standards. Still others suggest that the Court's accommodative approach will do little to encourage repressive states to change their politics.[4] Thomas Smith, for instance, contends that the Security Council's Chapter VII powers, which provides the Security Council with the mandate to use action with respect to the threats to the peace, breaches of the peace, and acts of aggression, "should become the principle source of enforcing the ICC's provisions against state intransigence."[5] This is a topic that I shall explore in further detail in chapter 8 when I discuss a potential cooperative arrangement between the ICC and the Security Council.

Here, it should be noted that a strong majority of Arab state delegations at the Rome Conference opposed the deferral powers of the Security Council. Articles 13 and 16 of the ICC Statute, for instance, enable the Security Council to refer and defer matters it deems a threat to international security, respectively. Arab states objected that the Security Council's exclusive competence over the crime of aggression would allow the permanent member states of the Security Council to use their veto power to block the investigation and prosecution of one of their own nationals. This is not to say that *only* Arab states opposed the role of the Security Council. In fact, many states, including Latin American and Asian states, opposed the Security Council's role in triggering the action to investigate perpetrators of gross human rights violations. Instead, it points to the need for studying the political and legal conflicts between domestic and international law.

As we saw in chapter 2, the primary objective of the Court is to investigate only the worst perpetrators of gross human rights violations (see the preamble of the ICC Statute). But the duty to prosecute will also require Arab states to abide by all the rules, procedures, and elements of crimes of the ICC Statute. Whether or not Arab states will carry out this duty, however, is an inherently political question, since presumably it will require Arab state governments to implement legal and constitutional safeguards against human rights abuses and other forms of repression (e.g., forced disappearances and torture).

What this suggests is that the repressive state practices of some Arab Islamic states will continue to expose the likelihood of further conflict between domestic and international law, and, more importantly, the need for further adaptation to the ICC. Indeed, any analysis of this conflict reflects the important role played by Islam in many Arab states, including the recognition of Islam as a source of legislation, and the implementation of *shariah* federal courts.[6] Here, Islamic values reflect the devotion to the five pillars of Islam (the teachings of Mohammed in the Sunna text and Hadith, prayer, pilgrimage to Mecca, fasting, and Zakat Tax or alms giving) and a commitment to applying Islamic law (*shariah*). As such, they encompass a wide range of interpretations of Islam within the Muslim community (*ummah*), which derive from the *Sunnah* and *Quran* (the written sacred texts of Islam) and define the procedural and substantive elements of Arab state constitutions.

Arab State Sovereignty

In order to address what these elements mean for projecting the core values of Islamic law through the ICC, it is important to assess, in systematic fashion, the juridical meaning of Arab state sovereignty. Traditional conceptions of sovereignty hold that sovereignty is an internationally recognized entitlement to rule over a territorially defined set of borders.[7] Here, the ontological structure of the state is what represents the fixed apparatus of sovereignty. Within this apparatus, sovereignty is treated as both a natural and unchanging concept, in that it is based on the fixed recognition of territorial borders. In challenging this static concept of sovereignty, some IR theorists have interpreted sovereignty as a social construct which "emerges as a product of knowledgeable practices by human agents including citizens, non-citizens, theorists, and diplomats. It is neither natural, nor even fully completed."[8] In other words, since the meaning of sovereignty remains contingent on fixed, arbitrary borders, conventional notions of sovereignty fail to register the impact of customs and knowledge (access to information). Still, the contestability of this concept should not restrict our application of the traditional conception to the Arab world, for many Arab states, as we shall see, rely on strict interpretations of sovereignty to legitimize their power.

In the descriptive analysis below, sovereignty is defined as an internationally recognized legal right which entitles a state entity to exercise authority over a territorially defined set of borders. All the sovereign Arab states referred to in this section belong to the Arab League, which was established in 1945.[9] Membership with the League confers both legitimacy and the identity. And while most constitutions of Arab states either refer to the state as an independent sovereign Arab state, which recognizes Islam as the state religion and Arabic the official language, some declare themselves as "Arab Islamic states."[10] Such a term, as it is understood here, is meant to convey the fundamental bond that exists between *shariah* and state rule, as well as the peoples and monarch. What generally typifies this form of sovereignty is the submission of the people to the king/sultan/sheik in exchange for social public order and beneficence (hereditary succession).[11]

Another form consists of a republican or pluralist arrangement. For example, the sovereignty of Yemen, which also adopts *shariah* as the principal source of legislation, is not defined *per se* by the union of prince and the peoples, but rather by the republican and pluralist order of the state, comprised of decision-making bodies of non-elected political parties and organizations.[12]

Perhaps the most extreme version of an Arab Islamic state is the Arab state of Sudan, whose constitution recognizes the supreme authority of "God over both sovereignty and the state" (see Article 4 of the Constitution of the Republic of Sudan).

Unlike the monarchial form of sovereignty of other Arab Islamic states, sovereignty in this setting is subordinated to God's will. This underscores an overtly rigid interpretation of *shariah* in which the state routinely rejects any compromise or concessions to secular norms or forms of law, including minimalist standards of human rights. It is important to note here that putting God's will over the state and sovereignty of the people is what typifies a true Islamic state. This is exemplified in non-Arab Islamic states, such as Iran and the former state of Afghanistan, ruled by the Taliban, where the highest clerical rulers are in charge of enforcing the laws and rules in conjunction with God's will (e.g., Supreme Ayatollah and Council of Guardians). In this sense, while monarchial Islamic Arab states may be fundamentalist in character, they are not, as understood here, Islamic states *per se.*

From this vantage point, virtually all Arab states, with the exception of Lebanon and Syria, recognize Islam as the state religion and/or source of legislation; and Arabic as the official language. Lebanon, for instance, constitutes the only self-proclaimed secular state, in light of its Christian Maronite majority; while in the socialist Arabic state of Syria, Islam represents the religion of one part of the state: "the President of the Republic."[13] In this respect, Islam and the Arabic language constitute two essential features of the Arab world, which comprises a vast geographical region populated by a variety of linguistic and religious groups. For virtually all Arabs, the Arab world is considered as one single nation to which all Arab states and people belong.

In addition to these three types of Arab state sovereignty mentioned above, there is also Arab state sovereignty that resides strictly in the people's democratic will or democratic institutions such as multiparty elections and direct representation. Those state constitutions that recognize this type of sovereignty include Egypt, Algeria, Tunisia, Syria, Jordan, Mauritania, Lebanon, Comorros, and Djibouti. The distinctive feature of this type of sovereignty is the separation of governmental powers or the arguably stronger commitment to protecting individual political and civil rights. While there is no way of ascertaining the relationship between this type of sovereignty and the abuse of human rights, it is possible to see particular deviations from the democratic norm of human rights protection. Indeed, as we shall see in the last section, many democratic states have proved capable of inflicting systematic torture on its citizens.

In sum, there are four types of Arab state sovereignty identified here: state sovereignty that is subordinate to God (Supreme sovereignty); sovereignty that resides strictly in the state or hereditary rule (Monarchical); sovereignty that lies in the state in the form of political pluralism or non-elected state political parties and organizations (Republican); and sovereignty that resides in the people (Democratic). These four different types of sovereignty correspond roughly to differing degrees of state repression, which can also take the form of the state's (abuse of its) monopoly on the use of force (see table 7.1). Culturally, the differing degrees of repression reflect the effects stemming from the undeveloped criminal systems of Arab states, and *shariah* as an ambiguous form of constitutional rule.[14]

Sovereignty and Repressive State Rule

Now, it is true that Islamic criminal law recognizes many of the basic rights of defendants encoded in the ICC Statute, such as the right to freedom from arbitrary arrest, presumption of innocence, and the right to a public trial.[15] But such rights do not address the more pressing issue of the lack of specificity of the elements of crimes. In short, the effects that arise from the abuse of the state's monopoly of the use of force reveals the need to adapt *shariah* and criminal legal systems to international law, or rather the ICC Statute. It suggests that a flexible application of *shariah* to civil society can and should facilitate the adaptation of Islam to international law. Such an application is exemplified by Jordan's ratification of the ICC Statute; the only Arab state to ratify the statute.

As table 7.1 indicates, the relationship between supreme sovereignty and the state's monopoly on the use of force correlates with the rigid application of *shariah.* As noted earlier, supreme sovereignty imposes an excessively rigid form of *shariah* on the people with little, if any regard for due process or the basic rights of citizens. By comparison, monarchial sovereignty and republican sovereignty correspond to a somewhat less rigid application of *shariah.* While the former reflects how the bond between the monarch and his subjects provides certain provisional safeguards against the state's arbitrary imposition of *shariah* rule, republican sovereignty allows for some degree of political accountability.

TABLE 7.1
Relationship between Sovereignty and *Shariah*

Arab State Sovereignty	*Number of States*	*% of Arab League*	*Key Problems of State Form*	*Application of* Shariah
Supreme	1	5	Severe ethnic cleansing	Excessively Rigid
Monarchial	8	43	Mass torture Mass executions	Rigid
Republican	1	5	Unlawful detentions	Rigid
Democratic	9	47	Cases of mass torture Unlawful detentions	Flexible

Note: The above list of Arab states belonging to the Arab League excludes Iraq and Somalia. The official number of Arab League members, including Palestine, is 22.

Conversely, democratic sovereignty reflects a flexible application of *shariah* in which the judges of *shariah* appeals courts must actively balance *shariah* against the protection of basic political liberties of Muslim citizens. Again, this is not to say that the democratic Arab Islamic states lack repressive practices. As we shall see, corruption and a lack of accountability continues to persist in Egypt and Tunisia, two of the more liberal states. Yet, when democratic and political reforms are undertaken to curb high levels of repression and corruption, there may be a stronger likelihood for ratifying the ICC Statute.

Negotiation and Mutual Accommodation

Turning to the various strategies employed by the ICC authorities at the Rome Conference, we find that there were many important conflicts between Arab states' ethical convictions and ICC provisions. Below, I document the particular conflict concerning women's rights; then discuss the events of the differences surrounding the crime of aggression (see chapter 6). The aim of this section is to demonstrate, in rather descriptive fashion, the continued importance of mutual accommodation as a political strategy, especially as this concerns the ICC's flexible juridical power. The idea here is that more mutual accommodation will spur continued cultural adaptation and further harmonization between the ICC's universal morality and Islamic ethics (worldview). In the following section, I will provide a substantive assessment of the ethical convictions of Arab states and the importance of Islamic ethics for promoting the juridical power of the ICC.

The Crime of Enforced Pregnancy

At the Preparatory Committees held between 1996–1998, Arab states, along with the Holy See delegation and other Catholic countries (e.g., Ireland and several Latin American countries), adopted a proposal that would restrict the scope of gender-related crimes in the ICC Statute. The main aim of the proposal was to replace the crime of forced pregnancy with "forcible impregnation." Despite the similarities between these terms, the two crimes contained different elements or rules defining the parameters and penalties for the crime. For instance, whereas forcible impregnation referred to the single act of forcing women into pregnancy, forced pregnancy was a "broader concept involving keeping a woman pregnant," even in cases of rape or incest.[16]

Although a majority of state delegations rejected the proposal, many Arab states feared that the permanent inclusion of forced pregnancy would force them to adopt national laws legalizing abortion. In their view, the proposal threatened to undermine the state's ability to govern its own national affairs by allowing the ICC to interfere in domestic legal matters. In this way, the disagreement seemed to point to the potential conflict between state politics and the ICC's jurisdictional reach.

Ultimately, the disagreement would resurface at the negotiations at the Rome Conference, where German and Canadian delegations introduced a proposal outlining a broader range of elements of crimes against humanity, including rape, sexual slavery, enforced prostitution, forced pregnancy, enforced sterilization, and other forms of sexual violence of comparable gravity. As discussed in chapter 2, a crime against humanity refers to any of the forgoing acts when committed as part of a widespread or systematic attack against any civilians with knowledge of the attack. Although Arab state delegations accepted this definition for rape and torture, they did not believe that forced pregnancy constituted a systematic, organizational attack against its civilians. Rather, the crime, in their view, was more akin to a war crime.

It is worthwhile to note here that many Arab state delegations at the Rome Conference initially insisted on the nexus between crimes against humanity and war. The issue raised in this debate was whether crimes against humanity were inherently linked to a systematic attack against the civilian population, and whether the Prosecutor should be given jurisdiction over atrocities regardless of whether they stemmed from conflict. Most Arab state delegations, such as Saudi Arabia and Syria, contended that the nexus between these crimes and war was necessary to prevent the Prosecutor from interfering in the local affairs of the state. Despite their initial opposition, Arab states agreed with the majority of state delegations that "there was no inherent nexus of a crime against humanity and war."[17]

To challenge the German and Canadian proposal, therefore, Arab states drew up their own counter-proposal that excluded the provision on forced pregnancy and restricted the definition of sexual violence to rape.[18] But a majority of state delegations voted down the Arab state proposal, arguing that it was too restrictive of the statutory character of the ICC. Once again, this left many Arab states deeply concerned that the provision would allow the ICC to extend its jurisdiction over matters that were of national concern, including the judicial authority to determine the scope of the crime of abortion (e.g., a woman's life or health).[19]

Not surprisingly, the rift between Arab (and Catholic) states and the West threatened to further divide state delegations. Negotiators at the Rome Conference needed to seek a compromise that would resolve this discrepancy between religious values and the provisions of the ICC. Thus, it was decided that the inclusion of forced pregnancy in Article 7(2)(f) would be balanced against a clause stipulating non-interference with the national customs of the state. The provision reads that

> forced pregnancy means the unlawful confinement of a woman forcibly made pregnant, with the intent of affecting the ethnic composition of any population or carrying out other grave violations of international law. This definition shall not in any way be interpreted as affecting national law relating to pregnancy.

The compromise provision effectively accommodated both the religious and rule of law concerns of several state delegations. Yet, here it could be argued that the opt-out clause of the provision severely weakens the accountability principle and that one should expect little, if any voluntary compliance with the former clause of the provision.[20] On the other hand, one might argue that the opt-out clause provides a typical diplomatic compromise to the conflict between national customs and the treaty statute. After all, it is quite common for international treaties to go out of their way to ensure that nothing in the statute will unduly affect national laws. In this respect, it seems only realistic to expect that Arab Islamic states will use this opt-out clause to defend and preserve their culture against the extension of the ICC's jurisdiction.[21]

Aggression and Non-Accommodation

Another significant point of debate at the Rome Conference concerned the crime of aggression and the political implications of including a comprehensive definition and the elements of this crime in the ICC Draft Statute. As discussed earlier in chapter 6, the debate revolved principally around the issue of whether the ICC or the Security Council could determine the conditions under which state leaders had committed aggression. As such, it highlighted the concern over the politicization of the ICC via the permanent members' veto power in the Security Council, and the U.S. contention that the role of Security Council needed to be included within the framework of the ICC. Arab states, in this respect, feared that the veto power would block the investigation and prosecution of their own nationals, thereby undermining the independence and legitimacy of the Court.

At the Rome Conference, Arab state delegations (e.g., Syria) were among the most vocal supporters of a comprehensive definition of the crime of aggression. For instance, some Arab states referred to the crime of aggression as "the mother of all crimes," a term used at the Nuremberg Trials to describe Nazi aggression. Others, such as the Syrian delegation, characterized it as "supreme crime."[22] In fact, the Syrian delegation went so far as to threaten its continued support of the ICC Treaty unless the Arab state proposal was adopted, or some working definition included in the statute.

The Arab state proposal was based on two international precedents: International Military Tribunal (IMT) and the General Assembly Resolution 3314 (XXIX).[23] Again, the International Military Tribunal (IMT) was one of the first tribunals to punish for war crimes and crimes against humanity, including the planning, preparation, initiation or waging of a war of aggression, and the participation in a common plan or conspiracy for the accomplishment of any of the forgoing. Arguably, the International Military Tribunal established an important baseline for future meetings in the General Assembly regarding the crime of aggression.[24] As we saw in chapters 1 and 6, this would eventually culminate in the General Assembly's Resolution 3314 (XXIX), which provided a definition of aggression.[25]

The resolution defined aggression in terms of the use of armed force against the sovereignty and territorial integrity of another state. Article 3 of the resolution, for instance, enumerates seven acts of aggression, with the first act (3[a]) stipulating the following: "an invasion of or attack by the armed forces of a State of the territory or any military occupation, however temporary, resulting from such invasion or attack or any annexation by the use of the force of the territory of another State or part thereof." Furthermore, Article 2 required that each case be interpreted according to its unique circumstances, but that only the Security Council reserved the ultimate right to judge whether or not a crime of aggression had been committed.

One of the issues of the crime of aggression discussed at the Rome Conference was whether the Security Council should be allowed to become a triggering mechanism for prosecution. At issue was whether the Security Council's determination of acts of aggression should become a 'prerequisite' for the Prosecutor's competence.[26] As table 7.2 shows, a majority of Arab states opposed this option regarding the Security Council's powers of referral and deferral. Instead, many preferred as their first choice the Prosecutor's capacity to determine when the acts of aggression had occurred. Those that wished to limit the powers of the Security Council within the ICC (the power to defer a case applies to United Arab Emirates, Mauritania, and Egypt) tended to prefer the Prosecutor and General Assembly as the primary mechanisms for triggering an investigation of a crime of aggression.

By comparison, some states preferred to have the Security Council remain entirely separate from the ICC. This is represented by the most prevalent preference ordering: p>g>s (where the Prosecutor = p, General Assembly = g, the Security Council = s, and Human Rights Commission = h). The second most prevalent pattern shows p>s>g; while a single country pattern of Sudan is indicated by p>g>h. Of the few Arab states that did agree to a limited role of the

TABLE 7.2
Arab State Preferences (at the Rome Conference) Regarding the Triggering Mechanisms for Prosecution on the Crime of Aggression

Countries	*Prosecutor*	*Security Council*	*General Assembly*	*Human Rights Commission*
Algeria	primary	tertiary	secondary	
Bahrain	primary	tertiary	secondary	
Comorros	primary	tertiary	secondary	
Djibouti	primary	tertiary	secondary	
Egypt	secondary	primary	tertiary	
Iraq	exclusive			
Jordan	exclusive			
Kuwait	primary		secondary	
Lebanon	primary	tertiary	secondary	
Libya	secondary	no	primary	
Mauritania	primary	secondary	tertiary	
Morocco				
Oman	primary	tertiary	secondary	
Qatar	primary	no	secondary	
Saudi Arabia	primary	no		
Sudan	primary	no	secondary	tertiary
Syria			exclusive	
Tunisia	primary	tertiary	secondary	
UAE	primary	secondary	tertiary	
Yemen	primary	tertiary	secondary	

Source: United Nations Diplomatic Conference of Plenipotentiaries on the Establishment of an International Criminal Court, Rome 15 June–17 July 1998.

Security Council, however, most supported the Security Council's limited right to referral, while a few even backed a 12-month *non-renewable* right to defer a case (e.g., Egypt and Oman).

In short, the varying preference orderings suggest that the Arab state delegations remained largely split over the role of the Security Council. Some even remained adamantly opposed to incorporating the Security Council into the ICC. The Syrian delegation, for instance, argued that the Court's competence was a necessary means of resolving the "history" of political complications involving Security Council inaction, including the nearly 200 cases in which the Security Council failed to make a determination.[27] Similarly, Libya rejected any inclusive role for the Security Council in the ICC, arguing that it would introduce a political element that would "run counter" to the complementarity principle.[28] In particular, they criticized the Security Council's failure to condemn the 1986 U.S. attack on its country, despite the fact that the General Assembly's adoption of Resolution 41/39 had declared the attack to be an act of aggression.

But while most Arab states insisted that the crime of aggression was primarily a state crime, they remained reluctant to consider the individualistic nature of this crime. For the most part, they preferred to focus on its statist nature, with a view to maintaining the strict separation of the U.N. and ICC powers. Politically speaking, this suggested that most Arab states, along with other delegations, recognized the General Assembly's ability to counteract the political effects of the permanent members' veto powers. As noted above, the permanent members of the Security Council can always use their veto power to shield one of their own military personnel from prosecution for the crime of aggression.

At the first meeting of the Preparatory Commission (1999), Arab states introduced a proposal on the crime of aggression, which restricted the definition of the crime of aggression to the seven acts of aggression encoded in the GA Resolution (Article 3) (see chapter 1).[29] Curiously, the proposal excluded Article 4 of the GA Resolution, which allows the Security Council to declare 'other' acts of aggression. In seeking to establish a complete and definitive list of acts of aggression under Article 5(2), Arab states may have sought to exclude the discretionary power of the Security Council altogether.

But it is also true that a complete list would include gaps that "would encourage the aggressor to exploit the definition, while leaving little room to determine whether pre-emptive self-defense would be lawful under the Charter."[30] In the end, it was decided that the proposal was a matter for the Assembly of States Parties (the decisionmaking body of the ICC) to take up at their first meeting in September 2003, in New York (see chapter 6).[31] Thus, while the delegations at the Rome Conference voted on the inclusion of the crime of aggression (see Article 5(d) of the statute), many remained deeply divided over the issue of whether the Security Council's determination of acts of aggression would be binding on the Court.[32]

In sum, the conflict between Arab and Western states underscores some of the potential limits for relying on accommodation to resolve the differences between the ICC and these states. The next section moves beyond these limitations by examining how the Islamic world view overlaps with and, in some cases, exposes the need for further adaptation of Islamic criminal law to the provisions in the ICC Statute.

State Repression and Cultural Adaptation

As we saw earlier, one of the ways that negotiators at the Rome Conference sought to resolve the conflict between Arab states' views on forced pregnancy and ICC provisions was to reinforce the primacy of national customs. This was in response to Arab state objections that the Court would interfere with the state's capacity to regulate its own internal affairs. Such objections underscored the idea that new national laws on abortion would ultimately contravene *shariah*, since it would allow women to hold a right in contradistinction to the state.[33] Given this idea, I shall examine the relationship between the application of *shariah* and the state's monopoly on the use of violence, by assessing two factors: the criminal legal systems of Arab states vis-à-vis international criminal law, and *shariah* as an obscure form of constitutional rule.

Shariah

Shariah consists of the legal codes, principles, and rules to which all jurors, state clerical leaders, and administrators must appeal when applying the rule of public law. On a personal level, it conveys the active pursuit of various spiritual and practical goals, including the protection of faith, life, intellect, lineage, property, and the elimination of corruption. Arab Islamic states that officially recognize *shariah* as the source of legislation assume the indivisibility of national decision-making and Islam.[34] In these and virtually all other Arab Islamic states, the judges of *shariah* appeals courts determine which criminal penalties to impose on Muslims accused of violating *shariah* codes, such as adultery and unlawful abortion.

So where does the conflict between *shariah* and the protection of individual rights arise? Earlier, I had identified the most extreme source of violence as the lack of state accountability to the people. An example of this was the constitutional provision on the supreme authority of God over state and sovereignty, which reflected the Sudanese government's ability to justify (or conveniently deny) virtually any form of brutal repression. Note that in the context of Article 24 of Sudan's constitution, which provides that the right to religion "shall be exercised in a manner that does not harm public order . . . ," the notion of public order becomes especially suspect and problematic since the struggle to maintain public order can become the basis for pursuing God's will at the expense of individual human rights.

Thus, it is not surprising that this constitutional element can intensify into the most brutal forms of violence. This is illustrated by the recent joint operation in the Darfur region of Sudan between government troops and Arab troops, in which 136 men were detained and then systematically massacred shortly thereafter.[35] Such an event reflects an ongoing pattern of violence involving the government's tacit support of the Janjaweed, a loose band of lawless militia on horses, which has conducted a campaign of ethnic cleansing by purging "villages of their darker-skinned black African inhabitants."[36]

For modern Islamic scholars, Islamic state violence underscores the larger issue of whether Islamic values can be effectively reconciled to today's international criminal justice system. According to M. Cherif Bassiouni, Arab Islamic states have generally failed to adopt a "progressive codification of Islamic criminal justice (procedure and administration), which could sift through and distill the law and practices of Islam and adapt it to a contemporary framework which would keep faith with the past, while setting the foundations for the future."[37] Moreover, the lack of procedural rules calls attention to the vague codification of crimes, such as torture. This problem has recently come to light in Libya, where the government has unlawfully detained and tortured seven Eritrean nationals suspected of terrorism. Here, the main problem stems from Libya's vague penal codes on torture, which proscribe torture, but fail to define the crime.[38]

Another important feature of the undeveloped criminal law systems in some Arab Islamic states is the absence of the rule of law, in particular, the lack of an independent judiciary to provide the necessary oversight of the government's actions and practices. In the case of Libya, the Peoples of the Court has repeatedly ignored accusations of the torture, and failed in the process to comply with moral standards set forth in Article 14 of the International Covenant of Civil and Political Rights. Thus, while several Arab Islamic state constitutions contain provisions of the rule of law and impartiality (see Article 58 of the Oman constitution), the judiciary in these states continue to turn a blind eye to accusations of torture.

Perhaps more important, the lack of rule of law continues to persist in the liberal, democratic Arab states such as Tunisia. Considered by many as one of the most liberal and democratic Arab states, Tunisia has, over the years, convicted defendants on the basis of dubious confessions.[39] In addition to Tunisia, Egypt, which declares itself a democratic socialist Arab nation, has also instituted an emergency draconian law to deal with Islamic militants, which allows the government to routinely torture suspected terrorists in order to extract confessions. Accordingly, one might expect *shariah* to limit these actions by the state actions, or at least prompt the court system to consider the legality of such actions.

However, in the case of Egypt, the Egyptian Supreme Court continues to struggle over the issue of implementing *shariah*. The decision, for instance, by the Egyptian Supreme Constitutional Court to suspend Article 2 of the Egyptian constitution, which established *shariah* as the basis of criminal punishment in Egyptian society, leaves open the question of whether *shariah* can serve as a reasonable basis of the will of the Egyptian people. As Claude Lombardi notes, it remains uncertain "if the Egyptian people will accept the judge's revised theory of *shariah*, which draws on influential thinkers of Islamic history to develop a working framework of principles."[40]

One might also consider the case of Saudi Arabia. Here, *shariah* remains somewhat rigid, even though it provides the only check on the judge's powers. As Article 46 of the Saudi Arab constitution provides: "The judiciary is an independent authority. There is no control over judges in the dispensation of their judgments expect in the case of the Islamic Shariah." Given this rigidity, the criminal system in Saudi Arabia allows the government to detain individuals without any judicial body to provide oversight of detention. Such a practice has become common in Saudi Arabia, as regards the Saudi government attempts to counter the rising terrorism against the Saudi state.

The question that, then, arises is whether *shariah* constitutes a cultural obstacle to adaptation. Some influential modern Islamic scholars contend that *shariah*, as it presently exists in many Arab Islamic states, still represents an "unfinished form of constitutional rule."[41] For An-Naim, developing *shariah* will require state leaders and Islamic clerical authorities to reinterpret the non-constitutive nature of *shariah*. In other words, *shariah* cannot in itself provide the essential source of constitutional changes to bring Islam into line with the modern evolution of international law (basic human rights protection). Only the *Sunnah* and *Quran*, in his view, offer the sources to develop the constitutional safeguards against human rights abuses. To clarify *shariah* in this setting, therefore, means that the clerical state leaders need to interpret the spirit and words of these texts, with a view to formulating a comprehensive system of specific codes (*shariah*). In particular, such leaders can and should reinterpret the relevant content of the broad principles of equality contained in the Sermon of the Prophet, which eliminates all forms of inequality in the social life of Muslims.[42]

Nonetheless, given the ambiguities of *shariah* as a form of constitutional rule, Arab Islamic states face the challenge of incorporating all the ICC's legal standards into their domestic criminal systems, including the elements of gender violence. Thus, for instance, any law or ordinance that declares a woman's testimony to be inadmissible in crimes, such as rape, will need to be revoked.[43] Also, state governments will need to address the constitutionality of cruel punishment and the death penalty, both of which continue to be practiced in several countries, including Saudi Arabia, Oman, Yemen, Kuwait, and Sudan. To be sure, ratification will almost certainly force the criminal systems of law in Arab Islamic states to be reconciled to a modern legal framework consistent with the spirit of Islam.

On the other hand, the challenge of adaptation reveals an important chance to adapt *shariah* to international law. In particular, Arab states need to see the ICC's incomplete list of new elements of crimes (crimes against humanity and aggression) as an opportunity to shape the content of modern international law, rather than reacting against it by applying a rigid form of *shariah*. This is why, as I have contended, cultural adaptation provides an important context from which the relationship between Islam and the serious international crimes will evolve.

Jihad

Perhaps the most important religious source in this respect is the duty to *defend* Islam against state aggression. The duty to defend represents one of more controversial principles of *shariah.* Generally speaking, *jihad* consists of two levels of meaning. On the most essential level, it expresses the personal and spiritual struggle for fulfillment of Muslims; while, on another level, it reflects the radical, military struggle against Western hegemony in the Arab world. When *jihad* is invoked as a military struggle against the infidels of the West, there is often the tendency to prioritize this latter level.

For many Islamic scholars, however, this type of invocation obscures and misrepresents the Muslim's personal spiritual fulfillment.[44] Here, it is possible to view the military aspects of *jihad* as a strictly strategic feature of Islam. Chaiwat Satha-Anand, for example, argues that the violent, militaristic meaning of *jihad* constitutes a lesser form of *jihad.* As he states, "Islamic justice requires inner *jihad* to guide the conduct of the lesser *jihad* in both its objectives and its conducts."[45]

One could also argue that militaristic *jihad* is the reflection of a rigid and oftentimes uncompromising interpretation of Islam. Islamic scholars from the medieval period (the *ulema*), for instance, distinguished between *Dar al-Islam,* referring to the lands occupied by Muslims, and *Dar al-harb,* which represents the land or territory occupied by non-Muslims, in order to study the threat of war and aggression against non-Muslims.[46] Compared to the clash of civilizations thesis in international relations, which holds that the clash of values stems from anarchy and fear, this rigid distinction between *Dar al-harb* and *Dar al-Islam* leaves little, if any, room for long-term cooperation.[47] More often than not, the result is that Arab state politics can and often will conflict with international law.

Modern Islamic scholars, however, argue that the traditional distinction between *Dar al-harb* and *Dar al-Islam* ignores Mohamed's emphasis on the realm of *Dar al-sulh* (the making of alliances).[48] Mohamed, it could be said, saw treaty making as the supreme safeguard against war, or the threat of unlawful invasion by the infidels into Arab lands. What this suggests is that *jihad* represents a strictly defensive orientation to other states; that is, a fundamental need to preserve the Islamic faith against attacks by the infidel, a need which requires a firm commitment to inner peace.

This raises the question as to whether this commitment envisions inaction and action as mutually exclusive. In other words, does U.N. Security Council inaction (to stop aggression) amount to a declaration of war by tacitly granting impunity to the transgressors of the principle of *jihad*? At the Rome Conference, it will be remembered, many Arab states argued against the role of the Security Council in determining the acts of the crime of aggression. Assertions that the Security Council had repeatedly failed to act on matters related to aggression conveyed many Arab states' deep-seeded suspicions of the Security Council's role in the ICC. Here, it could be argued that Arab states perceived Security Council inaction as a betrayal of *jihad*. In this way, the Security Council's irresponsibility could be considered a violation of the very principle uniting Islamic and international law (in *dar al-sulh*): namely, the defensive ethic of *jihad* that embodies Article 51 of the U.N. Charter (self-defense as the pretext for authorizing the use of force).

But it is also true that *jihad* encompasses only the defensive ethics of state behavior; not the individual actions of state leaders. This may explain why the Arab state proposal mentioned earlier included only state acts of aggression enumerated in the 1974 GA Resolution. Still, it is precisely this issue of the individual nature of the crime to which *shariah* must adapt, lest it fall prey to the U.S. and British contention that the ICC is not needed for matters where the U.N. Charter already authorizes the use of force against (only) state aggression. In other words, for *jihad* to play a more influential and convincing role in the ICC, it needs to be reconciled to the human elements of this crime. As George Fletcher points out, "the purpose of the ICC is almost exclusively to punish human offenders, and to vindicate the status of the victims."[49] In short, it seems that the most promising rationale for eliminating present and future conflicts between Islamic and international law is to encourage Arab state leaders to make not just short-term concessions to the secular customs of the ICC Statute, as proposed by An-Na'im, but to grant long-term, permanent concessions that reflect the adaptation of *shariah* to the ICC.

Conclusion

In this chapter, I focused on the tensions between Arab states and the ICC by examining the differences between the inflexible juridical system of many Arab states (the often rigid application and enactment of *shariah*) and the flexible juridical authority of the ICC, which emphasizes mutual accommodation and bargaining as a condition of adopting and enacting its legal rules and decisions. Clearly, the ICC Statute provisions will conflict with Islam where cases arise, and these cases will likely involve serious international crimes. But it is also true that the Islamic ethics of international law, while, in many respects fully compatible with international criminal law, also reveals the need for promoting the internal politicization of the ICC's juridical power.

As I argued in this chapter, more mutual accommodation will be needed to spur further cultural adaptation. Indeed, as the case of Sudan now suggests, there may be problems with applying and enacting ICC provisions in cases involving nationals of non-states parties. In this way, the effects of noncompliance with the judgment of the ICC will require dynamic political strategies to advance the ICC's role in promoting international peace and security. The next chapter examines a more elaborate and concerted attempt to promote the ICC's political dimension: a policymaking framework that links together the legitimacy of the ICC and the U.N. Security Council.

Notes

1. Abdullah An-Na'im, "Islamic Law, International Relations and Human Rights: Challenges and Response," *Cornell International Law Journal* 32, no. 3 (1987): 320. An-Na'im theorizes that the concessions made to international law should be short-term. This is because, in his view, Muslims cannot be expected to ultimately conduct their own affairs according to the secular customs and norms of international law. In other words, Muslims must be assured that their attempts to reconcile their religious customs to international law do not replace Islamic law. The problem with stressing the temporary nature of concessions, however, is that it fails to ensure that some Islamic states will change their constitutions (ratification) as a condition for erecting permanent constitutional safeguards against state abuse. Thus, by emphasizing the permanence of concessions, I am not suggesting that the proscriptive norms and rules of the ICC will replace Islam. Instead, I am stressing how the adoption of new constitutional safeguards will reflect long-term cooperation with the ICC.

2. Farhad Malekian, *The Concept of Islamic Criminal Law: A Comparative Study* (London: Graham & Trotman/Martinus Nijhoff, 1994), 3.

3. For a critical discussion of the role of *shariah,* see Max Rodenbeck "Islam Confronts Its Demons" *New York Review of Books,* LI(7): 14–18.

4. See, e.g., Ruti Teitel, "The Universal and the Particular in International Criminal Justice," *Columbia Human Rights Law Review* 30, no. 2 (1999): 285–303; Thomas Smith, "Moral Hazard and Humanitarian Law: The International Criminal Court and the Limits of Legalism," *International Politics* 39, no. 2 (2002): 175–192.

5. Smith, "Moral Hazard and Humanitarian Law: The International Criminal Court and the Limits of Legalism," 275. Article 39 provides the general scope of Chapter VII. It states: "The Security Council shall determine the existence of any threat to the peace, breach of the peace, or act of aggression and shall make recommendations, or decide what measures shall be taken in accordance with Articles 41 and 42, to maintain or restore international peace and security."

6. The constitutions of each of the Arab states, with the exception of Lebanon, recognize Islamic values as fundamental political principles of state society and as binding norms of federal *shariah* courts.

7. See, e.g., F. H. Hinsley, *Sovereignty*, 2nd edition (Cambridge: Cambridge University Press, 1986).

8. T. J. Biersteker and C. Weber, *State Sovereignty as Social Construct* (Cambridge: Cambridge University Press, 1996), p. 18.

9. The Arab states identified here include Algeria, Bahrain, Comorros, Djibouti, Egypt, Iraq, Jordan, Kuwait, Lebanon, Libyan Arab Jamahiriya, Morocco, Oman, Qatar, Saudi Arabia, Syria, Sudan, Tunisia, the United Arab Emigrates, Comoros, Mauritania, and Yemen.

10. This category includes Saudi Arabia, Bahrain, Kuwait, Oman, and Yemen.

11. Those states practicing this form of sovereignty include Saudi Arabia, Oman, Jordan, Morocco, Bahrain, UAE, Kuwait, and Qatar. It should be noted that Qatar's sheik, Hamad bin Khalifa al-Thani, has recently proposed changes to the country's constitution, including the introduction of democratic liberties, such as the right to freedom of expression, assembly, religion, and property. See "Qatar: Vote on Constitution," *New York Times* (April 29, 2003): A14.

12. See, e.g., the Yemen Constitution, Art. 5.

13. See, e.g., the Syrian Constitution, Art. 3(1).

14. See Bassam Tibi, *The Challenge of Fundamentalism* (Berkeley: University of California Press, 2002).

15. Malekian, *The Concept of Islamic Criminal Law: A Comparative Study*, 167.

16. Christine Steains, "Gender Issues," in Roy Lee, ed. *The International Criminal Court: The Making of the Rome Statute, Issues, Negotiators, and Results* (The Hague: Kluwer Publishers, 1999), 784.

17. Steven R. Ratner and Jason S. Abrams, *Accountability for Human Rights Atrocities in International Law*, 2nd Edition (Oxford: Oxford University Press, 2001), 56.

18. Darryl Robinson, "Article 7(1)(g)—Rape, Sexual Slavery, Enforced Prostitution, Forced Pregnancy, Enforced Sterilization, or Any Other Forms of Sexual Violence of Comparable Gravity," in Roy Lee, ed. *The International Criminal Court: Elements of Crimes and Rules of Procedure and Evidence* (Ardsley, NY: Transnational Publishers, 2001), 93.

19. Still, in some Arab Islamic states, such as Yemen, the government has undertaken steps to promote gender equality and freedom by stipulating certain exceptions to non-abortion laws.

20. Not all Arab states agreed that forced pregnancy should be excluded from the ICC Statute. Interestingly, the Jordanian delegation reasoned that since forcing a woman to bear a child of a rapist could be considered a severe form of torture, the pain and suffering from this torture constituted an element of crimes against humanity.

21. On the other hand, in many Latin American states, where there is a significant Catholic influence, the latter provision of 7(2)(f) will probably have little or no effect, since many of these countries have already implemented national laws on abortion. For a discussion of this issue, see Kristin Boon, "Rape and Forced Pregnancy Under the ICC Statute," *Columbia Human Rights Law Review* 32, no. 3 (2001): 666.

22. United Nations, *United Nations Diplomatic Conference of Plenipotentiaries on the Establishment of an International Criminal Court*, Rome, 15 June–17 July 1998. Volume II (New York: United Nations Publications, 1998).

23. The proposal was submitted by Algeria, Bahrain, Iraq, Kuwait, Lebanon, Libya, United Arab Emirates, and Yemen, and reissued on 8 July 1998. See A/CONF. 183/C.1/L.56.

24. United Nations G.A. Res. 95(I) U.N. GAOR, 1st Sess., at 188, U.N. Doc A/Res/95.

25. United Nations G.A. Res. 3314 (XXIX), U.N. GAOR, 29th Sess., Annex para. 10, Supp. No. 31, U.N. A/9631 (1974)

26. The other two elements discussed concerned whether occupation or annexation constituted an essential element, and if drug trafficking, terrorism, and attack on U.N. personnel amounted to essential elements of the crime of aggression. With the exception of attacks on U.N. personnel, Arab states unanimously favored the inclusion of these elements in the crime of aggression.

27. United Nations, *The Establishment of the International Criminal Court*, 184.

28. United Nations, *The Establishment of the International Criminal Court*, 178.

29. The proposal was submitted by Bahrain, Iraq, Lebanon, the Libyan Arab Jamahiriya, Oman, the Sudan, the Syrian Arab Republic, and Yemen. See Preparatory Commission, First Meeting of the Preparatory Commission for the International Criminal Court. PCNICC/1999/DP.11.

30. Antonio Cassese, "The Statute of the International Criminal Court," *European Journal of International Law* 10 (1999): 147.

31. See Resolution on the Continuity of Work in Respect of the Crime of Aggression. ICC-ASP.1/Res.1 and Note Article 3 of the resolution calls on the working group to draw up proposals that can be reviewed by the assembly at the review conference.

32. See C. K. Hall, "The First Five Sessions of the UN Preparatory Commission for the International Criminal Court," *American Journal of International Law* 94, no. 4 (2000): 787; Benjamin Ferencz, "Can Aggression Be Deterred by Law," *Pace International Law* 11, no. 2 (1999): 341–36; Nico Kirsch and Ved Oosterveld, "Legality, Morality and the Dilemma of Humanitarian Intervention after Kosovo," *European Journal of International Law* 13, no. 1 (2002): 567.

33. According to M. Cherif Bassiouni, these rights include: the "Protection of life, honour and property; Freedom of thought, expression, belief, and worship; Freedom of movement throughout the country; Freedom of Assembly and association; Freedom of engaging in any profession or occupation and the right to own, acquire and dispose of property; and equality of opportunity in all walks of life, and equal right of benefiting from all public institutions." See M. Cherif Bassiouni, "Sources of Islamic Law, and the Protection of Human Rights in the Islamic Criminal Justice System," in M. Cherif Bassiouni, ed. *The Islamic Criminal Justice System* (London: Oceana Publications, Inc., 1982), 23.

34. *Siyash shariyyah* or *shariah* oriented policy, for instance, is the policymaking component of *shariah*. Generally, *Siyash* aims to specify the necessary punishment of criminal offenses where such offenses are not clearly spelled out under *shariah*.

35. See the Human Rights Watch, "Sudan: Government and Militias Conspire in Darfur Killings," April 23. http://hrw.org/english/docs/2004/04/23sudan8487.htm.

36. Marc Lacey, "In Sudan, Militiamen on Horses Uproot a Million," *New York Times* (May 4, 2004): A1.

37. Bassiouni, "Sources of Islamic Law, and the Protection of Human Rights in the Islamic Criminal Justice System," 46.

38. Amnesty International, "Libya's Time to Make Human Rights a Reality," April 27, 2004.

39. See Human Rights Watch, Bush Should Call for End to Repression, February 14, 2004. http://hrw.org/english/docs/2004/02/13tunisi7478.

40. Clark Lombardi, "Islamic Law as Source of Constitutional Law in Eqypt: The Constitutionalization of the Sharia in Modern Arab States," *Columbia Journal of Transnational Law* 37, no. 2 (1998): 118.

41. See, e.g., An-Na'im, "Islamic Law, International Relations and Human Rights: Challenges and Response," and Ali Mazrui, "Islamic and Western Values," *Foreign Affairs* 76, no. 5 (1997): 118–132. Concerning the incompatibility between democratic policymaking and fundamentalism, Tibi states: "Most of the activists of Islamic fundamentalism know little about Islamic sharia and are unaware that should they seize power, they will not find a coherent legal system at hand that they may apply to a situation, conditions and events overnight as events will demand. This of course opens the way to arbitrary totalitarian politics and governance, in the name of Islam sharia." See Tibi, *The Challenge of Fundamentalism*, 171.

42. Malekian, *The Concept of Islamic Law: A Comparative Study*, 169.

43. In Pakistan, for instance, the government enacted the Hadud Ordinance (1979), which made inadmissible a woman's testimony on hudd crimes, including rape. On this issue, see Rafit Hassan, "Is Islam a Help or Hindrance to Women's Development," in Johan Meulman, ed. *Islam in the Era of Globalization* (London: Routledge Press, 2002), 190.

44. M. Al-Ghunaimi, *The Muslim Conception of International Law and the Western Approach* (The Hague: Kluwer, 1968).

45. Chaiwat Satha-Anand, "The Non-violent Crescent: Eight Theses on Muslim Non-violent Action," in Abdul Aziz Said, Nathan C. Funk, and Ayse S. Kasayifc, eds. *Peace and Conflict Resolution in Islam* (Lanham, MD: University Press of America, 2001), 200.

46. M. Kamali, *Freedom, Equality, Justice in Islam* (Cambridge: Islamic Texts Society, 2001), 142.

47. A 'clash of values' derives from Samuel Huntington's famous thesis on a 'Clash of Civilizations', which holds that an incommensurability of civilized values will outstrip the state's ability to manage intrastate conflict. While an incommensurability of values can lead to conflict, this does not mean that certain universal rules, such as human rights law, will fail to mediate the conflict within the framework of the state or international institutional structure.

48. See Satha-Anand, "The Non-violent Crescent: Eight Theses on Muslim Non-violent Action."

49. Fletcher refers to these conflicting purposes in terms of a prospective and retrospective aim. While prospective refers to "the purpose of the Court to look backward to the commission of the crime and to apply sanctions in order to do justice; retrospective denotes the Court's use of power to deter the occurrence of crimes within its jurisdiction." See George Fletcher, "Comments on Panel Entitled the International Criminal Court: Contemporary Perspectives and Prospects for Ratification," *New York Law School Journal of Human Rights* 15, no. 1 (2000): 523.

8

A Cooperative Arrangement with the U.N. Security Council

> In legislative politics, the supply of information and purposive-rational choice of means are interwoven with the balance of interests and compromise formation: with the achievement of ethical self-understanding . . . and with moral justification and tests of legal coherence.
>
> —Jürgen Habermas, *Between Facts and Norms*

LET US NOW TURN to the relationship between the ICC and United Nations. In our discussion of the conflict between the United Nations and ICC, it became evident that certain issues still divide the ICC and Security Council and that these two institutions will need to cooperate further with each other in order to promote international peace and security. The issue that we need to address here is whether a structural arrangement between the ICC and the United Nations will externally politicize the ICC (geopolitical interests), or rather undermine the independence and integrity of the ICC. This chapter addresses this issue by examining the potential parameters of an arrangement requiring a flexible application of the ICC's rules of procedure. Again, by flexible application, I am referring to the self-directed application of the ICC rules, which is designed to counter or neutralize the negative impact of the Security Council's geopolitical interests.

A cooperative arrangement between the ICC and U.N. Security Council, therefore, would be based on the adoption of various principles that would legalize politically legitimate humanitarian interventions.[1] The main principles in this case are contained in the International Commission of Intervention and State Sovereignty Report (ICISS) (December 2001), which addresses the important balance between international intervention and state sovereignty, including the responsibility to protect. Although the report contains few, if any concrete guidelines for Security Council action, it does provide an arguably important basis for a swift and effective international response to humanitarian disasters. Not only does it set forth the just war principles of self-defense and the use of military force as an option of last resort, it also recommends that the international community grant *prima facie* responsibility to state and regional authorities.

Formulating a cooperative arrangement will require analysis of the structural and policy implications of this report for a cooperative relationship between the ICC and Security Council. Here, I shall assume that the ICISS report provides a substantive normative framework for amending the U.N. Charter, since it sets forth principles consistent with the Charter's spirit (e.g., the responsibility to protect). In this way, I will address the broader issue as to whether a humanitarian-based criteria for military intervention, coupled with other proposed U.N. Security Council reforms (e.g., increased membership, global jury mechanisms), is sufficient to overcome the obstacles posed by the geopolitical interests of the U.N. Security Council, as well as fears of the high costs of intervention.[2] As the case of Darfur shows, member states of the Security Council will likely defer to regional authorities when their political interests are at stake; even where these regional authorities clearly lack the resources to stop the mass killings. An increase in the number of developing countries on the U.N. Security Council might mean added pressure on the permanent members to refer a situation to the ICC.[3] At the very least, such reform suggests the possible benefits of a cooperative relationship between the ICC and Security Council.

The main argument in this chapter is that the ICC needs be seen as an important source of legitimacy of Security Council action and vice versa. A cooperative relationship between the Security Council and ICC, I contend, would involve mutual political and moral benefits for both governing institutions. Working together, the ICC and Security Council will lead the international community in mounting an effective response to humanitarian crises. Thus, an indictment by the ICC Prosecutor against agents of a violent government will increase pressure on the Security Council to authorize, or at least threaten, humanitarian intervention against the government concerned, by enhancing the transparency of the threat posed by perpetrators of genocide, crimes against humanity, and war crimes. The threat of Security Council action will in turn make people take the ICC's indictments more seriously and help the Prosecutor to stand up to a hostile government and help the Court gain actual custody of indicted individuals. In this way, Security Council resolutions will confer added legitimacy on ICC indictments. I shall refer to this potential process of added legitimacy as a *mutual legitimacy push.* Unlike a 'legitimacy pull' towards compliance with international rules, which assumes that compliance derives principally from the desire to become and remain a member of an international club, a mutual legitimacy push constitutes the evolving normative benefits of mutual assistance or collaboration between institutional players.[4]

In the first section of the chapter, I analyze the debate on humanitarian intervention, then address the concept of legitimacy and the moral efficacy of the ICC's proscriptive norms. I move on to discuss the relevance of the ICISS report, as well as the issue of timing that involves the conflict between the need for a quick response to humanitarian disasters and the ICC's slow time schedule for investigating and prosecuting perpetrators of gross human rights offenses. Here, I show how this arrangement of mutual cooperation might look, illustrating in further detail the specific assistance that each of these institutions would lend each other when responding to a humanitarian emergency. Lastly, I conclude that such cooperation will not politicize the ICC, and that a new legislative body in the ICC needs to be considered for adding legitimacy to the Security Council, and vice versa.

Humanitarian Intervention

The literature on humanitarian intervention during the post-Cold War encompasses a vast array of case studies and theoretical approaches. At the core of the post-Cold War debate on humanitarian intervention is the issue of state sovereignty; more specifically, whether the international community can effectively suspend the norm of non-intervention in order to intervene on behalf of a severely abused peoples.[5] Many legal scholars argue that the imperative for collective intervention should be seen as a necessary trade-off between the violent consequences of action and the heinous results of *not* acting.[6] Others argue that while genocide has raised the stakes to intervene and has demonstrated the evolution of the norm of humanitarian intervention, it has not led to a fundamental change in international customary law.[7] Nor, for that matter, does it constitute a peremptory norm rule under international law (*jus cogens*).[8] Because state sovereignty remains a peremptory norm, it follows that nonintervention remains the standard by which to evaluate the legitimacy of intervention, in particular, the costs and consequences of suspending this norm.[9]

Those skeptical of the U.N.'s role in intervention also focus on the obstructive role played by geopolitical interests in the U.N. Security Council, notably the use of the Security Council veto to block the legalization of politically legitimized interventions. As some have argued, there remains the question of whether a new humanitarian council can provide the basis for the determination of a humanitarian emergency, much less the means by which intervention should be carried out.[10]

Much of the problem stems from the Security Council's mixed willingness to respond to humanitarian emergencies. In the spring of 2000, for instance, the Security Council took the unprecedented initiative to intervene militarily to stop the massacre of East Timorese in East Timor.[11] By contrast, it has demonstrated a relatively lackluster willingness to take action against the Sudanese government to prevent further ethnic cleansing in the Darfur region, where an estimated 70,000 civilians have been killed and millions have been driven from their homes.[12] More than anything, the Darfur crisis has raised the question as to whether the international community can respond effectively to the very worst humanitarian emergencies.

On this question, some have argued that U.S. national security should be seen as a plausible means of leveraging support for humanitarian intervention within the United Nations.[13] Still, others argue that the heavy reluctance to intervene on humanitarian grounds requires the revision of the outdated rules of the Charter, such as non-intervention and the equality of sovereign states.[14] What is needed, they claim, is a new set of procedures and rules that would remove the formal barriers to taking swift and decisive action (e.g., nonintervention and the sovereign equality of states). The issue here, however, is not whether the emerging norm of intervention has eroded state sovereignty, but rather if new institutional bodies are needed to legitimize humanitarian intervention. Mohammed Ayoob, for instance, argues that the geopolitical interests of the permanent U.N. Security Council members can and should be overcome through an alternative institutional body. Concerning this point, he states that

> It is . . . impossible to prevent consideration of national interest from intruding upon decisions regarding international intervention for ostensibly humanitarian purposes. This immediately complicates the problem of deciphering international will, for one is never sure whether decisions taken on behalf of the international community are truly the result of altruistic motives or are driven by the national interests of states that have a stake in intervening in particular crises and locales.[15]

Accordingly, Ayoob insists on the need to operate outside the U.N. Security Council via the establishment of a Humanitarian Council comprised of 50 member nation states (one-third of whom would be U.N. Security Council members) and a majority vote to launch a humanitarian intervention (no veto).[16] Whether or not this will remove the threat posed by geopolitical interests, however, is not altogether certain.

For its part, the United Nations has continued to debate the topic of Security Council reform, proposing among other things, an increase in the permanent membership from five to seven states (two of the "gang of four": India, Germany, Brazil, Japan) and the number of seats to 24.[17] What is more, Kofi Annan, the U.N. Secretary-General, has repeatedly pressed member states to reevaluate the role of the Security Council in responding effectively to humanitarian emergencies.[18] In his Statement on U.N. Reform, delivered on March 21, 2005, Annan recommended the establishment of three councils, which would deal with international peace and security, economic and social issues, and human rights.

This sweeping proposal comes on the heels of the publication of the International Commission of Intervention and State Sovereignty Report (ICISS) in December 2001, which, as noted earlier, addresses the important balance between international intervention and state sovereignty, including the responsibility to protect. As I will show, such principles provide the basis of a mutual legitimacy push and the justification for institutional reform in both the ICC and U.N. Security Council. Before we proceed to discuss this proposed course of action, let us briefly re-examine the concept of legitimacy and its importance for understanding the limitations and possibilities of an effective cooperative arrangement between the ICC and Security Council.

Functional Legitimacy and the Role of Impartiality

The Concept of Legitimacy

As we saw in chapter 5, legitimacy has become an important normative tool for addressing the effects of displaced juridical authority at the global level. Legitimacy, in a functional sense, is typically defined "as the moral and legal right to rule which is based on law, custom, hereditary or the consent of the government."[19] According to this definition, a norm is legitimate if it is adopted by international institutions that enjoy a high degree of perceived fairness.[20] As Thomas Franck notes, legitimacy is "a system of rules which conduces to a fairly high level of perceived obligation among members . . . it reflects the 'rules' capacity to obligate and secure the community's behavior, while sovereign states characterize obedience to the law."[21] In this respect, legitimacy constitutes the pull towards institutionalized norms that are perceived to be fair.[22] For example, it could be argued that the EU, which has implemented many novel human rights legislation in the form of minority rights protection and social redistribution, enjoys a strong degree of political legitimacy.

Legitimacy, then, is functional when states desire to be recognized as a member of a community. As Franck notes: "the rules of international system obligate—to the extent that they do primarily because they are like the house rules of a club . . . it is the desire to be a member of the club, to benefit by the status of membership, that is the ultimate motivator of conformist behavior."[23] States, in this respect, are no different from individuals who fulfill their daily routines: they learn to conform to the rules and to impose self-constraints on their own behavior. This self-enforcement mechanism, in Franck's view, explains why state leaders voluntarily comply with international rules in the absence of an official sovereign to enforce these rules. For states can ill afford to ignore the consequences of non-compliance, since this would mean incurring the ill effects of disrepute, including economic sanctions. Indeed, as Abram and Antonia Chayes point out: "when states choose to deviate from accepted norms they almost out of necessity must respond in order to show that the facts are not what they seem to be."[24] This is especially true of cases involving the transparency of rules and norms, that is, where the access to information or knowledge exposes more readily the deviation from certain norms.

Still, there remains the problem of directly linking legitimacy with conformity to legal rules and norms. For what makes rules and institutions legitimate are not simply the interest to abide by these rules. If this were the case, then there would be submission to the rules, and little, if any, capacity to shape these rules. Thus, one could argue that the desire to conform to rules is not sufficient to validate these rules as legitimate. Values must be taken into account. As Jean Marc Coicaud states:

> Belief in legality necessitates two complementary conditions. In the first place, legal statements have to be in agreement with the constitutive values of the identity of society. These values being at once the sources and the guarantees of right, law can pass for being legitimate only on the condition that it be their emanation. It is therefore when legality expresses the identity of the group that it becomes possible to present legitimacy as conformity to the law.[25]

As this passage suggests, values constitute the political and social resources of one's identity. It is only when values can shape the law that one begins to truly identify with these rules as legitimate. Thus, on the one hand, legitimacy provides an external standard for assessing the ways of correcting deviations from the rules. On the other hand, legitimacy remains a problematic concept since conformity to the law does not directly confer legitimacy, but is the product of one's ability to draw on his or her beliefs and values to shape the legal rules.

Functionalizing the Political Legitimacy of the ICC

Given that legitimacy remains a contested concept, it is important to see the ICC's legitimacy as a formative dimension of its development. Here, the procedural features of this dimension refer to how the ICC's legitimacy is predicated upon the ICC Judiciary's capacity to eliminate undue delays and to ensure that states meet the high evidential standards for investigating and prosecuting perpetrators of gross human rights violations. More precisely, the ICC's legal neutrality in this respect depends on the Prosecutor's ability to exercise his or her discretionary power in a consistent manner, especially in politically sensitive cases where its potential decision to defer to national courts may be perceived as unfair to certain victims. In this way, the ICC's legitimacy lies in the impartial and effective application of the ICC Statute.

As noted earlier, the primary mission of the Court is twofold: to ensure that the worst perpetrators of gross human rights violations are held accountable for their crimes, and to allow all states parties *prima facie* to try perpetrators of gross human rights violations in their own national courts. Thus, on the one hand, the ICC's mission provides the basis of accountability for all serious perpetrators of gross human rights abuses. On the other hand, its complementarity regime ensures that it will operate on a relatively slow schedule when investigating and prosecuting such perpetrators. To recall, the principle of complementarity ensures that states will be allowed *prima facie* to prosecute, but stipulates that the Court can intervene where the national court has proved unwilling and unable to investigate or prosecute.[26]

In chapter 2, we discussed how the ICC Prosecutor may be expected to defer to national Courts for political reasons, which may, in this case, foster the perception of the Court's unwillingness to uphold the rule of law on the national and global level. Again, the political overtones of certain cases (or the ICC Prosecutor's discretionary power) constitutes a politically problematic dimension of the ICC's legitimacy, since it suggests that state power might place undue limits on its moral mission of holding accountable the worst perpetrators of gross human rights offenses.

As the increasing number of ratifications suggests, many states have come to embrace the ICC as a legitimate and important institution. Whether this will be enough to effectively address the challenge posed by the Bush Administration's opposition remains an open-ended issue. On the other hand, as we saw in chapter 6, U.S. opposition does constitute a considerable challenge to the ICC. At the very least, it points to the tensions between upholding the ICC Statute and U.S. influence over the Security Council, and shows how the use of the U.S. veto will likely drive a wedge between the Security Council and the ICC with respect to humanitarian intervention.

On the other hand, the United States may be willing to concede to Security Council resolutions that refer a situation to the ICC, as the Darfur crisis illustrates.[27] Here, the Security Council adopted Resolution 1593, referring the situation of the Darfur crisis to the ICC.[28] The resolution calls for the Sudanese government to cooperate and assist the ICC, and the ICC jurisdiction to apply only to nationals of states parties (Articles 3 and 6). This was meant to assure the United States that its military personnel would not be investigated, nor prosecuted by the ICC.[29] Certainly, the Bush Administration's determination to address the genocide in Sudan underscores the importance of issue linkage or the benefits of bargaining between the United States and the United Nations. In chapter 6, we discussed how this bargaining could become part of a strategy of enhancing the U.S. informative role in the Security Council on matters related to peacekeeping and gross human rights abuses.

In this way, increased bargaining makes it possible to realize the benefits of further reform in the United Nations, especially if such reform leads, in turn, to increased pressure for such bargaining. Thus, for instance, an increase in the permanent membership of the Security Council may mean added diplomatic pressure being placed on the United States to accept the ICC's role in a humanitarian crisis. On the other hand, closer ties between the ICC and Security Council also raise the prospects for the politicization of the Court; hence the intrusive role of the Security Council in the proceedings of the ICC. To recall, the issue of the role of the Security Council was passionately debated at the Rome Conference (1998), especially in the context of who would determine when acts of the crime of aggression had occurred.[30]

In short, Security Council reform remains a delicate approach for changing the attitudes of its members toward the ICC. This is one main reason for stressing the ICC's role as neutral arbiter in conflicts and for showing the ways in which this perceived neutrality can be situated within a cooperative arrangement of the ICC and Security Council. Such reform also points to the need for convincing opponents of the ICC that the ICC can play a positive political role in resolving humanitarian crises and vice versa. As we shall see, U.N. and ICC reform needs to proceed upon a basis in which each institution shares the common objective of facilitating an efficient response to humanitarian emergencies.

The Role of the ICISS Report

The need for a swift response to humanitarian emergencies constitutes one of the key focal points of Security Council reform. As is well known, the Security Council failed to act in a timely manner to stop the slaughter of 800,000 innocent civilians in Rwanda in the spring of 1994. Equally so, China's and Russia's veto presented a legal obstacle to U.S.-led NATO plans to intervene in Kosovo to prevent further ethnic cleansing of the Kosovar Albanians by Milosevic's forces (this prompted NATO to launch the invasion without U.N. authorization). Yet, it was out of these events of the Kosovo War that the Independent

International Commission on Kosovo (IICK) subsequently concluded that the intervention was "legitimate but illegal" and recommended the suspension of the veto in the Security Council, as well as the adoption of a General Assembly Directive to improve the United Nation's response to humanitarian crises.

Following these recommendations, the Canadian government decided to commission a panel of human rights scholars and practitioners to study the "critical gap" between state sovereignty and international intervention.[31] In December 2001, the ICISS published its report on intervention, which, as noted earlier, set forth several moral principles and rules, including the responsibility to protect that stipulated, *inter alia*, threshold criteria for military intervention as an option of last resort.

Generally speaking, the responsibility to protect calls on the international community to act, only when the state and regional authorities have proved unable to stop the crisis. It also provides for a coercive criteria or the use of military force as an option of last resort to facilitate a rapid and concerted response to ethnic cleansing. More than anything else, it is this coercive factor that highlights the problematic time gap between the ICC and Security Council action. In this section, I claim that humanitarian-based criteria, one closely modeled after the ICISS report, will help to establish the normative basis of an effective cooperative arrangement between the ICC and Security Council. Along with other proposals, it will provide the centerpiece for Kofi Annan's recent recommendation to establish a new council to deal with abuses of human rights.[32]

Principles and Rules

The ICISS report provides an important basis for a coordinated response to humanitarian emergencies that will close what many scholars have referred to as the "critical gap" between the inevitability of grave human suffering and the U.N. Charter principles. One of the ways it proposes doing this is by amending Chapter VII of the Charter, which provides the Security Council with the mandate to use coercive measures (e.g., military, economic sanctions, and blockades) to counter the threat posed by state aggression to international security.

For instance, the United Nations has launched various humanitarian interventions (e.g., Northern Iraq [1991], Somalia [1992] and East Timor [2000]). In these and other cases, however, the Security Council lacked a set of humanitarian guidelines or humanitarian criteria for determining the threat to international peace and security. For the most part, the justification for intervention was defined largely in terms of the threat posed by civic anarchy to regional security or neighboring states. One of the unstated aims of the ICISS report, however, is to establish the basis of an effective humanitarian response and to provide a set of widely agreed upon moral principles for determining the dire threat posed by civic anarchy and gross human rights violations.

Perhaps the most critical principle of the report is the duty to protect populations at risk. Such a principle, as suggested earlier, lies at the core of the report's interpretation of sovereignty. The report, for instance, defines sovereignty as the "responsibility in which states are responsible for the functions of protecting the safety and lives of citizens and promotion of their welfare, and response to the disasters internally and to the international community through the UN."[33] As such, the duty to protect begins on the state level, but rises to the international level when the state proves unwilling or unable to offer basic protection to its civilians.[34]

In short, when states remain unwilling or unable to fulfill their responsibility to protect their civilian populations from undue harm, then regional organizations will have "the duty to protect communities from mass killing, women from systematic rape, and children from starvation."[35] Should regional organizations prove unable or unwilling, then the duty shall rise to the international level where a broader community of states have a responsibility to protect the population at risk." To this end, the report encourages the participation of developing states, which may need to be reassured that the willingness of the international community will not serve as the basis of Western imperialism.

In addition, the report lists three main components of the international duty to protect: 1) the responsibility to prevent disasters, 2) to react to the disaster with the threat of force, and 3) to rebuild the affected society. In respect of the reactive component, the report sanctions the use of force only in the most extreme cases, such as "large scale loss of life, actual or apprehended with genocidal intent or not, which the product of deliberate state action or state neglect or inability to act or failed state situation; and large scale ethnic cleansing actual or apprehended, whether carried out by killing forced expulsion, acts of terror or rape."[36]

Despite these principled recommendations, the report remains vague with respect to the specific policy initiatives needed to amend the Charter and to overcome the obstacles posed by the veto. Thus, on the one hand, the report provides an important set of working principles for amending the Charter by "making humanitarian intervention a more acceptable concept."[37] On the other hand, it fails to describe the specific conditions under which humanitarian crises will rise to the level of international responsibility. Here, it could be argued that the ICISS report was never directly intended to provide a specific blueprint for U.N. action. Perhaps, for this reason, we need to see the ICISS report in very broad terms, that is, as a generalized normative framework that would work in conjunction with other proposed mechanisms to facilitate a response to humanitarian disasters.

The ICISS Report and the ICC

One way of considering the ICISS report in this light is to realize the shared normative dimensions between the report and the ICC Statute. The reason why this is important is that it allows us to gain some understanding of the underlying principles that will shape and inform a cooperative arrangement between the ICC and Security Council. Again, the ICISS Report asserts that a new approach to intervening on humanitarian grounds would have to meet various objectives. Such objectives include the need to establish clearer rules, procedures and criteria for determining when and how to intervene; and to establish the legitimacy of military intervention when necessary and after all other approaches have failed.[38] In the case of the latter, the report contains several basic core moral principles, some of which are embodied in international conventions, most notably the 1948 Genocide Convention, the Geneva Conventions, and Additional Protocols.[39]

By comparison, the ICC Statute contains various rules and conditions for intervening in the judicial affairs of states. Article 17(2 and 3), which, as noted earlier, comprises the complementarity regime, contains not only the provisions of partial or complete state collapse, but also the conditions for intervening into the judicial affairs when state/judicial authorities either fail to furnish the necessary evidence or cause an undue delay of more than 30 days. Once again, if state leaders prove unwilling to accept its own unwillingness, as determined by the ICC Prosecutor, then the ICC Judiciary has the duty to intervene in the judicial affairs of the state, regardless of the political overtones of its request.

By comparison, the ICISS threshold criteria for military intervention contains many provisions similar to those found in the ICC Statute including

1. those actions defined by the framework of the 1948 Genocide Convention that involve large scale threatened or actual loss of life;
2. the threat or occurrence of large scale loss of life, whether the product of genocidal intent or not, and whether or not involving state action;
3. different manifestations of "ethnic cleansing" including the systematic killing of members of a particular group in order to diminish or eliminate their presence in a particular area;
4. the systematic physical removal of members of a particular group from a particular geographical area; acts of terror designed to force people to flee;
5. the systematic rape for political purposes of women of a particular group (either as another form of terrorism or as a means of changing the ethnic composition of that group).[40]

In the context of conditions 1–3, the ICC Statute encodes the elements of the core crimes, which specify the nature of the crime and the parameters of intent to commit the crime. As suggested earlier, the specification of these crimes is what underscores the determinacy of the ICC's proscriptive norms against genocide, war crimes, and crimes against humanity. By determinacy, I mean the causal impact of these norms on the behavior of state leaders: the perceived capacity of the ICC to invoke the rules of procedures and evidence to hold accountable the worst perpetrators of gross human rights violations.

From this it follows that when a perpetrator of gross human rights violations becomes the primary cause of a grave humanitarian crisis, the ICC should invoke its duty to investigate or prosecute. If one of the perpetrators in this context is charged with the crime of genocide before the United Nations considers taking action, then the ICC's indictment may help to provide further evidence regarding the extent and nature of the threat posed by the individual. This of course does not mean that the U.N. Security Council will act on this evidence. As Thomas Franck argues, an additional mechanism may be needed to turn this evidence into action or to establish a binding verdict.

Franck, for instance, proposes that a "global jury" mechanism might help to resolve the disparity between action and the availability of evidence/information. Not only would it help to adduce the facts of the crisis on the ground, but it would provide an impartial and binding mechanism for determining a humanitarian emergency. In effect, it would "rest on those having extraordinary recourse to an unlawful remedy to prevent a much greater wrong."[41] But even if the Security Council acts on the ICC's indictment and/or international rest warrant, it still must enforce these actions. And it must do so in a way that "does not weaken the bonds of restraint that restrict war making by the state."[42] One of the initiatives proposed by Richard Falk is to establish a voluntary peace enforcement capability within the framework of the United Nations. As he argues, the objective "would be to loosen the bonds that now tie intervention to the vagaries of geopolitics, encourage democratize debate on issues of intervention, and give the organized international community a decisive role and responsibility in both redefining the relationship between human rights and state sovereignty."[43]

In short, the ICC indictment of perpetrators of genocide, crimes against humanity, or war crimes might justify and even facilitate other proposals to induce Security Council action. It is out of this mutual respect and procedural interaction that a cooperative relationship between the ICC and Security Council may begin to take shape. The next section provides a sketch of the institutional parameters of this cooperative framework along with a hypothetical example showing how this cooperative relationship will likely work.

The ICC and Security Council: Mutual Benefits or Politicization?

Policy Mechanisms and Objectives

As noted earlier, cooperation between the ICC and Security Council will depend on the ways in which each of these institutions will lend assistance to each other when responding to humanitarian emergencies. This section examines two types of assistance: information gathering and institutional reengineering. It argues that information sharing within the Security Council alone may not be sufficient to promote what I have been referring to as a mutual legitimacy push, much less resolve the issue of timing, or the need for speeding up the ICC's time schedule.

The first type of assistance underscores the ICC as an important source of evidence for justifying military intervention as an option of last resort. It should be noted here that Article 15(2) allows the ICC Prosecutor to discuss and consult with the Secretary-General and Security Council on various matters related to investigations. Such evidence could, however, be used to increase the transparency of selective enforcement.[44] The ICISS Report, for instance, refers to several organizational sources of information that could provide evidence of large-scale killing, including the International Red Cross, Human Rights Commission, and the fact-finding missions commissioned by the Security Council. But the report is also careful to stress that the gathering of evidence must proceed in a neutral and impartial manner. This applies primarily if not exclusively to NGOs such as the International Red Cross, which has traditionally sought to remain neutral in all conflicts, with the possible exception of incidences of genocide.

On the other hand, the ICC's strict evidential standards ensure that investigations and prosecutions will be conducted in an effective and proper manner. As a result, there is little reason to believe that the ICC would compromise its neutrality by sharing information with a broad coalition of states. In fact, one of the primary aims of the Court is to screen out evidence and information provided by NGOs that does not meet the ICC Statute's strict evidential standards. In this respect, the ICC might work more closely together with the United Nation's fact-finding missions when gathering its information and evidence.[45]

Certainly, then, the sharing of information remains an important procedural and logistical objective. But it is not, as some would believe, a sufficient condition for bringing together the ICC and Security Council. In other words, the exchange of information and evidence does not guarantee that the ICC will respond swiftly. Nor does it ensure that particular permanent members will look beyond their political or national interests, especially if the permanent member states have maintained close relations with so-called rogue states. For this reason, some institutional reengineering within the ICC is needed to bring together the ICC and Security Council; yet in a way that does not externally politicize the Court.

As table 8.1 shows, the ICC compares favorably to the Security Council in a number of ways. As cells 3 and 4 indicate, the ICC's policy of requesting surrender represents the most overt, albeit restrictive form of the Court's intervention into the judiciary affairs of a state. Compared to the Security Council's Chapter VII powers, enforcement of the ICC's request of surrender is predicated upon state cooperation and international pressures. Here, it should be noted that Chapter VII, if invoked in the context of a new set of guidelines, might provide the substantive basis of civic reconstruction and peace-building measures in war-torn areas (e.g., East Timor, Cyprus, Bosnia and Herzegovina, Afghanistan, Cambodia, and Kosovo),[46] including the dispatch of a Rapid Deployment Force to stop and prevent humanitarian emergencies.[47]

Alan Kuperman, for instance, argues that a rapid deployment force could have prevented several hundreds of thousands of deaths in Rwanda.[48] To the extent that the ICC could validate NGO reports on the ground, the ICC's information gathering would arguably pressure the Security Council to act and vice versa. It would reflect an informative link that would address the political overtones of the ICC's complementarity principle in hard cases, while prompting member states of the Council to act militarily to stop humanitarian emergencies.

Yet, as with any new legal cooperative arrangement, there would need to be a reworking of the decision-making process. This would require a more efficient working relationship between the ICC judiciary and the Assembly of States Parties. The corollary of this relationship would be the creation of a decision-making body within the Assembly of States Parties whose task it would be to address a humanitarian crisis in a manner that overcomes the time restrictions imposed by the principle of complementarity (chapter 6). Such a novel body within the Assembly of States Parties would function much

TABLE 8.1
Types of Prevention in the ICC and Security Council

Organs	*Non-Intervention*	*Intervention*
ICC	Cell 1 -Reputation	Cell 3 -Admissibility
Security Council	Cell 2 -Preventive Diplomacy -Economic Sanctions	Cell 4 -Use of Military Force -Stabilization -Rapid Deployment

like the Security Council, albeit without the veto. Its operations would be based on two policy objectives: namely, the ICC judiciary's obligation to share relevant evidence with this body, and a two-thirds vote in this specialized body to overturn the time restrictions imposed by Article 17 (complementarity). The main criteria for determining what constitutes a special case would be determined largely by international pressures and mounting media exposure of gross human rights violations.[49]

Because the body would be called upon at any time to address a humanitarian emergency, it would not be restricted by the time lag between the biannual meetings of the Assembly of States Parties. The Security Council could, in turn, ensure the ICC that it will not invoke Article 16 of the ICC Statute, which allows the Council to defer on an investigation for up to 12 months. In addition, the Security Council (the relevant member states that were involved in the ICC meeting) could use the moral and technical arguments raised at the special convocation of this new organ of Assembly of States Parties to substantiate the need for an immediate response to humanitarian emergencies. Such a cooperative relationship between the ICC and Security Council would nonetheless mean the possibility of added legitimacy and effectiveness for both institutions *via* the creation of a new specialized body, or efficient mechanism, within the ICC.

Hypothetical Example

So how will this mutual legitimacy push be more fully realized? And why might member states, especially the permanent five, prove willing to dilute their veto power? The Darfur crisis, it will be recalled, called attention to the Security Council's limited role in referring a situation to the ICC. However, its action also confirmed U.N. support for the ICC's role in humanitarian crisis. This, at the very least, has offered an important glimpse into the cooperative relationship between the ICC and Security Council. On the other hand, such action does not exhibit the full range of a legitimacy push; more precisely, the second stage of interaction, which refers to the active connection between the ICC indictment (which may or may not be based on, or induced by Security Council referral of a situation) and additional proposed mechanisms such as a global jury. As already suggested, the link between these mechanisms will likely induce, albeit not guarantee Security Council military action, by encouraging the permanent five to recognize the validity of humanitarian intervention.

Consider the case of Syrian occupation in Lebanon. Let us assume that the Syrian government does not fully meet the U.N. demands expressed in Security Resolution 1551, for reasons related to Israel's unjust and unforeseen bombing of several Islamic sites where the terrorists are thought to be hiding. In retaliation for these missile strikes, the Syrian government decides to offer clandestine support to several gangs whose orders are to slaughter the Jews still residing in the area. Here, the complete and gross failure to comply with Security Council Resolution 1551 would likely stir up passionate calls for intervention in order to stop the massacre of innocent civilians. Either the Security Council could adopt a resolution referring the situation to the ICC, as it has in the Darfur crisis. Or, the ICC could operate through its own emergency organ, notably the second policy objective mentioned above.

If the ICC indictment, for instance, exposes the excesses of the perpetrators crimes, then the U.N. Security Council may be further induced to adopt another resolution calling for economic sanctions; or, if it deems necessary, to carry out military action to stop the killing. However unrealistic this Syrian and Israeli conflict may be, it is important to see the speculative value of this hypothetical scenario: namely, the possibilities for converging the operations and legitimacy of the ICC and the Security Council, though in a way that does not allow the Security Council to manipulate the proceedings of the ICC.

In sum, a mutual legitimacy push would reflect a more constructive informative "link" between the ICC and Security Council. Such a policy link would, in turn, reflect the strategic advantages of a special legislative body within the ICC, which would, in turn, help to meet the "challenge of balancing the moral imperative to use force to rescue imperiled humanity against the pragmatic question of whether force will succeed and do more harm."[50]

Conclusion

In the coming years, it will be important to address the ICC's role in global politics. The sharing of information between the ICC and Security Council, and the creation of a new institutional body within the Assembly of States Parties would indirectly address certain logistical limitations on Security Council inaction. As is well known, the United Nations does not possess a standing army. Rather, it must depend on state cooperation to acquire troops. Proposals to correct this defect have stressed the need to resurrect the 1950 General Assembly initiative of a voluntary peace enforcement mechanism.

Still, there is little way of ascertaining whether the Security Council will act to stop all severe humanitarian emergencies. Certainly, U.N. leaders and officials will need to reengineer the Security Council in a way that addresses the relevance of the veto powers in respect to an effective response to humanitarian emergencies. This will likely "involve a genuinely collective communitary, interventionary judgement guided predominantly by considerations of the public good."[51] Such considerations will invariably turn on complex notions of the rule of law and make a cooperative relationship between the ICC and Security Council an arguably important focal point of humanitarian intervention.

Notes

1. There are several general principles that would provide the normative basis for intervention, including the degree of violence and state unwillingness to comply with international norms of human rights protection. See Lori F. Damrosch, "The Inevitability of Selective Response? Principles to Guide Urgent International Action," in Albrecht Schnabel and Ramesh Thakur, eds. *Kosovo and the Challenge of Humanitarian Intervention: Selective Indignation, Collective Action, and International Citizenship* (New York: United Nations Press, 2000), 406–407.

2. For a detailed discussion of these costs, see Michael Barnett, *Eyewitness to a Genocide: The UN and Rwanda* (Ithaca, NY: Cornell University Press, 2002).

3. It should be noted that while the U.N. Security Council can refer a "situation," only the ICC Prosecutor and states parties can refer a "case."

4. Thomas Franck, *The Power of Legitimacy Among Nations* (New York: Oxford University Press, 1990), 38.

5. A discussion of the new post-Cold War priorities for humanitarian intervention and implications for state sovereignty can be found in Gene Lyons and Michael Mastanduno, eds. *Beyond Westphalia: State Sovereignty and International Intervention* (Baltimore: Johns Hopkins University, 1995); see also Friedrich Kratochwil, "Sovereignty as Dominium: Is There a Right of Humanitarian Intervention?" Gene Lyons and Michael Mastanduno, eds. *Beyond Westphalia: State Sovereignty and International Intervention* (Baltimore: Johns Hopkins University, 1995), 1–20.

6. See, e.g., Tom Farer "Intervention in Unnatural Humanitarian Emergencies: Lessons of the First Phase," *Human Rights Quarterly* 18 (1996): 1–22; Fernando Teson, "Collective Humanitarian Intervention," *Michigan Journal of International Law* 17 (1996): 323–371; Richard Falk, "The Complexities of Humanitarian Intervention: A New World Order Challenge," *Michigan Journal of International Law* 17 (1996): 492–493; Thomas Weiss and Jarat Chopra, "Sovereignty under Siege: From Intervention to Humanitarian Space," in Gene Lyons and Michael Mastanduno, eds. *Beyond Westphalia: State Sovereignty and International Intervention* (Baltimore: Johns Hopkins University, 1995), 87–115; David Caron, "Iraq and the Force of Law: Why Give a Shield of Immunity?" *American Journal of International Law* 87 (1991): 89–92.

7. See, e.g., Jack Donnelly, "State Sovereignty and International Intervention: The Case of Human Rights," in Gene Lyons and Michael Mastanduno, eds. *Beyond Westphalia: State Sovereignty and International Intervention* (Baltimore: Johns Hopkins University, 1995), 115–146; op. cit., Jack Donnelly, "Genocide and Intervention," *Journal of Human Rights* 1 (March 2002): 91–111; see also Steven D. Krasner, "Sovereignty and Intervention," in Gene Lyons and Michael Mastanduno, eds. *Beyond Westphalia: State Sovereignty and International Intervention* (Baltimore: Johns Hopkins University, 1995), 228–249.

8. On this point, see Michael Byers and Simon Chesterman, "Changing the Rules About Rules? Unilateral Humanitarian Intervention and the Future of International Law," in J.L Holzgrefe and Robert Keohane, eds. *Humanitarian Intervention: Ethical, Legal, and Political Dilemmas* (Cambridge: Cambridge University Press, 2003), 177–203.

9. Jane Stromseth, "Rethinking Humanitarian Intervention: The Case for Incremental Change," in J. L. Holzgrefe and Robert Keohane, eds. *Humanitarian Intervention: Ethical and Legal Dilemas* (Cambridge: Cambridge University Press, 2003): 245.

10. Counter-arguments to Ayoob's proposal can be found in B.S. Chimni, "A New Humanitarian Council for Humanitarian Interventions?" *The International Journal of Human Rights* 6, no. 1 (Spring 2002): 103–112.

11. For a detailed discussion of the issues surrounding the intervention, see James Traub, "Inventing East Timor," *Foreign Affair* 79 (2000): 74–89.

12. Scott Straus "Darfur and the Genocide Debate," *Foreign Affairs* 84 (January/February 2005): 123–133.

13. See, e.g., Tom Farer, "Humanitarian Intervention Before and After 9/11: Legality and Legitimacy," in J.L. Holzgrefe and Robert Keohane, eds. *Humanitarian Intervention: Ethical and Legal Dilemmas* (Cambridge: Cambridge University Press, 2003); Andy Knight, "The Future of the UN Security Council: Questions of Legitimacy and Representation in Multilateral Governance," in Andrew F. Cooper, John English, Ramesh Thakur, eds. *Enhancing Global Governance: Towards Global Governance* (New York: United Nations University Press, 2002), 19–37.

14. See, e.g., Richard Falk, "Legality to Legitimacy: The Revival of the Just War Framework," *Harvard International Review* 24 (2004): 40–45; Nicholas J. Wheeler, "Decisionmaking-making Rules and Procedures for Humanitarian Intervention," *The International Journal of Human Rights* 6, no. 1 (Spring 2002): 127–138; B.S. Chimni, "A New Humanitarian Council for Humanitarian Interventions?" *The International Journal of Human Rights* 6, no.1 (Spring 2002): 103–112; Lori Fisher Damrosch, "The Inevitability of Selective Response? Principles to Guide Urgent International Action," in Albecht Shnabel and Ramesh Thakur, eds. *Kosovo and the Challenge of Humanitarian Intervention: Selective Indignation, Collective Action, and International Citizenship* (New York: United Nations Press, 2000), 405–419.

15. Ayoob, 85.

16. Ayoob, 95

17. It should be noted that there is little agreement as to which of these two should be granted a permanent seat. The United States, for instance, continues to object to the permanent membership of Germany. Some of the details of this proposal can be found in Kofi Annan Statement on U.N. Reform, March 21, 2005. Available at http://www.undispatch.com/archives/2005/03annan_statement.html. Wikipedia. (2005).

18. Maggie Farley, "Annan Acts to Prevent Genocide," *Denver Post* (April 17, 2004): 2A.

19. Karen Mingst, *Essentials of International Relations* (New York: W.W. Norton, 1999), 249.

20. H.L.A. Hart, "International Law," in Robert J. Beck, Anthony Clark Arend, and Robert D. Vander Lugt, eds. *International Rules: Approaches from International Law and International Relations* (New York: Oxford University Press, 1996), 75–93;

Christopher Gelpi, *The Power Assessing the Role of Norms in Crisis Bargaining* (Princeton: Princeton University Press, 2003), 14–16.

21. Thomas Franck, *The Power of Legitimacy Among Nations* (New York: Oxford University, 1990), 40.

22. Anthony Arend, "Toward an Understanding of International Legal Rules," in Robert J. Beck, Anthony Clark Arend, and Robert D. Vander Lugt, eds. *International Rules: Approaches from International Law and International Relations* (New York: Oxford University Press, 1996), 21.

23. Franck, *Power of Legitimacy Among Nations*, 40.

24. Abram Chayes and Antonio Chayes, *The New Sovereignty: Compliance with International Regulatory Agreements* (Cambridge, MA: Harvard University Press, 1995), 118.

25. Jean-Marc Coicaud, *Legitimacy and Politics* (Cambridge: Cambridge University Press, 2002), 23.

26. See, e.g., ICC Statute, Article 17(2–3).

27. International Herald Tribune, "UN will refer crimes to Court in Hague," April 2, 2005.

28. United Nations Resolution 1593, adopted on March 31, 2005, by the Security Council at its 5158th meeting.

29. In the end, the United States agreed to abstain from the voting of the resolution, even though it had adamantly opposed any role of the ICC in the crisis.

30. See, e.g., Mauro Politi and Giuseppe Nesi, *The International Criminal Court and the Crime of Aggression* (Aldershot: Ashgate Publishing Inc, 2004).

31. International Commission on Intervention and State Sovereignty, The Responsibility to Protect: Report of the International Commission on Intervention and State Sovereignty (2001). Available at http://www.dfait-maeci.gc.ca/iciss-ciise/report-en.asp>.

32. Kofi Annan, "Statement on UN Reform-3-21-05." Available at http://www.undispatch.com/archives/2005/03annan_statement.html.

33. International Commission on Intervention and State Sovereignty, 13.

34. International Commission on Intervention and State Sovereignty, 17.

35. International Commission on Intervention and State Sovereignty, 18.

36. International Commission on Intervention and State Sovereignty, 32.

37. Ian Williams, "Righting the Wrongs of Past Interventions: A Review of the International Commission on Intervention and State Sovereignty." *The International Journal of Human Rights* 6, no. 1 (2002): 108.

38. International Commission on Intervention and State Sovereignty, 11.

39. United Nations (1948a) Convention on the Prevention and Punishment of the Crime of Genocide, Dec. 9, 1948, U.N.T.S. 277.

40. International Commission on Intervention and State Sovereignty, 17.

41. Thomas Franck, "Interpretation and Change in the Law of Humanitarian Intervention," in J.L. Holzgrefe and Robert Keohane, eds. *Humanitarian Intervention: Ethical, Legal, and Political Dilemmas* (Cambridge: Cambridge University Press), 2003, 227.

42. Richard Falk, "Legality to Legitimacy: The Revival of the Just War Framework," *Harvard International Review* 24 (2004): 42.

43. Falk, "Legality to Legitimacy," 44.

44. For a concise overview of the literature on preventive diplomacy, see Fen Osler Hampson, "Preventive Diplomacy at the United Nations and Beyond," in Fen Osler Hampson and David M. Malone, eds. *From Reaction to Conflict Prevention* (Boulder: Lynne Rienner Publishers, 2002), 139–158.

45. At its first meeting in September of 2002, the Assembly of States Parties addressed the issue of the relationship between the United Nations and the ICC. In the Draft Relationship Agreement between the Court and the United Nations, the Assembly of States Parties discussed the issues of the immunity of U.N. personnel from ICC jurisdiction and financial matters. Despite efforts to discuss the compatibility between these two organs, several sticking points remained regarding whether the Security Council could act in an efficient manner, and whether the obstacles (power interest intrusion and bias) of the veto power of the Permanent members could be surmounted.

46. A good discussion of how the comprehensiveness of peace-building measures and preventive diplomacy have stretched the U.N. resources too thin, or led to the failure to design a more effective overall coordinating strategy to manage the political and economic costs, can be found in Edward Luck, "Prevention: Theory and Practice," in Fen Osler Hampson and David M. Malone, eds. *From Reaction to Conflict Prevention* (Boulder: Lynne Rienner Publishers, 2002), 139–158.

47. Boutros-Boutros Ghali, *Building Peace and Development: Report on the Work of the Organization from the Forty-eight to the Forty-ninth Session of the General Assembly* (New York: United Nations Publications, 1994).

48. Alan Kuperman, "Rwanda in Retrospect," *Foreign Affairs* 79 (2000): 94–118.

49. See Mohammed Ayoob, "Humanitarian Intervention and State Sovereignty."

50. Nicholas J. Wheeler, "Decisionmaking-making Rules and Procedures for Humanitarian Intervention," *The International Journal of Human Rights* 6, no. 1 (2002): 129.

51. Richard Falk, "The Complexities of Humanitarian Intervention: A New World Order Challenge," *Michigan Journal of International Law* 17 (1996): 492–493. It is argued that the Security Council was never designed as a collective security arrangement because of the geopolitical concerns of the permanent members. On this point, see Anthony C. Arend and Robert J. Beck, *International Law and the Use of Force: Beyond the UN Charter Paradigm* (London: Routledge Press, 1993); B.S. Chimni, "A New Humanitarian Council for Humanitarian Interventions?"

9

Conclusion: Toward a New Global Political Order

> Power goes far to create the morality convenient to itself, and coercion is a fruitful source of consent. But when all these reserves have been made, it remains true that a new international order and a new international harmony can be built upon only the basis of an ascendency which is generally accepted as tolerant and non-oppressive, or any other rate, as preferable to any practicable manner.
>
> —E.H. Carr

THUS FAR, I HAVE FOCUSED on the ICC's global juridical power by investigating the intersection of power, politics, and ethics. This final chapter seeks to build on these investigations by examining and speculating upon the potential synthesis of decisionism and political cosmopolitanism, or the possibilities of uncovering the political substance of a global authority. The aim here is to place the ICC's juridical power in the context of a larger trend (transformative) toward an ethical and political convergence at the global level.

In the previous chapter, we examined the prospects of a global cooperative arrangement between the ICC and the United Naions. In doing so, we learned how geopolitics can and often does detract from the political will to intervene on humanitarian grounds. The question that arises here is whether we can understand the ICC's flexible juridical power in terms of the political (or lack thereof) substance of collective decision making and enforcement. In other words, if an effective decision-making framework is needed for swift and decisive action, then how will the normative pressure to act merge or conflict with the decisive and absolute need to intervene on humanitarian grounds? Will a new normative framework for making a decision reflect a new, stricter form of ethics or revolutionary enforcement mechanism?

Naturally, there will always be high costs associated with intervention, and it would be somewhat naïve to ignore these costs when calculating when and when not to intervene. But it is also true that the normative commitment to stop gross human rights abuses has engendered a growing interest and concern in a decisive framework for action. In this chapter, I shall address this growing concern by formulating a theory of decisionist ethics, or the growing fusion of universal morality with decisionism at the global level. In this way, the theoretical task we face is one of working toward a synthesis of two mutually opposing approaches to promoting peace and stability: namely, a soft, global form of decisionism that harnesses the substance of liberal principles to the absolute dictates of action (under emergency situations) and international peace (see chapter 5).

Another way of understanding this task is to realize the difficult problem of balancing the forces of coercion and consent within a global interventionist framework. For, as E.H. Carr notes,

> Power goes far to create the morality convenient to itself, and coercion is a fruitful source of consent. But when all these reserves have been made, it remains true that a new international order and a new international harmony can be built upon only the basis of an ascendency which is generally accepted as tolerant and non-oppressive, or any other rate, as preferable to any practicable manner.[1]

For Carr, it is only when morality gravitates to the international level that we become aware of the limits and prospects of our ethical commitment to promote global justice. It could thus be said that now, more than ever, international legal scholars need IR theory to develop a more systematic political understanding of the ICC that focuses on its role in the emerging normative global *political* order. As Martin Shaw notes, "humanitarian agencies and campaigns are more formal organizations, with clearly articulated goals and structures designed to achieve them, they are more capable of articulating consistent globalist policies than are social movements."[2]

Nevertheless, the task of understanding and justifying decisionist ethics will require a reinterpretation of the global dimension of decisionist ethics, more specifically, a critical reassessment of Carl Schmitt's theory of decisionism, which posits that the absolute power of the state leader is needed to preserve the political unity of the state in times of severe crisis. The theoretical challenge is to show how Schmitt's theory provides a conceptual space for bridging together the above approaches while also exposing the falseness of his anti-liberal/humanitarian and authoritarian views. Not only will we need to turn Schmitt's theory on its head in this respect, but we will also need to overcome its authoritarian conclusions by exploring the dialectical implications of the global.

The Normative Basis of a New Global Political Order: The Role of Humanitarian Intervention

Turning our attention to humanitarian intervention, it is important to note that proposed global legal mechanisms, such as a global jurying mechanism, end up exposing the limitation of procedural ethics (to mediate between moral principles or guidelines and the political realities on the ground). This, however, detracts from the need for more theoretical analysis to resolve the gap between decisionist and normative ethics. In other words, such procedures need to be situated within the theoretical spectrum between decisionism and cosmopolitanism, where it becomes possible to reconcile the hard decision needed to uphold the normative demands or obligations of stopping severe human rights abuses.

In short, we need to work beyond the procedural issue of whether extraordinary mechanisms can be devised to bridge the gap between the rules of the Charter and the political legitimacy of humanitarian intervention.[3] Or alternatively, whether the recent instances of humanitarian intervention reflect a new normative consensus on humanitarian intervention: an evolution of norms within international customary law, or *opinio juris* (convictions that turn into legally binding obligations).[4] For such approaches can only underscore the need for "collective legitimation," which, as Gene Lyons and Michael Mastanduno point out, is "a political decision that is made in accordance with generally accepted procedures and is consistent with generally accepted norms of behavior."[5]

As already noted, the political dimension of the ICC constitutes an important component of an emerging global political order. On the other hand, the need for a reliable standing international enforcement mechanism also presupposes the need for effective global governance: at the very least, a strong and enduring ethical commitment to legitimizing the authority of institutions. For Carl Schmitt, it was the looming threat of severe political stability and disorder that legitimized the absolute authority of the sovereign and the concomitant power to preserve the constitutional will of the people.[6] The instantiation of this authority, in turn, underscored the necessity of a hard, political decision. By revealing the latent dialectical logic of Schmitt's theory via globalization, it is possible to see the global dimension of decisionism as the content design of decisionist ethics, whereby a global authority, preferably the

United Nations in this case, is needed to stop and prevent the grave political instability caused by humanitarian emergencies. Global decisionism, in this sense, posits that legal neutrality remains inadequate to understand the possibilities for a global political and ethical order.[7] Interpreting Schmitt's thought from a dialectical standpoint is to understand the normative implications of his anti-positivist views for the ICC's political role in the international realm.

So what are the parameters of the political in the newly emerging global order? And how should we understand the political substance of this decision made at the global level? How does a global decisionism move us beyond a strict interpretation of state sovereignty as the primary locus of power and enforcement? In addressing these questions, I shall first assess in greater detail some procedural views on the global political order; then turn to Schmitt's theory of political sovereignty and its evolution into the global realm.

The Concept of the Political in an Age of Globalization

Before turning to these questions, however, let us return to our earlier discussion of Thomas Franck's global jurying mechanism. Franck, it will be recalled, believed that international judicial institutions had not only become prescriptive in their political intentions, but also *intrinsically* prohibitive. As he states:

> When law permits or even requires behavior that is widely held to be unfair, immoral or unjust, it is not only persons but also the law that suffers. So, too, if law prohibits that which is widely believed to be just and moral. Consequently, it is in the law's self-interest to narrow the gap between itself and the common sense of what is right in a specific situation.[8]

What Franck is asserting here is that such a global jury mechanism would become a legitimate basis for justifying intervention (chapter 8). This would, in turn, equate with, or at the very least, facilitate a political decision to intervene in humanitarian emergencies. But does such legitimacy actually reflect the political substance of the decision to intervene? Or, does such legitimacy accord with the ability to act effectively and appropriately outside the limitations of existing U.N. law? Indeed, even if such a mechanism provides a fair and legitimate triggering mechanism for intervention, it remains quite uncertain if this will lead to effective political action, or facilitate an authoritative political decision, for that matter. After all, it is quite possible that the global jury may reach a negative verdict that prevents intervention into the worst emergencies.[9]

The question arises, then, is whether the international community can expect to develop a reliable and effective enforcement mechanism for stopping humanitarian emergencies. Those who maintain that international criminal courts constitute a viable option for enforcing peace and security must contend with the issue as to how this would lead to a fair and manageable trade-off between stopping the violence and minimizing the violence caused by the intervention. It is this failure to take stock of this issue that, as Anne Orford argues, reflects a legal "myopia," or the inability to look beyond the need for action to counter the heinous consequences of inaction.[10] Far from constituting a revolutionary movement, according to Orford, the focus on a human rights enforcement regime underscores the conservative appeal of violent, often overlooked repressive means to uphold the ideals of human rights. In short, by opposing action to inaction, legal scholars tend to ignore the importance of long-term preventative or entrenched measures of changing the society (before that society enters into a severe crisis phase). Certainly, stronger ethical commitments are needed to institutionalize this moral and political will of the international community to foster the legitimization of juridical and military power. What I argue, however, is that the trend toward exceptionalism amounts to a fundamental shift in our thinking about the political substance of humanitarian intervention.

Schmitt's Theory of Decisionism and Political Sovereignty

In order to theorize about the political substance of humanitarian intervention, we need to understand the conceptual link between Schmitt's concept of the political and the evolution of state sovereignty into the global realm. Schmitt's formulation of the concept of the political is based on three major ideas: the rejection of the rule of law, political unity/sovereignty, and the need for distinguishing between constitutionalism and democracy. According to Schmitt, humanity constitutes an "essentially ideological instrument of imperialist expansion . . . that excludes the concept of the enemy, because the enemy does not cease to be a human being."[11] The fact that humanity cannot wage war (since it has no enemy) suggests that humanitarian wars are ultimately "driven by the utmost inhumanity and potential destructiveness."[12] Curiously, some present-day humanitarian critics of the Kosovo War arrive at the same conclusion of the destructiveness of humanitarian wars, even though none of them share the anti-democratic views of Schmitt. For instance, Robert Hayden argues that NATO's violation of international law transformed human rights from a protest against state violence to one of "the application of massive violence on states deemed to be inferior."[13]

Schmitt's rejection of liberalism is rooted in the idea that neutrality ultimately contradicts the purpose that it sets out to accomplish: namely, to preserve a permanent peace among nation states. This was illustrated by the

League of Nations' prohibition of war and aggression (e.g., the Kellogg Briand Act 1928), which had the effect of removing the constraints imposed by the friend/enemy distinction.[14] In Schmitt's view, then, the rule of law is another way of expressing the empty, formalistic character of international law, which fails to ensure that a political decision can be made under extenuating circumstances such as a state emergency.

This is not to say that democratic nation states are inherently incapable of waging an effective war, but rather, that in times of crisis, negotiating and debating tends to undermine decisive action. It does so by placing the rules of war (or rights of individuals) ahead of the absolute need to preserve the unity of the people via the leader's ability to trump or dissolve the constitution. It was nonetheless this need for an absolute decision to save the peoples and the constitution from unchecked power that underscores the political sovereignty of the nation state: the convergence of the absolute power of the sovereign leader and the political unity of the nation.

Ultimately for Schmitt, constitutionalism sets into motion laws that had restricted, and even ran counter to the political unity (sovereignty) of the peoples.[15] As he states in his essay on Democracy and Parliamentarism:

> An intervention based on the concept of monarchial legitimacy is illegal in democratic theory only because it violates the principle of the people's self-determination. By contrast a restoration of free self-determination achieved through intervention, the liberation of a people from a tyrant, cannot violate the principle of non-intervention in any way, but only creates the preconditions for the principle of non-intervention.[16]

Preserving the democratic will of the peoples in times of crisis requires the sovereign to stand outside the law, that is, to act as the absolute mediator between the particular circumstances and the preservation of the peoples' democratic will. The idea here is that absolute state power is needed in times of crisis to preserve the political unity of the state and the viability of the constitution.[17] As this would indicate, Schmitt reached a rigid, even dangerous, conclusion concerning the need to rise above the rule of law. Concerning this idea, Hiener Bielefeldt theorizes that

> Neutrality serves as an antidote to all sorts of biases and discrimination . . . rather than being an expression of evasiveness, the principle of neutrality can be used as a critical standard within that liberal fight for political justice. For the principle of neutrality calls for permanent self-reflection and public critical debate in order to articulate ever new experiences of oppression and discrimination and to discover potential biases even behind purportedly universal validity claims.[18]

Far from being disengaged, neutrality, according to Bielefeldt, constitutes an active element in the reasoning process of state decision making; for it validates and shapes the content of the decision-making process. Yet, as I have argued, it is not so much that Schmitt ignores the content of democratic values, but that, in times of crisis, the sovereign ruler must rise above these principles in order to undo the crisis that the formalism of these principles has engendered (inaction). This, however, does not necessarily mean that a new constitution should exclude liberal principles; nor that Schmitt adamantly ruled out the possibility of future liberal constitutionalism. Rather, it suggests the transformative dimension of the interaction between peace and crises: the need for an absolute solution to restore stability and the viability of these principles. Certainly, one may disagree with this latter statement. However, it is quite plausible that Schmitt believed in the temporality of a state of emergency, and, by extension, the temporary suspension of democratic principles.

In this way, we need to distinguish between a crisis and the permanent dissolution of the values that brought the state into the crisis in the first place. Schmitt, in this case, failed to clarify this idea as to how the sovereign decision restores a stable balance between democracy and liberal constitutionalism; that is, how it regenerates the forces of constitutionalism, whose own dynamics remain inseparable from the forces of democratic and liberal values. In effect, what I am arguing here is that Schmitt's theory employs a dialectical logic to validate the liberal crisis of the constitutional state and to preserve the negative forces that gave rise to the preservation of the state. Unless Schmitt believed that this decision permanently dissolved liberal constitutionalism, then it makes little sense to speak of the permanent dissolution of liberal and democratic values.

This, of course, challenges the idea that Schmitt possessed the ability "to perceive the political as an independent, dynamic variable, outside the state and beyond the law . . . for sovereignty is by no means divided, which would contradict its concept, but remains durably suspended between the federation and the member states."[19] As we shall see, the changing global conditions at the global level enable us to conceptualize the parameters of a global decisionism, even if this framework remains immanent and rudimentary in relation to state sovereignty. The following section assesses how this merging global trend provides a space for reinterpreting the decisional value of humanitarianism, while at the same time exposing the Schmittian flaw that humanitarian wars are inherently destructive globalizing wars.

Beyond State Sovereignty: The Hard Legitimization of Global Juridical Power

As noted earlier, Schmitt believed that human rights constituted an instrumental tool of universal or destructive wars.[20] I have already mentioned some loose parallels between Schmitt's ideas and the new emerging global political system, including the political unity of the peoples and the absolute need to stop humanitarian emergencies. Here, however, I shall discuss how global decisionism inverts this conclusion to reflect the ICC's role in shaping the new global political order. As we saw in chapter 8, many of the proposed global mechanisms for bridging the gap between legitimacy and legality fall within the ambit of the exceptionalism recognized under the U.N. Charter. Such exceptionalism is expressed in Articles 24 and 25 of the Charter (under chapter VII), which allow, *inter alia*, the Security Council to trump state sovereignty.

This, however, is contradicted be the fact that Article 39 leaves out any humanitarian-based criteria to validate the use of force to preserve the severely disaffected peoples of a collapsed or failing state. To understand this shortcoming of the Charter is to realize how the principles of nonintervention and sovereign equality of states restricts the politics of decisionism at the global level. Again, the question that arises here is whether we can begin to make a plausible fit between Schmitt's decisionism, which is averse to human rights, and the apolitical nature of these Charter principles. This, of course, will depend on our ability to link global change with the limits to Schmitt's theory of decisionism. What I am proposing, then, is that globalization has eroded or unbundled state sovereignty in ways that enable us to weave new normative strands through Schmitt's theory. Globalization, in other words, has released the normativity of Schmitt's decisionism onto the global level in the form of an ethics of decisionism (humanitarian intervention). In this sense, the moral responsibility to preserve the lives and political unity of a peoples becomes the driving force for a decisionist ethics.

As we saw in chapter 8, a cooperative arrangement between the ICC and the Security Council represents the ICC's capacity to mediate between the politics of inaction (and its unethical consequences) and decisionism (action). A mutual legitimacy push in this sense would underscore the value orientation of decisionist ethics and the logical idea that a global authority must be able to apprehend the value of his or her decision on behalf of the democratic will of the people. Thus, decisionist ethics is not simply about legitimating power by illiberal means. As Jean-Marc Coicaud states: "relations of forces are indissociable from a dynamic in which collective beliefs regarding the organization of life in society become involved in the triggering, development and the outcome of confrontations. It is therefore not power alone, understood in the physical sense, that decides events."[21]

Nonetheless, within the framework of Schmitt's theory of decisionism, it becomes increasingly difficult to maintain the link between state dictatorship and democracy, since it is precisely such state authority that undermines the democratic will and political substance of the state.[22] Because genocide fractures the notion of the political unity of the people, it also, by extension, problematizes the statist concept of political sovereignty. It is precisely this particular limit of Schmitt's theory that creates a new space for understanding an immanent global decisionism: the capacity of a global authority to complement, or in some circumstances replace, the state as the absolute authority to restore political unity. In this context, the absolute need to preserve the basic human rights of severely disaffected people legitimizes the global decision to operate outside the traditional legal scope of the U.N. Charter.

More importantly, it represents an emergent spectrum of political legitimacy at the global level. At one end of the spectrum lies the U.N. Security Council's Chapter VII powers to suspend the principle of nonintervention (with all the political obstacles that come with this, including the veto); at the other, is the pure exceptionalist goal or decisionist framework for concentrating power in the Secretary-General who could act directly on behalf of the peoples of the severely disaffected state. Whether this latter end constitutes a realistic alternative at the present time—especially since it would entail radical change to the balance of power among the different organs of the United Nations—remains an empirical issue.[23]

Accordingly, it is important to see this changing global political reality in terms of the *projection* of a flexible application of the political to the global level. Schmitt, however, was decidedly ambiguous on the notion of global political order, or even on the political unity of the peoples. On this point, Ellen Kennedy notes that "the people are finally the subject (in both senses) of politics; its real initiator. . . ."[24] Within this context, it is possible to interpret a severely disaffected peoples as the subject of global politics: an initiator of the political decision at the global level; or alternatively, as the critical link between the ICC's awareness of itself as a political institution and a stable global political order. On the other hand, it is this link between the body public and international action that implies the increasing fluidity of the global political order and allows globalization to serve as the basis for a new form of decisionist ethics.

In *Nomos of the Earth*, for instance, Schmitt theorizes that the rise of the United States as a new global humanitarian hegemon represents the emergence of a new destructive world order: the end of what he referred to as the peaceful period of the *jus European publicum* or the stabilizing effects of the nation state system in Europe. This, however, should raise suspicion in Schmitt's conception, since it was Nazi Germany and its calls for war that turned into total war and annihilation.[25] Thus, Schmitt's denunciation of world order (orchestrated by the United Nations) remains unconvincing, especially since he fails to provide any coherent reasons to explain the emergence of a new world order.[26] As Jean Francois Kervegan points out: "rather than heading toward a universalism, always a disguise for power politics, a new pluralism should be based on the coexistence of several imperial powers, each equipped with its own Monroe Doctrine."[27]

In terms of the ICC, an emergent global link between decisionism and political cosmopolitanism would reflect a dual function: to counter the political effects of the old Charter rules (geopolitical interests); and to show how the institutionalization of proscriptive norms against genocide and crimes against humanity mediates between the collective political decision and the occurrence of gross human rights abuses. The latter suggests that the ICC, although playing a key role in the new global political order, would serve to complement the influence of other international organizations and non-state actors in promoting international peace and security (see chapter 3). Clearly, security and geopolitical concerns will play a key role in limiting the influences of this enforcement network. On the other hand, it is difficult to ignore the influence of these actors and their role in constructing a new global political order.

One way of demonstrating the link between globalization and the decision to act is to assess how the non-sovereign or non-state actors presuppose a broader and more fluid conception of political unity within the United Nations; more specifically, the evolving link between humanitarian emergencies and the growing influence of NGOs and the media as agents in the international decision-making process. This was a point discussed in chapter 3, when we examined the pragmatic character of the ICC. The question that this raises here in terms of the ICC's role in constructing a global political order is how the ICC's political dimension will provide the possibilities for understanding and concretizing the self-directed application of international rules. Can we overcome, for instance, the rigid effects of U.S. opposition to the ICC (chapter 5)? And will the ICC's juridical power remain flexible enough to ensure its continued development and positive impact on global politics? Both of these questions will need to be addressed if we are to advance a more developed understanding of the ICC's political dimension. At the very least, they should suggest the important and unexplored parameters of the ICC's formative role in global politics.

Notes

1. E.H. Carr, *The Twenty Years Crises: 1919–1939,* 2nd Edition (London: Macmillan, 1946), 236.

2. Martin Shaw, "Global Voices: Civil Society and the Media in Global Crises," in Tim Dunne and Nicholas J. Wheeler, eds. *Human Rights in Global Politics* (Cambridge: Cambridge University Press, 1999), 229.

3. To re-emphasize a point made earlier: the political legitimacy of interventions became a central issue after the Independent International Commission determined that the U.S.-led NATO invasion of Kosovo was illegal but legitimate. See, e.g., Gareth Evans and Mohamed Sahnoun, "The Responsibility to Protect," *Foreign Affairs* 81, no. 6 (November/December 2002): 99–110; Tom Farer, "Humanitarian Intervention Before and After 9/11: Legality and Legitimacy," in J.L. Holzgrefe and Robert Keohane, eds. *Humanitarian Intervention: Ethical and Legal Dilemmas* (Cambridge: Cambridge University Press, 2003); J.L. Holzgrefe and Robert Keohane, eds. *Humanitarian Intervention: Ethical and Legal Dilemmas* (Cambridge: Cambridge University Press, 2003); Nicholas J. Wheeler, "Decisionmaking-making Rules and Procedures for Humanitarian Intervention," *The International Journal of Human Rights* 6, no. 1 (2002): 127–138.

4. Jane Stromseth, "Rethinking Humanitarian Intervention: The Case for Incremental Change," in J.L. Holzgrefe and Robert Keohane, eds. *Humanitarian Intervention: Ethical and Legal Dilemmas* (Cambridge: Cambridge University Press, 2003), 246–247.

5. Gene Lyons and Michael Mastanduno, "Introduction: International Intervention, State Sovereignty and the Future of International Society," in Gene Lyons and Michael Mastanduno, eds. *Beyond Westphalia: State Sovereignty and International Intervention* (Baltimore: Johns Hopkins University, 1995), 8.

6. See, e.g., William Scheuerman, "International Law as Historical Myth," *Constellations: An International Journal of Critical and Democratic Theory* 11, no. 4 (December 2004): 537–550; Chantal Mouffe, "Carl Schmitt and the Paradox of Liberal Democracy," in Chantal Mouffe, ed. *The Challenge of Carl Schmitt* (London: Verso, 1999), 38–53; David Dyzenhaus, *Carl Schmitt, Hans Kelsen and Herman Heller in Weimar* (Oxford: Clarendon Press, 1997); Paul Hirst, "Carl Schmitt's Decisionism," in Chantal Mouffe, ed. *The Challenge of Carl Schmitt* (London: Verso, 1999), 7–17.

7. Note that liberalism, for Schmitt, provided the basis for globalizing the enemy, that is, of waging a war of total destruction in the name of humanity, which, in turn, reflected the total elimination of the constraints imposed by the friend/enemy distinction. Schmitt based this idea on his concept of the political, which derives from friend/enemy distinction and how this distinction discloses the possibilities for war. As Schmitt states, "the political is the most intense an extreme antagonism, and every concrete antagonism becomes that much more political the closer it approaches the most extreme point, that of the friend-enemy grouping." See Carl Schmitt, *The Concept of the Political*, George Schwab, trans. (Chicago: University of Chicago Press, 1996), 29.

8. Franck, 227.

9. Of course, the international community would also have to be informed of the procedures and conditions for carrying out any verdict of a global jury. They may wish, as we discussed in chapter 8, to consult the report published by International Commission on Intervention and State Sovereignty.

10. Anne Orford, *Reading Humanitarian Intervention: Human Rights and the Use of Force in International Law* (Cambridge: Cambridge University Press, 2003), 10.

11. Schmitt, *The Concept of the Political*, 54.

12. Schmitt, *The Concept of the Political*, 55.

13. Robert Hayden, "Biased Justice: Humanitarianism and the International Criminal Tribunal for the Former Yugoslavia," in R.G.C. Thomas, ed. *Yugoslavia Unraveled* (Lanham, MD: Lexington Books, 2003), 261.

14. To the extent that the possibilities of war underscores humankind's instincts for self-preservation and war, Schmitt's criticism of liberal neutrality echoes Friedrich Nietzche's critique of slave morality: namely, the self-imposed detachment from one's vital instincts that hinders one from overcoming the political constraints imposed on one's will to power.

15. On this point, see Heiner Bielefeldt, "Carl Schmitt's Critique of Liberalism: Systematic Reconstruction and Countercriticism," in David Dyzenhaus, ed. *Law as Politics* (Durham, NC: Duke University Press, 1998), 23–36.

16. Carl Schmitt, *The Crisis of Parliamentary Democracy*, Ellen Kennedy, trans. (Cambridge: MIT Press, 1985), 31.

17. Carl Schmitt, *Political Theology: Four Chapters on the Concept of Sovereignty*, George Schwab, trans. (Cambridge: MIT Press, 1985), 50.

18. Bielfeldt, 31.

19. Hauke Brunkorst, "The Right to War: Hegemonial Geopolitics or Civic Constitutionalism," *Constellations: An International Journal of Critical and Democratic Theory* 11, no. 4 (December 2004): 512–526.

20. As Paul Hirst notes, "to overlook this outside substantive element is to ignore the fact that all laws have an outside, that they exist because of a substantiated claim on the part of some agency to be the dominant source of binding rules. . . ." See Hirst, "Carl Schmitt's Decisionism," 117.

21. Jean-Marc Coicaud, *Legitimacy and Politics* (Cambridge: Cambridge University Press, 2002), 169.

22. Given Schmitt's own tacit participation in the Nazi regime and the peremptory norm of nonintervention at the time, it is easy to see why he saw genocide as falling within the narrow scope of state legitimacy or stability.

23. Here, we need to stress the comparison between this and other forms of synthesis, including Amitai Etzioni's normative synthesis between Eastern and Western values. Like a normative synthesis, the synthesis between decisionism and political cosmopolitanism remains equally formative; it requires further theoretical and empirical analysis to demonstrate its emergent dynamics and patterns.

24. Ellen Kennedy, "Hostis Not Inimicus: Toward a Theory of the Public in the Work of Carl Schmitt," in David Dyzenhaus, ed. *Law as Politics* (Durham, NC: Duke University Press, 1998), 23–36.

25. Scheuerman, 542–543.

26. Jean-Francois Kervegan, "Carl Schmitt and 'World Unity'" in Chantal Mouffe, ed. *The Challenge of Carl Schmitt* (London: Verso, 1999), 54–74.

27. Kervegan, "Carl Schmitt and 'World Unity,'" 61.

Bibliography

Abbott, Kenneth W., Robert Keohane, Andrew Moravcsik, Anne-Marie Slaughter, and Duncan Snidal. "The Concept of Legalization." *International Organization* 54, no. 3 (2002): 401–19.

Abul-Ethem, Fahad. "The Role of the Judiciary in the Protection of Human Rights and Development: A Middle East Perspective." *Fordham International Law Journal* 26 (2003): 761–70.

Akhaven, Payam. "Beyond Impunity: Can International Criminal Justice Prevent Future Atrocities?" *American Journal of International Law* 95 (2001): 7–31.

Albert, Mathias, and Lena Hilkermeier, eds. *Observing International Relations.* London: Routledge, 2004.

Al-Ghunaimi, M. *The Muslim Conception of International Law and the Western Approach.* Hague: Kluwer, 1968.

Amstutz, Mark R. *International Ethics.* Lanham, MD: Rowman & Littlefield Publishers, 1999.

An-Na'im, Abdullahi Ahmed. "Islamic Law, International Relations and Human Rights: Challenges and Response." *Cornell International Law Journal* 32, no. 3 (1987): 317–35.

Arend, Anthony. "Toward an Understanding of International Legal Rules." In Robert J. Beck, Anthony Clark Arend, and Robert D. Vander Lugt, eds. *International Rules: Approaches from International Law and International Relations, 289–310.* New York: Oxford University Press, 1996.

Arend, Anthony C., and Robert J. Beck. *International Law and the Use of Force: Beyond the UN Charter Paradigm.* London: Routledge Press, 1993.

Aristotle. *Politics.* Oxford: Oxford University Press, 1974.

Assembly of States Parties. *Continuity of Work in Respect of the Crime of Aggression.* Res. ICC-ASP.1/Res.1 (2002).

———. *Draft Paper on the Definition and Elements of the Crime of Aggression.* ICC-ASP/2/10 (2003).

Axelrod, Robert. *The Evolution of Cooperation.* New York: Basic Books, 1984.

Ayoob, Mohammed. "Humanitarian Intervention and State Sovereignty." *The International Journal of Human Rights* 6, no. 1 (2002): 81–102.

Baghramian, M., and A. Ingram, eds. *Pluralism: The Philosophy and Politics of Diversity.* London: Routledge Press, 2000.

Balakian, Peter. *The Burning Tigris: The Armenian Genocide and America's Response.* New York: Harper Collins Publishers, 2003.

Ball, Howard. *Prosecuting War Crimes and Genocide: The Twentieth-Century Experience.* Lawrence: University of Kansas Press, 1999.

Barnett, Michael. *Eyewitness to a Genocide: The UN and Rwanda.* Ithaca, NY: Cornell University Press, 2002.

Barringer, Felicity. "U.N. Renews U.S. Peacekeeper's Exemption from Prosecution." *New York Times* (June 13, 2003): A18.

Barry, Brian. *Justice as Impartiality.* Oxford: Clarendon Press, 1995.

Bass, Gary. *Stay the Hand of Vengeance: The Politics of War Crimes Tribunals.* Princeton: Princeton University Press, 2000.

Bassiouni, M. Cherif. "Accountability for Violations of International Humanitarian Law and Other Serious Violations of Human Rights." In M. Cherif Bassiouni, ed. *Post-Conflict Justice,* 3–54. Ardsley, NY: Transnational Publishers, 2003.

———. "Negotiating the Treaty of Rome on the Establishment of an International Criminal Court." *Cornell International Law Journal* 41 (2000): 57–89.

———. "Proposed Guiding Principles for Combating Impunity for International Crimes." In M. Cherif Bassiouni, ed. *Post-Conflict Justice,* 255–82. Ardsley, NY: Transnational Publishers, 2003.

———, ed. *The Statute of the International Criminal Court.* New York: Transnational Publishers, 1998.

———. "Sources of Islamic Law, and the Protection of Human Rights in the Islamic Criminal Justice System." In M. Cherif Bassiouni, ed. *The Islamic Criminal Justice System,* 3–54. London: Oceana Publications, Inc., 1982.

———. "The Universal Model: The International Criminal Court." In M. Cherif Bassiouni, ed. *Post-Conflict Justice,* 813–28. Ardsley, NY: Transnational Publishers, 2003.

———. "World War I: The War to End All Wars and the Birth of a Handicapped International Criminal Justice System." *Denver Journal of International Law and Policy* 30 (2002): 244–90.

Beccaria, Cesare. *On Crimes and Punishments.* Trans. Henry Paolucci. Indianapolis: Bobbs-Merrill Educational Publishing, 1963.

Beck, Robert J. "International Law and International Relations: The Prospects for Interdiscplinary Collaboration." In Robert J. Beck, Anthony Clark Arend, and Robert D. Vander Lugt, eds. *International Rules: Approaches from International Law and International Relations,* 3–33. Oxford: Oxford University Press, 1996.

Becker, Elizabeth. "U.S. Suspends Aid to 35 Countries Over New International Court." *New York Times* (July 2, 2003): 16A.

Beitz, Charles. "Justice and International Relations." In Charles R. Beitz, Marshall Cohen, Thomas Scanlon, and A. John Simmons, eds. *International Ethics*, 292, 294. Princeton: Princeton University Press, 1983.

Bellamy, Richard. "Dealing with Difference: Four Models of Pluralist Politics." In Michael O' Neill and Dennis Austin, eds. *Democracy and Cultural Diversity*, 198–217. Oxford: Oxford University Press, 2000.

Berdal, Mats. "Lessons Not Learned: The Use of Force in Peace Operations." *International Peacekeeping* 7 (2000): 55–72.

Berlin, Isaiah. *The Crooked Timber of Humanity*. Princeton: Princeton University Press, 1990.

Berlin, Isaiah, and Ramin Jahanbegloo. *Conversations with Isaiah Berlin*. New York: Charles Scribner's Sons, 1991.

Bielefeldt, Heiner. "Carl Schmitt's Critique of Liberalism: Systematic Reconstruction and Countercriticism." In David Dyzenhaus, ed. *Law as Politics*, 23–36. Durham, NC: Duke University Press, 1998.

Boas, Gideon, and William A. Schabas, eds. *International Criminal Law Developments in Case Law of the ICTY*. Leiden, Boston: Martinus Nijhoff Publishers, 2003.

Bodley, Anne. "Weakening the Principle of Sovereignty in International Criminal Law: The International Criminal Tribunal for the Former Yugoslavia." *International Law and Politics* 31 (2000): 417–71.

Bolton, John R. "From the U.S. House of Representatives. Committee on International Relations and the American Service member's Protection Act of 2000." Hearing on 25 July. Washington D.C.: Government Printing Office, 2000.

———. "The Risks and the Weaknesses of the International Criminal Court from America's Perspective." *Virginia Journal of International Law* 41 (2000): 186.

Boon, Kristin. "Rape and Forced Pregnancy Under the ICC Statute." *Columbia Human Rights Law Review* 32 (2001): 626–75.

Boutros-Ghali, Boutros. *Building Peace and Development: Report on the Work of the Organization from the Forty-eight to the Forty-ninth Session of the General Assembly*. New York: United Nations Publication, 1994.

Brackman, Arnold C. *The Other Nuremberg: The Untold Story of the Tokyo War Crimes Trials*. New York: Morrow, 1987.

Brock, Lothar. "World Society From the Bottom Up." In *Observing International Relations: Niklas Luhman and World Politics*, edited by Mathias Albert and Lena Hilkermeier. London: Routledge, 2004.

Broomhall, Bruce. *International Justice and the International Criminal Court: Between Sovereignty and the Rule of Law*. Oxford: Oxford University Press, 2003.

Brown, Chris. "World Society and the English School: An 'International Society' Perspective on World Society." *European Journal of International Relations* 7 (2001): 423–41.

Brown, Bertram S. "Unilateralism, Multilateralism, and the International Criminal Court." In Stewart Patrick and Shepard Forman, eds. *Multilateralism and US Foreign Policy: Ambivalent Engagement*, 323–44. Boulder and London: Lynne Reinner, 2002.

Brunkorst, Hauke. "The Right to War: Hegemonial Geopolitics or Civic Constitutionalism." *Constellations: An International Journal of Critical and Democratic Theory* 11, no. 4 (2004): 512–26.

Bull, Hedley. *The Anarchical Society.* New York: Columbia University Press, 1977.

Buzan, Barry. *From International to World Society.* Cambridge: Cambridge University Press, 2004.

Buzan, Barry, and Richard Little. "Reconceptualing Anarchy: Structural Realism Meets World History." *European Journal of International Relations* 2, no. 4 (Winter 1996): 403–38.

Buzan, Barry, Charles Jones, and Richard Little, eds. *The Logic of Anarchy.* New York: Columbia University Press, 1993.

Byers, Michael, and Simon Chesterman. "Changing the Rules About Rules? Unilateral Humanitarian Intervention and the Future of International Law." In *Humanitarian Intervention: Ethical, Legal, and Political Dilemma,* edited by J. L. Holzgrefe and Robert Keohane, 177–203. Cambridge: Cambridge University Press, 2003.

Campbell, Tom. *The Legal Theory of Ethical Positivism.* Aldershot: Dartmouth Publishing, Inc., 1996.

———. *Prescriptive Legal Positivism: Law, Rights and Democracy.* New York: UCL Press, 2004.

Caney, Simon. "International Distributive Justice." *Political Studies* 49 (October 2001): 974–97.

Caron, David D. "War and International Adjudication: Reflections on the 1899 Peace Conference." *American Journal of International Law* 94, no. 4 (2002).

Carr, Edward H. *The Twenty Years' Crisis, 1919–1939.* London: Macmillan, 1946.

Cassese, Antonio. "The Statute of the International Criminal Court." *European Journal of International Law* 10 (1999): 141–71.

Cervasio, Christine. "Extradition and the International Criminal Court: The Future of the Political Offense Doctrine." *Pace International Review* 11 (1991): 419–47.

Chan, Stephen. "Aspirations and Absent Methodologies in Universalism: Towards a Multicultural Normative Theory." In *Value Pluralism, Normative Theory, and International Relations,* edited by M. Lensu and J. Fritz, 59–75. London: St. Martin's Press, 2002.

Charlesworth, Hilary, C. Chinkin, and S. Wright. "Feminists Approaches to International Law." *American Journal of International Law* 85 (1993): 613–45.

Charney, John. "International Criminal Law and the Role of Domestic Courts." *American Journal of International Law* 95 (2001): 120–24.

Charvet, John. "Epilogue: Further Reflections on Value Pluralism in International Relations." In *Value Pluralism, Normative Theory and International Relations,* edited by M. Lensu and J. Fritz, 196–204. London: St. Martin's Press, 1996.

Chayes, Abram, and Antonio Chayes. *The New Sovereignty: Compliance with International Regulatory Agreements.* Cambridge, MA: Harvard University Press, 1995.

Chimni, B. S. "A New Humanitarian Council for Humanitarian Interventions?" *The International Journal of Human Rights* 6, no. 1 (Spring 2002): 103–12.

Clapham, Andrew. "The ICC Statute: Protecting the Sovereign Rights of Non-Parties." In *International Crimes, Peace, and Human Rights: The Role of the International Criminal Court,* edited by Dinah Shelton, 207–18. Ardsley, NY: Transnational Publishers, 2000.

———. "Issues of Complexity, Complicity and Complementarity: From the Nuremberg Trials to the Dawn of the New International Criminal Court." In *From Nuremberg to the Hague*, edited by Phillipe Sands, 30–67. Cambridge: Cambridge University Press, 2003.

Cochran, Molly. *Normative Theory in International Relations.* Cambridge: Cambridge University Press, 1999.

Coicaud, Jean-Marc. *Legitimacy and Politics.* Cambridge: Cambridge University Press, 2002.

Convention for the Creation of an International Court. (Opened for signing on November 16, 1937, League of Nations Doc. C. 547 CIIM, 384 (I) 1937.)

Crawford, James. "The ILC's Draft Statute for an International Criminal Tribunal." *American Journal of International Law* 88 (1994).

Cronin, Bruce. "Changing Norms of Sovereignty and Multilateral Intervention." In *Collective Conflict Management and Changing World Politics*, edited by Joseph Lepgold and Thomas Weiss, 159–80. Albany: State University of New York Press, 1998.

Crowder, George. *Liberalism and Value Pluralism.* London: Continuum Publishing, 2002.

Cutler, Claire. "Law in the Global Polity." In *Towards a Global Polity*, edited by Morten Ougaard and Philipp Higgot, 58–77. London: Routledge Press, 2002.

Damrosch, Lori F. "The Inevitability of Selective Response? Principles to Guide Urgent International Action." In *Kosovo and the Challenge of Humanitarian Intervention: Selective Indignation, Collective Action, and International Citizenship*, edited by Albecht Shnabel and Ramesh Thakur, 405–19. New York: United Nations Press, 2000.

Danner, Allison Marston. "Enhancing the Legitimacy and Accountability of Prosecutorial Discretionary at the International Criminal Court." *American Journal of International Law* 97, no. 3 (July 2003): 510–52.

Derrida, Jacque. *Spectres of Marx.* London: Routledge, 1994.

Dewey, John. *The Essential Dewey. Volume 2: Ethics, Logic, Psychology.* Bloomington: Indiana University Press, 1998.

Dillon, Michael. "Criminalising Social and Political Violence Internationally." *Millennium: Journal of International Studies* 2, no. 3 (1998): 538–65.

Donnelly, Jack. "Genocide and Intervention." *Journal of Human Rights* 1, no. 1 (March 2002): 91–111.

———. "State Sovereignty and International Interventions: The Case of Human Rights." In *Beyond Westphalia? State Sovereignty and International Intervention*, edited by Gene M. Lyons and Michael Mastanduno, 398–403. Baltimore: Johns Hopkins University Press, 1995.

Duffy, Helen. "National Constitutional Compatibility and the International Criminal Court." *Duke Journal of Comparative and International Law* 11 (2001): 5–38.

Dunne, Tim. *Inventing International Society.* Basingstoke: Macmillan, 1998.

———. "Sociological Interpretations: Instrumental, Legitimist and Coercive Interpretations of International Society." *Millennium: Journal of International Studies* 30, no. 1 (2001): 67–91.

Dyzenhaus, David. *Carl Schmitt, Hans Kelsen, and Herman Heller in Weimar.* Oxford: Clarendon Press, 1997.

Edkins, Jenny. *Postructuralism and International Relations.* Boulder, CO: Lynne Rienner Publishers, 1995.

Ellis, Mark S. "The International Criminal Court and its Implication for Domestic Law and National Capacity Building." *Florida Journal of International Law* 15, no. 2 (2002): 216–42.

Etzioni, Amitai. *From Empire to Community.* New York: Palgrave Macmillian, 2004.

Evans, Gareth, and Mohamed Sahnoun. "The Responsibility to Protect." *Foreign Affairs* 81, no. 6 (November/December 2002): 99–110.

Falk, Richard. "The Complexities of Humanitarian Intervention: A New World Order Challenge." *Michigan Journal of International Law* 17 (1996): 492–93.

———. *The Declining World Order: America's Imperial Geopolitics.* London: Routledge, 2004.

———. "Legality to Legitimacy: The Revival of the Just War Framework." *Harvard International Review* (Spring 2004): 40–45.

Farer, Tom. "Humanitarian Intervention Before and After 9/11: Legality and Legitimacy." In *Humanitarian Intervention: Ethical and Legal Dilemmas*, edited by J.L. Holzgrefe and Robert Keohane. Cambridge: Cambridge University Press, 2003.

———. "Intervention in Unnatural Humanitarian Emergencies: Lessons of the First Phase." *Human Rights Quarterly* 18 (1996): 1–22.

Farley, Maggie. "Annan Acts to Prevent Genocide." *Denver Post* (April 17, 2004): 2A.

Fehl, Caroline. "Explaining the International Criminal Court: A 'Practice Test' for Rationalist and Constructivist Approaches." *European Journal of International Relations* 10, no. 3, (September 2004): 357–94.

Ferencz, Benjamin. "Can Aggression Be Deterred by Law?" *Pace International Law* 11 (1999): 341–61.

Ferguson, Yale H., and Richard W. Mansbach. *Remapping Global Politics: History's Revenge and Future Shock.* Cambridge: Cambridge University Press, 2004.

Finch, George A. "The Nuremberg Trial and International Law." *American Journal of International Law* 41, no. 1 (January 1947): 20–37.

Finnemore, Martha. "Military Intervention and the Organization of International Politics." In *Collective Conflict Management and Changing World Politics*, edited by Joseph Lepgold and Thomas Weiss, 181–204. Albany: State University of New York Press, 1998.

Foucault, Michel. *Power/Knowledge.* Edited by Colin Gordon. New York: Random House, 1980.

Franceschet, Antonio. "The Rule of Law, Inequality, and the International Criminal Court." *Alternatives* 29, no. 3 (2004): 23–42.

Franck, Thomas. "Interpretation and Change in the Law of Humanitarian Intervention." In *Humanitarian Intervention: Ethical, Legal, and Political Dilemmas*, edited by J. L. Holzgrefe and Robert Keohane, 204–31. Cambridge: Cambridge University Press, 2003.

———. *The Power of Legitimacy Among Nations.* New York: Oxford University Press, 1990.

Fritz, Nicole, and Alison Smith. "Current Apathy for the Coming Anarchy: Building the Special Court for Sierra Leone." *Fordham International Law Journal* 25 (2001): 105–45.

Frost, Mervyn. *Constituting Human Rights.* London: Routledge Press, 2002.

Galipeau, Claude J. *Isaiah Berlin's Liberalism.* Oxford: Clarendon Press, 1994.

Gallón, Gustavo. "The International Criminal Court and the Challenge of Deterrence." In Dinah Shelton, ed. *International Crimes, Peace, and Human Rights: The Role of the International Criminal Court,* 93–104. Ardsley, NY: Transnational Publishers, 2000.

Galston, William. *Liberal Pluralism.* Cambridge: Cambridge University Press, 2002.

Grant, Ruth, and Robert Keohane. "Accountability and the Abuses of Power in World Politics." *American Political Science Review* 99, no. 1 (2005): 29–44.

Gray, John. "Where Pluralists and Liberals Part Company." In *Pluralism: The Philosophy and Politics of Diversity,* Maria Baghramanian and Attracta Ingram, 85–102. London: Routledge Press, 2000.

Habermas, Jürgen. *Between Facts and Norms.* Cambridge: MIT Press, 1996.

———. *Moral Consciousness and Communicative Action.* Cambridge: MIT Press, 1990.

———. *The Theory of Communicative Action,* Vol. 1. Boston: Beacon Press, 1984.

———. *The Theory of Communicative Action,* Vol. 2. Boston: Beacon Press, 1987.

Hall, C. K. "The First Five Sessions of the UN Preparatory Commission for the International Criminal Court." *American Journal of International Law* 94, no. 4 (2000): 773–89.

Hampson, Fen Osler. "Preventive Diplomacy at the United Nations and Beyond." In *From Reaction to Conflict Prevention,* edited by Fen Osler Hampson and David M. Malone, 139–58. Boulder: Lynne Rienner Publishers, 2002.

Harf, Barbara. "No Lessons Learned from the Holocaust? Assessing Risks of Genocide and Political Mass Murder since 1955." *American Political Science Review* 97, no. 1 (2003): 75–91.

Hart, H. L. A. "International Law." In *International Rules: Approaches from International Law and International Relations,* edited by Robert J. Beck, Anthony Clark Arend, and Robert D. Vander Lugt, 75–93. Oxford: Oxford University Press, 1996.

Hassan, Riffat. "Is Islam a Help or Hindrance to Women's Development?" In *Islam in the Era of Globalization,* edited by Johan Meulman, 189–210. London: Routledge Press, 2002.

Hawkins, Darren. "Universal Jurisdiction for Human Rights." *Global Governance* 9 (2003): 291–99.

Hayden, Robert. "Biased Justice: Humanitarianism and the International Criminal Tribunal for the Former Yugoslavia." In *Yugoslavia Unraveled,* R. G. C. Thomas. Lanham, MD: Lexington Books, 2003.

Hayner, Priscilla. "Fifteen Truth Commissions—1974 to 1994: A Comparative Study." *Human Rights Quarterly* (1994).

Held, David. *Democracy and the Global Order.* Palo Alto, CA: Stanford University Press, 1995.

Herman, Edward S. "Propaganda System One: From Diem and Arbenz to Milosevic." In *Yugoslavia Unraveled,* edited by Raju G. C. Thomas, 243–58. Lanham, MD: Lexington Books, 2000.

Herman, Edward S., and David Peterson. "CNN: Selling NATO's War Globally." In *Degraded Capability: The Media and the Kosovo Crisis*, edited by P. Hammond and E. S. Herman, 111–22. London: Pluto Press, 2001.

Higgot, Richard. "Contested Globalization: The Changing Context and Normative Challenges." In *How Might We Live?*, edited by Ken Booth, Tim Dunne, and Michael Cox, 95–110. Cambridge: Cambridge University Press, 2001.

Hirsh, Michael. "Peacekeeping's Hybrid Future." *Foreign Affairs* 79 (2000): 1–9.

Hirst, Paul. "Carl Schmitt's Decisionism." In *The Challenge of Carl Schmitt*, edited by Chantal Mouffe, 7–17. London: Verso, 1999.

Hoffmann, Stanley. "The Political Ethics of International Relations." In *Ethics & International Affairs*, edited by Joel H. Rosenthal, 27–48. Washington, DC: Georgetown University Press, 1999.

Holmes, John T. "The Principle of Complementarity." In *The International Criminal Court: The Making of the ICC*, edited by Roy Lee. The Hague: Kluwer Publishers, 2001.

Holzgrefe, J. L. and Robert O. Keohane, eds. *Humanitarian Intervention: Ethical, Legal, and Political Dilemmas*. Cambridge: Cambridge University Press, 2003.

Human Rights Watch. "The Criminal Justice System in the Kingdom of Saudi Arabia." At www.hrw.org./press/2003/05/saudimemo0503.htm.

———. "Report on International Justice: Europe Should Oppose U.S. Law on War Crimes Court." At www.hrw.org/press/2001/12/ASPAeu1210.htm.

———. "U.S. Hague Invasion Act Becomes Law." At www.hrw.org/campaigns/icc/docs/aspa20010202.htm.

Huntington, Samuel. "The Clash of Civilizations?" *Foreign Affairs* 72 (1993): 25–50.

Hurrell, Andrew. "International Society and the Study of Regimes: A Reflective Approach." In *International Rules*, edited by Robert J. Beck, Anthony Clark Arend, and Robert D. Vander Lugt. Oxford: Oxford University Press, 1996.

Hutchings, Kimberly, and Roland Dannreuther, eds. *Cosmopolitan Citizenship*. New York: St. Martin's Press, 1999.

International Commission on Intervention and State Sovereignty. "The Responsibility to Protect: Report of the International Commission on Intervention and State Sovereignty (2001)." At www.dfait-maeci.gc.ca/iciss-ciise/report-en.asp>.

International Law Commission. Draft Statute for an International Criminal Court. *Report of the International Law Commission on the work of its forty-sixth session*. 2 May–22 July 1994. Chapter II.B.I. United Nations General Assembly Official Records, 49th sess., Supp. no. 10, A/49/10 1994: 29–140.

International Military Tribunal at Nuremberg. *Charter of International Military Tribunal*. 8 August 1945. Art. 6, 59, Stat. 1547.

Kamali, Mohammad H. *Freedom, Equality and Justice in Islam*. Cambridge: Islamic Texts Society, 2002.

Kamminga, Menno. "Lessons Learned from the Exercise of Universal Jurisdiction in Respect of Gross Human Rights Offences." *Human Rights Quarterly* 23 (2001): 941–44.

Kant, Immanuel. *Kant's Political Writings*. Edited by Hans Reiss. Cambridge: Cambridge University Press, 1970.

———. "Perpetual Peace." In *The Theory of International Relations: Selected Texts from Gentile to Treitschke*, edited by M. Forsyth, H. M. A. Keens-Soper, and P. Savigear. London: Allen and Unwith, 1971.

Kennedy, David. "A New Stream of International Law Scholarship." In *International Rules: Approaches from International Law and International Relations*, Robert J. Beck, Anthony Clark Arend, and Robert D. Vander Lugt, 230–52. Oxford: Oxford University Press, 1996.

Kennedy, Ellen. "Hostis Not Inimicus: Toward a Theory of the Public in the Work of Carl Schmitt." In *Law as Politics*, edited by David Dyzenhaus, 23–36. Durham, NC: Duke University Press, 1998.

Kenny, Michael. "Isaiah Berlin's Contribution to Modern Political Theory." *Political Studies* 48 (2000): 1026–39.

Keohane, Robert. *After Hegemony*. Princeton: Princeton University Press, 1983.

———. "International Institutions: Two Approaches." *International Studies Quarterly* 32 (1988): 379–96.

———. "International Relations and International Law: Two Optics." *Harvard International Law Journal* 38, no. 2 (1997): 487–502.

Keohane, Robert, and Lisa Martin. "The Promise of Institutionalist Theory." *International Security* 20 (1995): 39–51.

Kerr, Rachel. *The International Criminal Tribunal for the Former Yugoslavia*. Oxford: Oxford University Press, 2004.

Kervegan, Jean-Francois. "Carl Schmitt and 'World Unity.'" In *The Challenge of Carl Schmitt*, edited by Chantal Mouffe, 54–74. London: Verso, 1999.

Kirsch, Nico, and Ved Oosterveld. "Legality, Morality and the Dilemma of Humanitarian Intervention after Kosovo." *European Journal of International Law* 13 (2002): 323–35.

Kissinger, Henry. "The Pitfalls of Universal Jurisdiction." *Foreign Affairs* 80 (2001): 92–95.

Knight, Andy. "The Future of the UN Security Council: Questions of Legitimacy and Representation in Multilateral Governance." In *Enhancing Global Governance: Towards Global Governance*, edited by Andrew F. Cooper, John English, and Ramesh Thakur, 19–37. New York: United Nations University Press, 2002.

Knoops, Ganz. *Surrendering to International Criminal Courts*. Ardsley: NY: Transnational Publishers, 2002.

Koremenos, Barbara, Charles Lipson, and Duncan Snidal. "The Rational Design of International Institutions." *International Organization* 55, no. 4 (2001): 761–99.

Krasner, Stephen D. "Structural Cause and Regime Consequences." In *International Regimes*, edited by Stephen D. Krasner. Ithaca, NY: Cornell University Press, 1983.

Kratochwil, Friedrich. *Rules, Norms, and Decisions: On the Conditions of Practical Reasoning in International Relations and Domestic Affairs*. Cambridge: Cambridge University Press, 1989.

Kuperman, Alan. "Rwanda in Retrospect." *Foreign Affairs* 79 (2000): 94–118.

Kymlicka, Will. *Multicultural Citizenship: A Liberal Theory of Minority Rights*. Oxford: Oxford University Press, 1995.

Joyner, Christopher. *International Law in the 21st Century: Rules for Global Governance.* Lanham, MD: Rowman & Littlefield, 2004.

Lee, Roy. "An Assessment of the ICC Statute." *Fordham International Law Journal* 25, no. 1 (2002): 750–66.

Lee, Roy S., ed. *The International Criminal Court: The Making of the Rome Statute.* The Hague: Kluwer Law International, 1999.

Leigh, Michael. "The United States and the Statute of Rome." *The American Journal of International Law* 95 (2001): 124–31.

Lephold, Joseph, and Thomas G. Weiss. "Collective Conflict Management and Changing World Politics: An Overview." In *Collective Conflict Management and Changing World Politics,* edited by Joseph Lepgold and Thomas Weiss, 3–30. Albany: State University of New York Press, 1998.

Linklater, Andrew. "The Problem of Harm in World Politics: Implications for the Sociology of States-System." *International Affairs* 78 (1999): 319–38.

———. *The Transformation of Political Community.* London: Polity Press, 1998.

Lombardi, Clark B. "Islamic Law as Source of Constitutional Law in Eqypt: The Constitutionalization of the Sharia in Modern Arab States." *Columbia Journal of Transnational Law* 37, no. 2 (1998): 81–123.

Luck, Edward C. "Prevention: Theory and Practice." In *From Reaction to Conflict Prevention,* edited by Fen Osler Hampson and David M. Malone, 139–58. Boulder, CO: Lynne Rienner Publishers, 2002.

Lyons, Gene, and Michael Mastanduno, eds. *Beyond Westphalia: State Sovereignty and International Intervention.* Baltimore: Johns Hopkins University, 1995.

Malekian, Farhad. *The Concept of Islamic International Criminal Law: Comparative Study.* The Hague: Graham & Trotman/Martinus Nijhof, 1994.

Mandel, Michael. "Politics and Human Rights in International Criminal Law: Our Case Against NATO and the Lessons to be Learned from It." *Fordham International Law Journal* 25 (2001): 95–115.

Mazrui, Ali. "Islamic and Western Values." *Foreign Affairs* 76 (1997): 118–32.

McDougal, M., and M. Lasswell. "The Identification and Appraisal of Diverse Systems of Public Order." *American Journal of International Law* 53 (1959).

Megret, Frederic. "The Politics of International Justice." *European Journal of International Law* 13 (2002): 1261–84.

Meintjes, Garth. "Domestic Amnesties and International Accountability." In *International Crimes, Peace, and Human Rights: The Role of the International Criminal Court,* edited by Dinah Sheldon, 83–92. Ardsley, NY: Transnational Publishers, Inc., 2000.

Meron, Theodor. *War Crimes Law Comes of Age.* Oxford: Clarendon Press, 1998.

Meyer, John, John Boli, George M. Thomas, and Francisco Romero. "World Society and the Nation State." *American Journal of Sociology* 103, no. 1 (July 1997): 144-81.

Miller, David. *On Nationality.* Oxford: Clarendon Press, 1995.

Mingst, Karen. *Essentials of International Relations.* New York: W.W. Norton, 1999.

Morris, Madeleine. "Complementarity and Conflict: States, Victims, and the ICC." In *The United States and the International Criminal Court,* edited by S. B. Sewall and Carl Kaysen. Lanham, MD: Rowman & Littlefield Publishers, Inc., 2000.

———. "High Crimes and Misconceptions: The ICC and Non-Party States." In *International Crimes, Peace, and Human Rights: The Role of the International Criminal Court*, edited by Dinah Sheldon, 203–6. Ardsley, NY: Transnational Publishers, Inc., 2000.

Mouffe, Chantal. "Carl Schmitt and the Paradox of Liberal Democracy." In *The Challenge of Carl Schmitt*, edited by Chantal Mouffe, 38–53. London: Verso, 1999.

Nadelman, Ethan A. "Global Prohibition Regimes: The Evolution of Norms in International Society." *International Organization* 44, no. 4 (1990): 525.

Nardin, Terry. "International Pluralism and the Rule of Law." In *How Might We Live?*, edited by Ken Booth, Tim Dunne, and Michael Cox, 95–110. Cambridge: Cambridge University Press, 2001.

———. "The Moral Basis of Humanitarian Intervention." *Ethics and International Affairs* 16 (2002): 57–70.

Neier, Aryeh. *War Crimes*. New York: Random House Publishing, 1998.

Newman, Edward. "Humanitarian Intervention, Legality and Legitimacy." *The International Journal of Human Rights* 6, no. 4 (2002): 102–120.

Nicholls, Clive. "Reflections on Pinochet." *Virginia Journal of International Law* 41 (2000): 140–52.

Nye, Joseph S. *Power in the Global Information Age: From Realism to Globalization*. New York: Routledge, 2004.

Orford, Anne. *Reading Humanitarian Intervention: Human Rights and the Use of Force in International Law*. Cambridge: Cambridge University Press, 2003.

Overy, Richard. "The Nuremberg Trials: International Law in the Making." In *From Nuremberg to the Hague*, edited by Phillipe Sands. Cambridge: Cambridge University Press, 2000.

Parekh, Bhiku. "Cosmopolitan and Global Citizenship." *Review of International Studies* 29 (2003): 3–17.

Paust, Jean. "The Reach of ICC Jurisdiction Over Non-Signatory Nationals." *Vanderbilt Journal of Transnational Law* 33 (2000): 1–15.

Pejic, Jelena. "Creating a Permanent International Criminal Court: The Obstacles to Independence and Effectiveness." *Columbia Human Rights Law Review* 29 (1999): 291–354.

Politi, Mauro, and Giuseppe Nesi. *The International Criminal Court and the Crime of Aggression*. Aldershot: Ashgate Publishing, Inc., 2004.

Posner, Richard. *Law, Pragmatism, and Democracy*. Cambridge: Harvard University Press, 2003.

Preparatory Commission. Draft Relationship Agreement Between the United Nations and the International Criminal Court. UN Doc. PCNICC/2001/WGICC-UN/L.1. October 4, 2001, Art. 5.

———. The First Meeting of the Preparatory Commission for the International Criminal Court. PCNICC/1999/DP.11.

Prosper, Pierre, and Roger Clark. "Justice Without Borders: The International Criminal Court." *Temple International & Comparative Law Journal* 17 (2003): 85–96.

Purvis, Nigel. "Critical Legal Studies in International Law." *Harvard International Law Journal* 392 (1991): 81–127.

Ralph, Jason. "International Society, the International Criminal Court and American Foreign Policy." *Review of International Studies* 31, no. 1 (2005): 27–44.

Ratner, Steven R. "Belgium's War Crimes Statute: A Postmortem." *American Journal of International Law* 97, no. 4 (2004): 888–97.

Ratner, Steven R., and Jason Abrams. *Accountability for Human Rights Atrocities in International Law: Beyond the Nuremberg Legacy*. 2nd ed. Oxford: Oxford University Press, 2001.

Rawls, John. *The Law of the Peoples*. Cambridge: Harvard University Press, 1999.

———. *A Theory of Justice*. Cambridge: Harvard University Press, 1971.

Raz, Joseph. *The Morality of Freedom*. Oxford: Oxford University Press, 1986.

Reisman, Michael W. "Legal Responses to Genocide and Other Massive Violations of Human Rights." In *Accountability for International Crime and Serious Violations of Fundamental Human Rights*, edited by M. Cherif Bassiouni and Madeline H. Morris, 77–78. Durham, NC: Duke University School of Law 1996.

Reus-Smit, Christian, ed. *The Politics of International Law*. Cambridge: Cambridge University Press, 2004.

———. "The Politics of International Law." In *The Politics of International Law*, edited by Christian Reus-Smit, 14–44. Cambridge: Cambridge University Press, 2004.

Riley, John. "Crooked Timber and Liberal Culture." In *Pluralism and the Philosophy and Politics of Diversity*, edited by Maria Baghramian and Attracta Ingram. London: Routledge Press, 2000.

Risse, Thomas, Stephen C. Ropp, and Kathryn Sikkink, eds. *The Power of Human Rights*. Cambridge: Cambridge University Press, 1999.

Roach, Steven C. "Arab States and the Role of Islam in the International Criminal Court." *Political Studies* 53, no. 1 (March 2005): 143–61.

———. *Cultural Autonomy, Minority Rights and Globalization*. Aldershot: Ashgate Publishing Inc., 2005.

———. "Humanitarian Emergencies and the International Criminal Court: Toward a Cooperative Arrangement between the ICC and the UN Security Council." *International Studies Perspectives* 6, no. 4 (November 2005): 431–46.

———. "Minority Rights and the Emergent International Right to Autonomy: A Historical and Normative Assessment." *International Journal on Group and Minority Rights* 11, no. 4 (2004): 411–32.

———. "U.S. Foreign Policy and the International Criminal Court: Towards a Third Way of Strategic Accommodation." *International Politics* 43, no. 1 (February 2006).

———. "Value Pluralism, Liberalism, and the Cosmopolitan Intent of the International Criminal Court." *Journal of Human Rights* 4, no. 4 (December 2005): 475–90.

Robertson, Geoffrey. *Crimes Against Humanity: The Struggle for Global Justice*. New York: The New Press, 1999.

Robinson, Darryl. "Serving the Interests of Justice: Amnesties, Truth Commissions and the International Criminal Court." *European Journal of International Law* 14 (2003): 481–505.

———. "Article 7(1)(g)—Rape, Sexual Slavery, Enforced Prostitution, Forced Pregnancy, Enforced Sterilization, or Any Other Forms of Sexual Violence of Comparable Gravity." In *The International Criminal Court: Elements of Crimes and Rules of*

Procedure and Evidence, edited by V Roy S. Lee, 93–94. Ardsley, NY: Transnational Publishers, 2001.

Rodenbeck, Max. "Islam Confronts Its Demons." *The New York Review of Books* LI, no. 7 (April 16, 2004):14–19.

Roht-Arriaza, Naomi. "Civil Society in Processes of Accountability." In *Post-Conflict Justice*, edited by M. Cherif Bassiouni, 97–114. Ardsley, NY: Transnational Publishers, 2003.

Rorty, Richard. *Philosophy and the Mirror of Nature*. Princeton: Princeton University Press, 1979.

Rosenau, James. *Turbulence in World Politics: A Theory of Change and Continuity*. Princeton: Princeton University, 1990.

Ruggie, John G. *Constructing a New World Polity*. Routledge Press, 1999.

Sadat, Leila Nadya. *The International Criminal Court and the Transformation of International Law: Justice for the New Millennium*. Ardsley, NY: Transnational Publishers, 2002.

———. "The Evolution of the ICC: From the Hague to Rome and Back Again." In *The United States and the International Criminal Court*, edited by Sarah B. Sewall and Carl Kaysen, 31–50. Lanham, MD: Rowman and Littlefield Publishers, 2000.

Saland, Per. "International Criminal Law Principles." In *The International Criminal Court: The Making of the Rome Statute*, edited by Roy Lee, 189–216. The Hague: Kluwer Publishers, 1999.

Sandholtz, Wayne, and Alec Stone Sweet. "Law Politics, and International Governance." In *The Politics of International Law*, edited by Christian Reus-Smit, 238–71. Cambridge: Cambridge University Press, 2004.

Sands, Philippe. "After Pinochet: The Role of National Courts." In *From Nuremberg to the Hague*, edited by Philippe Sands, 68–108. Cambridge: Cambridge University Press, 2003.

Satha-Anand, Chaiwat. "The Non-violent Crescent: Eight Theses on Muslim Non-violent Action." In *Peace and Conflict Resolution in Islam*, edited by Abdul Aziz Said, Nathan C. Funk, and Ayse S. Kasayifc, 192–221. Lanham, MD: University Press of America, 2001.

Schabas, William. *Genocide in International Law*. Cambridge: Cambridge University Press, 2000.

———. *Introduction to the International Criminal Court*. Cambridge: Cambridge University Press, 2004.

Schachter, Oscar. "General Course in Public International Law." *Recueil des Cours* 5 (1982): 1–395.

Scharf, Michael P. "Justice versus Peace." In *The United States and the International Criminal Court*, edited by Sarah B. Sewall and Carl Kaysen, 179–193. Lanham, MD: Rowman and Littlefield Publishers, 2000.

———. "The ICC's Jurisdiction over the Nationals of Non-Party States." In Sarah B. Sewall and Carl Kaysen, eds. *The United States and the International Criminal Court*, 213–36. Lanham, MD: Rowman and Littlefield Publishers, 2000.

Scharf, Michael P., and Nigel Rodley. "International Law Principles on Accountability." In *Post-Conflict Justice*, edited by M. Cherif Bassiouni, 89–96. Ardsley, NY: Transnational Publishers, 2003.

Scheffer, David J. "The U.S. Perspective on the ICC." In *The United States and the International Criminal Court*, edited by Sarah B. Sewall and Carl Kaysen, 115–18. Lanham, MD: Rowman and Littlefield Publishers, 2000.

Scheuerman, William. "International Law as Historical Myth." *Constellations: An International Journal of Critical and Democratic Theory* 11, no. 4 (December 2004): 537–50.

Schmemann, S. "U.S. Vetoes Bosnia Mission, Then Allows 3–day Reprieve." *New York Times* (July 1, 2002): 3A.

Schmitt, Carl. *The Concept of the Political.* Chicago: University of Chicago, 1996.

———. *Political Theology.* Translated by George Schwab. Cambridge, MA: MIT Press, 1985.

———. *The Crisis of Parliamentary Democracy.* Translated by Ellen Kennedy. Cambridge, MA: MIT Press, 1985.

Shanker, Thom, and J. Dao. "US Might Refuse New Peace Duties Without Immunity." *New York Times* (July 3, 2002).

Shaw, Martin. "Global Voices: Civil Society and the Media in Global Crises." In Tim Dunne and Nicholas J. Wheeler, eds. *Human Rights in Global Politics*, 229. Cambridge: Cambridge University Press, 1999.

———. *Theory of the Global State.* Cambridge: Cambridge University Press, 1992.

Simonovic, Ivan. "The Role of the ICTY in the Development of International Criminal Adjudication." *Fordham International Law Journal* 23 (1999): 440–59.

Slaughter, Anne-Marie. "International Law and International Relations Theory: A Dual Agenda." *American Journal of International Law* (1993).

Smith, Michael. "Humanitarian Intervention: An Overview of Ethical Issues." *Ethics and International Affairs* 12 (1998): 63–79.

Smith, Thomas. "Moral Hazard and Humanitarian Law: The International Criminal Court and the Limits of Legalism." *International Politics* 39 (2002): 175–92.

Smith, Steve, Ken Booth, and Marysia Zalewski, eds. *International Theory: Positivism & Beyond.* Cambridge: Cambridge University Press, 1996.

Stahn, Carsten. "The Ambiguities of Security Council Resolution 1422 (2002)." *European Journal of International Law* 14 (2002): 85–104.

Steains, Christine. "Gender Issues." In Roy S. Lee, ed. *The International Criminal Court: The Making of the Rome Statute, Issues, Negotiators, and Results*, 357–90. The Hague: Kluwer Publishers, 1999.

Stromseth, Jane. "Rethinking Humanitarian Intervention: The Case for Incremental Change." In *Humanitarian Intervention: Ethical and Legal Dilemmas*, edited by J.L Holzgrefe and Robert Keohane, 235–252. Cambridge: Cambridge University Press, 2003.

Straus, Scott. "Darfur and the Genocide Debate." *Foreign Affairs* 84 (January/February 2005): 123–33.

Teitel, Ruti. "The Universal and the Particular in International Criminal Justice." *Columbia Human Rights Law Review* 30 (1999): 285–304.

Tepperman, Jonathan. "Truth or Consequences." *Foreign Affairs* 81, no. 2 (March/April 2002).

Teson, Fernando. "Collective Humanitarian Intervention." *Michigan Journal of International Law* 17 (1996).

Tibi, Bassam. *The Challenge of Fundamentalism.* Berkeley: University of California Press, 2002.

Traub, James. "Inventing East Timor." *Foreign Affairs* 79, no. 4 (2000): 74–89.

Trimble, Phillip R. "International Law, World Order and Critical Legal Studies." *Stanford Law Review* 42 (1999).

United Nations. UN Security Res. 1422, 12 July 2002. UN Documents S/PV. 4567; SC/7445/Rev. 1.

———. Fifth Report of Secretary General on the United Nations Mission in Sierra Leone. S/2000/751, 31 July 2000.

———. The Rome Statute of the International Criminal Court. Adopted and opened for signature July 17, 1998. UN Doc. A/Conf. 183/9.

———. *United Nations Diplomatic Conference of Plenipotentiaries on the Establishment of an International Criminal Court.* Rome, 15 June–17 July 1998. Vol. II. New York: United Nations Publications, 1998.

———. *Building Peace and Development: Report on the Work of the Organization from the Forty-eight to the Forty-ninth Session of the General Assembly.* New York: United Nations Publications, 1994.

———. Revised Draft Statute for an International Criminal Court prepared by the Committee on International Criminal Jurisdiction, Annex, Report of the Committee on International Criminal Jurisdiction on its Session held form 27 July to 20 August 1953. United Nations General Assembly Official Records. 9th sess., Supp. no. 12, A/2645 (1954).

———. Universal Declaration of Human Rights adopted and proclaimed by United Nations General Assembly Resolution 217A(III) of 10 December 1948. United Nations General Assembly Official Records. 3rd sess., A/RES/3/217 (1948).

———. Convention on the Prevention and Punishment of the Crime of Genocide adopted and opened for signature by General Assembly Resolution 260A (III) of 9 December 1948. United Nations General Assembly Official Records. 3rd sess., 78 U.N.T.S. 277.

U.S. Congress. Supplemental Appropriations Bill. H.R. 4775, presented for signature by the U.S. President on 26 July 2002 and signed on 2 August 2002.

———. 106 Congress, 2nd sess., H.R. 4654; S 2726, 14 June 2000.

Vasquez, John A. "Ethics, Foreign Policy, and Liberal Wars: The Role of Restraint in Moral Decision Making." *International Studies Perspectives* 6, no. 3 (August 2005): 307–15.

Waldron, Jeremy. "Arguing a Universal Claim." *Columbia Human Rights Law Review* 30 (1999): 305–14.

Washburn, John. "The Negotiation of the Rome Statute for the International Criminal Court and International Lawmaking in the 21st Century." *Pace International Law Review* 11 (1999): 361–77.

Weber, Max. *Economy and Society.* Vol. 1. Berkeley: University of California Press, 1978.

———. *The Protestant Ethic and the Spirit of Capitalism.* London: Routledge, 1992.

Wedgwood, Ruth. "The Constitution and the ICC." In *The United States and the International Criminal Court,* edited by Sarah B. Sewall and Carl Kaysen, 119–36. Lanham, MD: Rowman and Littlefield Publishers, 2000.

Wedgwood, Ruth. "The International Criminal Court: An American View." *European Journal of International Law* 10 (1999): 93–107.

Weiss, Thomas, and Jarat Chopra. "Sovereignty Under Siege: From Intervention to Humanitarian Space." In *Beyond Westphalia: State Sovereignty and International Intervention*, edited by Gene Lyons and Michael Mastanduno, 87–115. Baltimore: Johns Hopkins University, 1995.

Weller, Marc. "Global Constitutionalism: UN Security Council Action." *International Affairs* 79 (2002): 693–711.

Wenar, Leif. "The Legitimacy of Peoples." In *Global Justice and Transnational Politics: Essays on the Moral and Political Challenges of Globalization*, edited by Pablo De Greiff and Ciaran Cronin, 65–67. Cambridge: MIT Press, 2002.

Wendt, Alexander. "Anarchy Is What States Make of It." *International Organization* 46 (1992): 391–425.

———. *Social Theory of International Politics*. Cambridge: Cambridge University Press, 1999.

Wheeler, Nicholas J. "Enforcing Human Rights." In *International Human Rights in the 21st Century: Protecting the Rights of Groups*, edited by Gene M. Lyons and James Mayall, 169–199. Lanham, MD: Rowman and Littlefield Publishers, 2003.

Wheeler, Nicholas J. "Decision-making Rules and Procedures for Humanitarian Intervention." *The International Journal of Human Rights* 6, no. 1 (2002): 127–38.

Wight, Martin. *Power Politics*. Edited by Hedley Bull and Carsten Holbraad. New York: Holmes and Meier, 1978.

Williams, Ian. "Righting the Wrongs of Past Interventions: A Review of the International Commission on Intervention and State Sovereignty." *The International Journal of Human Rights* 6, no. 3 (2002): 103–13.

Wippman, David. "The International Criminal Court." In *The Politics of International Law*, edited by Christian Reus-Smit, 151–88. Cambridge: Cambridge University Press, 2004.

Wippman, David. "Atrocities, Deterrence, and the Limits of International Justice." *Fordham International Law Journal* 23 (1999): 473–88.

Woetzel, Robert K. *The Nuremberg Trials in International Law*. New York: Stevens & Sons Limited, 1962.

Wright, Quincy. "The Law of the Nuremberg Trial." *American Journal of International Law* 41, no. 1 (January 1947).

Zappala, Salvatore. "The Reaction of the US to the Entry into Force of the ICC Statute: Comments on UN SC Resolution 1422(2002) and Article 98 Agreements." *Journal of International Criminal Justice* 1 (2003): 114–34.

Index

About the Author

Steven C. Roach is assistant professor in the Department of Government and International Affairs at the University of South Florida. He is author of *Cultural Autonomy, Minority Rights, and Globalization* and editor of *Critical Theory and International Relations: A Reader*. He has published numerous articles in peer-reviewed journals and is currently finishing a book on the evolution of critical international theory.

www.ingramcontent.com/pod-product-compliance
Ingram Content Group UK Ltd.
Pitfield, Milton Keynes, MK11 3LW, UK
UKHW012039150926
475560UK00001B/83

9 780742 541030